I Didn't Know I Needed This

I Didn't Know
I Needed This

THE NEW RULES FOR
FLIRTING, FEELING, AND
FINDING YOURSELF

ELI RALLO

HARVEST

An Imprint of WILLIAM MORROW

FIRST EDITION

Designed by Renata DiBiase
Art page ii © Mathieu – stock.adobe.com
Art pages 1, 121, 217 © ehaurylik – stock.adobe.com

Library of Congress Cataloging-in-Publication Data

Names: Rallo, Eli, author.
Title: I didn't know I needed this : the new rules for
   flirting, feeling, and finding yourself / Eli Rallo.
Description: First edition. | New York, NY : Harvest, [2023]
Identifiers: LCCN 2023033356 | ISBN 9780063298460
   (hardcover) | ISBN 9780063298491 (digital audio) | ISBN
   9780063298514 (audio) | ISBN 9780063298484 (ebook)
Subjects: LCSH: Dating (Social customs) | Flirting.
Man-woman relationships. | Couples.
Classification: LCC HQ801 .R24 2023 | DDC 306.73—dc23/eng/20230727
LC record available at https://lccn.loc.gov/2023033356

ISBN 978-0-06-329846-0

23 24 25 26 27 LBC 5 4 3 2 1

To all the versions of you and all the versions of me—past, present, and meant to be. It's time for us to meet the world.

Contents

Part 3

Preface

WHEN YOU'RE ABOUT to graduate from college, and an "adult" asks about your career aspirations, and you say "to write about love like Carrie Bradshaw," it's not a good look. At twenty-one, I knew I wanted to be a writer. But I didn't know how to make writing about sex and dating and relationships and exes a career—so, instead, I got a graduate degree. I headed to Columbia University and decided to get a master's in journalism to become a "real, serious writer." Columbia told me to delete my social media if I wanted to be a "real journalist." So I decided I wouldn't be a real journalist.

I'd be a fake one.

I started a podcast, talked about sex on Instagram, and wrote a newsletter about my boob job. I started giving advice to anyone about anything they had a question about. I started building a community.

And then, of course, there was TikTok. In a matter of months, I had nearly half a million people listening to my every word.

I started workshopping my lists of rules for everything from one-night stands to flirting to breakups to second dates and publishing them on my TikTok. These rules became bible for a global audience of young women. I was told I became an older sister to strangers. Young women in Perth and London and Brazil and Ohio call me "Mom" in my DMs daily. I built a community of young women who want to be listened to and heard and applauded—who, for whatever reason, take my word as exactly what they needed to hear. Someone recently told me I give such good advice

I could convince them to commit manslaughter, which is scary, but in a very cool way.

I leaned into being a fake journalist so hard and so truthfully and with so much vulnerability, I acquired 722,000 TikTok followers and counting, over 100,000 on Instagram, and the opportunity to do a TED Talk at my alma mater. I pinched myself when face-to-face with Tina Fey, I connected to Drew Barrymore, and I meet my followers out in New York daily.

Give my regards to Columbia J-school: I never deleted my sexually charged, unhinged internet presence, and I now have the ability to write the rules for a generation.

The crux of this is I've always been fervently creating. I occupied myself with imagination for hours as a child. I played a pretty convincing Helen Keller in a fourth-grade production of the play *The Miracle Worker*. I was sent to the school social worker for writing a short story in my writer's notebook of an orphan who poisoned herself to death in seventh grade. I begged my parents to allow me to go to college for theater. I wrote plays about women and sex and pushed myself to create things that would pass the Bechdel test—including a story about a boy meeting a girl named Salsa in a McDonald's who claimed to be Jesus Christ herself.

I have a degree in journalism and another in theater, but honorarily, I have a third one in the ins and the outs of dating and sex and ghosting and relationships.

I acquired this degree through an arduous ten-year program. None of the exams were open note, but I graduated with a 4.0. I am very good at loving, losing, ghosting, having good sex, having bad sex, breakups, heartbreak, and messing up in the name of my silly little heart. I am also very good at sharing these lessons.

In February 2018 I wrote in my iPhone notes, at 11:25 p.m., "I want to be a writer → decide what this means." I was lying in my sorority house's twin bunk beds, contemplating how the hell I'd ever be a writer, or what it meant to gain the title. Underneath the note I wrote "this one time at Jesus camp . . . ," because I thought it would be funny to write an essay about going to second base with a sixteen-year-old from Illinois in the dugout of a baseball field in high school at Jesus camp, while everyone else prayed somewhere nearby.

So, let us pray, I guess.

In college, I had my heart traumatized. I won't say broken, because upon reflection, heartbroken does not mean having your heart run over sixteen times with a three-ton truck driven by a so-ciopath in an improv group wearing glasses. After dumping me, he went on to emotionally manipulate me, convincing me he still loved me and wanted to be with me, just to end things again days later, blaming the reasons why we just wouldn't work on me. He made me think I was such a fuckup and a failure I hardly got out of bed second semester of my freshman year.

I love fearlessly and deeply. I am proud of how I love even though it fucks me over at least once a year. I love more than any-one could ever return to me and I know that to be true. The way I love has gotten me into trouble and into wonder. It has led me astray and walked me back home and told me "you're doing the best you can." And it has given me the ability to share my so-called wisdom with my peers. What gives me the authority to recom-mend how to live, or love? Nothing. I'm just willing to do so.

I've had my heart broken by a guy who told me he could make an exception to his rule that he would only date (religiously) Jewish girls for someone exceptional, but I wasn't. The same ex-boyfriend told me, via a Google Doc, that I was the best sex he ever had. I dated a closeted pro-lifer who got me to fall in love with him before telling me I was too crass to ever have a serious career (I think I took ninety-eight showers to wash that off me). As "revenge" I hooked up with his roommate (great move). I've been on more app dates than I can count. I met my boyfriend's parents dressed like Julia Fox. And I learned everything I know about sex from the Catholic Church's education system. (Just kidding, don't worry.)

In the age of the iPhone, we're not finding our advice in syndicated columns in our local newspapers. We're finding them on our apps on our phones. My TikTok and Instagram accounts have become a virtual advice column. And *I Didn't Know I Needed This* is an advice column that looks less like "Dear Abby" and more like your audacious older sister sitting on your bed with a handle of tequila and a box of tissues and a bottle of lube, saying, "If you like them . . . just tell them. Worst case it's a good story, best case, it's the rest of your life."

I Didn't Know I Needed This is a to-do list of self-appreciation and validation and answers to questions like: Who texts first after the first date? How do I find out who I am? How do I ask them to go down on me during sex? And what the fuck am I supposed to do with a broken heart?

This book is my scripture, one I've shared pieces of in three-minute videos and Instagram stories. *I Didn't Know I Needed This* will give you the rules for how to use your voice, how to fuck to finish, what to wear on a first date, and how to fall in love with yourself in such an intimate and truthful way that you will be fulfilled and invigorated. These are the rules for intimate and intimidating and fearless foreplay—in the bedroom and in life.

I am overwhelmed each time I read the DM and the comment: "Thank you so much for this. I didn't know I needed this." It never gets old.

What is better, though, is that I feel the very same way about all of you—our conversations through screen and now page. I didn't know I needed this either.

Part 1

Rules for Being Single

1. GIRL BOSS BUCKET LIST—you have so much time. USE IT.

2. Kissing is a handshake. It doesn't have to be that deep and should be done liberally.

3. Play around with some rebrands.

4. Keep your roster organized.

5. Simple: lie. Make up fun personas in the bar when you talk to strangers.

6. Double date—if you're going to potentially waste your time on a stranger, you may as well waste it with your friends.

7. Be IMPULSIVE while you aren't having to think about someone else and their emotions!

8. Date your city and date your friends.

9. The 10% rule (read on).

10. Be intentionally SELFISH.

11. There's no one way to be single.

12. Good vibrations—buy a vibrator. There's nothing you can do with a partner that you cannot do alone (sexy time) or with a friend (date night).

13. Get a body pillow to replace a partner.

14. Live like you're going to meet your soulmate in a year.

MY NAME IS Eli Rallo, and I am a recovering career serial dater. Everyone say, "Hi, Eli."

.

I took myself out on a date for the first time when I was twenty-two years old. I'd never been very good at being alone. If given the choice to eat alone, sleep alone, go to the gym alone, or to do each of those activities with someone else, I'd almost always choose the latter. Partnership—in a friend, a lover—was a safety blanket that protected from the unruly beast I saw in myself.

You would never willingly spend time with someone you don't like, and that's how it felt to live inside my skin—constantly spending time with someone I loathed. Wishing I was anywhere else.

But a few months prior, hungover in the Chicago O'Hare airport, I decided I was sick of spending time with my worst enemy. Eli. I wanted to learn to view myself like a friend I was elated at having an afternoon with, uninterrupted. Self-loathing was tiring and dim. I wanted to fall in love with the person I saw in the mirror, the person I always found a way to be too busy for.

Months later, in my bedroom half dressed, I noticed the fruits of my labor in my face—I looked soft and loved and pleased. I looked how I usually did in the few white hot moments stumbling home from some guy's apartment—validated. But I hadn't slept with anyone or gone on any dates. This was a glow that said *I like the person that I am.*

I'd been working so hard on intentionally enjoying my time alone, on feeling desired and validated by myself, I decided that challenging myself to enjoy an evening out in my own company was the perfect final test.

I put on a pair of soft gray jeans, a sweater, a jacket, a little makeup. I packed my tote bag—a book, a notebook, a pair of headphones, my wallet and keys, and lip gloss.

I'd purposefully not chosen a destination. I wanted to exist outside of my comfort zone in more ways than one. Not having a plan felt uncomfortable, like an itchy sweater or a rigid dining room chair. That's what I needed. I took the stairs down two at a time, a pit growing in my stomach, almost convincing me to turn back.

Why did I need to do this? Why did I need to take myself out on a date? Why couldn't I just sit with myself at home? Why couldn't using my vibrator and going to bed be sufficient? Were other people who were comfortable with themselves going out alone? Did hot people go on dates by themselves? Do people who regularly get laid go out alone? Hadn't I done enough work?

Deep down I felt that taking myself on this date would be a graduation ceremony. I wanted to officially mark my growth—that over the past year, my fears of singlehood and loneliness and unpopularity and solitude had slowly diminished, to the point that they were almost invisible. I felt fulfilled and pretty and okay, all without notifications from dating apps, nights half asleep next to my high school crush, or tearful phone calls from an ex.

I wanted to celebrate alone—the way it felt to be a little happier. A little lighter.

I liked who I was. I wanted to hold on to that. I wanted to hold on to her. Into the next relationship or just the next day.

I wanted to be a woman who liked herself.

I was still nervous as I traversed the streets and ducked into the subway downtown. Arriving in the East Village, I felt pairs of stranger's eyes on me like I never had before. Of course, nobody was looking at me—nobody knew I was going to dinner alone and, more importantly, nobody cared. But it felt like they must've known. I spent an hour walking down the same five streets, scoping out where I would look the least awkward. I had chosen a Friday night because I knew it meant more couples, more friend groups, more loneliness—a bigger challenge than eating alone on a Monday.

I finally decided on a sushi place with a little bar.

"Just one," I said as I approached the hostess's stand. I figured they'd sit me at the bar. But instead the hostess led me to a small table. I liked the space—I put out my notebook and my book while I mulled over the menu.

I ordered champagne. I was celebrating, after all. Celebrating me, celebrating this life—one where, even if I was all alone, I was fulfilled. I was content. I was having a good fucking time.

The bubbles exploded on my tongue. I felt an instant buzz. It wasn't weird to be alone. I was all I had, and yet all I needed.

It felt good.

Cheers.

I used to walk down the gray streets of Manhattan's Upper West Side with tunnel vision, refusing to allow my eyes to stumble upon happy couples sharing bowls of pasta or walking hand in hand. I looked at my feet or my cell phone, aimlessly scrolling through Hinge matches. My perpetual anxiety and self-doubt was a sickness I believed could be remedied by a prescription that was, to me, addictive. The Rx: a boyfriend. Having a partner was morphine to me. Under the belief that someone else's love or lust could distract me from my own self-loathing, I claimed the label "relationship type" with ease.

But the truth: I was terrified of being alone.

In 2019, my therapist, Heather, pointed out that I hadn't been single since junior year of high school and asked me what I feared so much about being single.

"I don't fear being single. I'm single right now and I love it," I said, trying to convince us both.

Next to me, my phone buzzed—a Snapchat from the guy I was "talking to"—whatever that means. Even when I didn't have a boyfriend, I always made sure to have *someone* feeding me affirmation.

Heather said I should work to affirm and validate myself before seeking out a partner to do so. I remember sitting there being sort of pissed at her. Who was she to tell ME, a *FEMINIST*, that I was afraid to be single? Of course I wasn't *afraid* of being alone—I was a powerful woman with a moon in Cancer, making me naturally emotional. My national anthem was Dua Lipa's "New Rules" because I no longer felt inclined to text my ex for a late-night hookup—and clearly this alone made me a strong, powerful woman.

Four years later, I realized that she was right.

.

In 2016, my freshman year of college, my boyfriend Ezra broke up with me in a church parking lot after a very fast, eighteen-year-old sugar-rush, naive relationship of three months. I was devastated. Standing in the snow, he started to cry, hardly coming up with a why, though his words felt rehearsed. He said he felt like I hadn't sought out my own life at college. How could I have, being that he asked me to be his girlfriend a month after I arrived on campus? But, sometimes the truth fucking hurts, and here was the truth: all I had were *his* friends and *his* social life and our nights together. The cups of vodka, the rehearsed laughing, my shaky hands unzipping his pants. I hadn't branched out, joined the newspaper or any student groups, and I, a self-proclaimed writer, hadn't written a thing since beginning my freshman year.

Who are you without him? a voice in my head asked as I stormed off. I didn't know, but I lied to myself instead—I was fine. The truth: I didn't know who that inner woman was and I didn't want to find out. I feared her. She felt like a stranger I met once and immediately hated without even giving her a chance. The love that

Ezra had for me, however fleeting and sparse, had kept my engine going. Now, I had no gas and I was stalling in the middle of the road. I was *single*, and I was determined to be that way for as brief a time as possible.

So instead of dedicating the aftermath of our breakup to figuring out who I was or how to love myself—or even to just *enjoying* my freshman year of college—I fixated on the issue he had cited in his little rehearsed breakup speech: that he and I could never be together because I had no real identity outside of us. The solution seemed pretty clear to me: if I could prove I had self-love and worth without him, then he would love me again. Love yourself before you love someone else . . . foolproof, right?

Wrong.

I wasn't even sure if I had really liked him, or if he just served as the validation I needed—that because of his attention, I blossomed into a real person, not just the idea of one. With Ezra as my boyfriend, I finally felt pretty, sexy, thin enough. Cool enough and smart enough to be wanted. I distinctly recall forcing myself to get over red flags because having someone who treated me terribly felt better to me than having nobody at all. Months later, I was single and pining after a man I had CONVINCED myself to fall in love with, plotting just how I'd get him back.

At age eighteen, I lived in a shitty little house built on the foundation that I'd grown comfortable with—that a boyfriend made me worth something. That a partner made me viable. That I wasn't whole but, rather, searching for a "missing piece." When I failed at working on Broadway, or becoming an author, at least someone would take care of me. And even if I was utterly miserable, I wouldn't be alone. I feared solitude more than I feared never being the woman the little girl inside of me knows I am.

This worldview, and the feelings it conjured up, weren't fully my fault. Our society is built on an American dream of white picket fences and nuclear, heterosexual families, where women and men know their place and play their parts. In 2023, I think we can all agree that this is pretty outdated. But what hasn't really changed, what is buried deep within the core of our happy families and manicured lawns and dinnertimes, is that our society still teaches women to aspire to partnership. Subconsciously, we feed girls the idea, from birth, that marriage = the end goal. Nobody really ever says it outright, but it's learned in subliminal ways.

I love my parents. But in high school they taught my brothers how to invest the money they'd earned from waiting tables and summer jobs. They did not teach me the same lessons. And while nobody ever said to my face, "You're going to be taken care of by a man"—or maybe even thought that explicitly—the unspoken expectation seemed to be that someone else would take care of me, while my brothers should learn to take care of themselves (and someone else, too).

Women couldn't own their own credit cards until 1974—the year my mother was born. It wasn't until the year 1900 that a married woman could enter contracts, file lawsuits, and receive her own inheritance. The first woman to become CEO of a Fortune 500 company was Katharine Graham in 1972. And of course, all this only applied, for the most part, to cisgender, heterosexual white women.

When I was a kid, I never saw anyone truly push back against the way our society was set up. So by young adulthood I was completely unaware of the ways I had been impacted. Being single to me was like the boarding gate at an airport, a place to wait before my flight would take off. And I'd rather be on standby than not be at the airport at all.

Every time Ezra and I slept side by side, postbreakup, after a drunken night, he'd tell me he loved me and then take it back, like some sort of sadistic ritual. I would then tell him things to make it seem like I really liked myself, so then maybe he'd be inclined to realize how much he loved me too. But if the only reason you're trying to heal is for someone else's approval, you won't ever heal.

It's not so much about our actions, but the intentions and energy behind them. So as you can imagine, it didn't work. I didn't fix my inner aching, my disgust for myself. And I didn't get the guy. I got a diagnosis for depression, binge eating disorder, and further off path than I'd ever been before.

•

There's no one way to be single. You can be actively dating, you can be not dating at all, you can be hooking up with people, you can be recovering from a breakup. All those states of singledom are equal in value. There's no "right" way to be single. But there's certainly a wrong way, and I was pretty good at it. The wrong way to be single is to be in denial, because you've decided that being single is a waiting room for a relationship. Being single is a final destination. I wish I'd known that.

One night second semester of freshman year, I met a guy at a club. I thought he was hot enough to make Ezra, who was at the same bar that night, jealous. So I took him home. The exchange was boring. After it was over, I asked him to leave. I sat on my dorm room floor and called Ezra with a bubbly energy. I thought I'd done the right thing. I told him what happened to try to make him jealous, but he just sounded glad I was trying to move on. Imagine calling your ex and saying, "I hooked up with the guy I left with," to hear him say, "Good for you." I was doing what I believed a single person was "supposed to do"—have casual, meaningless nights, focus on herself, be sexy and flirty and fine. So why couldn't I get what I wanted? Why didn't I feel fine? Ezra told me he'd see me soon, that he couldn't hear me that well. He must've still been at the club. I put my head in my hands and sobbed.

•

In the cast of characters that is my life, my best friend, Sadie, is front and center. She's a redheaded Sagittarius who has never once in her life put up with bullshit or dated someone just so she wouldn't be alone. She is blunt and headstrong, cool like a glass of ice water speckled with condensation. She has taught me more about relationships than anyone else in my life. Through our entire friendship she's reminded me she'd rather be single than with someone she wasn't head over heels for—and for a while, I couldn't relate. As I jumped from boyfriend to boyfriend throughout college, Sadie stayed single save for one high school lover (by choice) and she loved it. I envied her but figured I wasn't bold or cool or brave enough to ever mimic her lifestyle. I wrote her off as an anomaly.

In August 2019, we arrived at our senior-year house in Ann Arbor, Michigan, and unpacked our bedrooms. Our first night there, I poured us vodka lemonades as she fiddled with our speaker. She looked at me and said, "We're staying single all year." She was declarative and grave, and her blue eyes somehow convinced me. It would be fun, she said. I needed to be single, for once. She sparkled when she spoke. And she was right. But I had no clue how and couldn't admit that to her. Furthermore, my true battle was that I didn't *want* to be alone with myself. Since age fifteen I'd hopped from one partner to the next, and in the quick spurts between each, I'd grasped at anything to fill the void and avoid myself. I'd succeeded at acquiring a handful of boyfriends who treated me less than favorably, and I convinced myself I preferred the hurt to being with just me—a stranger. I didn't know how to look at my best friend and say, *Sadie, I'm terrified of being alone with myself. Or, I know you love me, but I don't know why you do.*

So instead we pinkie swore on our pledge, and one thing I always do is stick to my word. This would be my first real step into figuring out what it was to be single. The process would be not a step, not a mile, but a marathon.

You have to start somewhere.

We made a bucket list of all the things we most wanted to do while we were single together. It lived in our iPhone notes and we put green emoji check marks next to our completed tasks. We kissed as many people as we could and rebranded ourselves into the coolest versions of us we could imagine, keeping neat, organized rosters that we'd talk about over Chipotle on the weekends. Our rosters were a revolving door of people we entertained for fun and not for anything serious, because we wouldn't allow ourselves to be serious with anyone—re: the pledge. This was our fleeting youth—we believed naively. This was our moment to not care, because caring would enter the picture at graduation. We developed the roster between class and dating apps and people we met out. We made sure to keep degrees of separation between our roster members to keep ourselves free from drama. It was never about just being single—it was about prioritizing ourselves, each other, and the memories we could make free from romantic distraction— and it started to become sort of fun. I liked who I was when I wasn't worried what a boyfriend thought of my decisions. I liked who I was when I didn't have to tell someone where I was off to, or stay up late on the phone arguing or sexting. I liked who I was when I wasn't allowed to have a boyfriend, but I didn't like who I was when our game was over and we turned on the lights and I was still alone.

While you're out having a good time with your friends, here's some ways to keep it fun and light:

- Tell that group of people you just met that you and your best friends are fraternal twins who were separated at birth, and now you've reunited at college and are roommates.

- Set up a dating app date on the same day as one of your friends, or set up a first date with someone and ask them if they have a friend who'd like to join as a double date with one of your friends.

  RULE
  6

- Say yes to life. This is a moment for you to be fully, whole-heartedly, intentionally selfish.

  RULE
  7

Despite the fun I was having, I learned quickly that *casual* was not the word anyone would use to describe me. I am not a casual person. Casual hookups and sex and flings were incongruous with the formalities that had governed my former life. I did them anyway—thinking in supposed tos—and they made me feel horrible. Not because I didn't like hookups and fun, drunken nights, but because I was *forcing* myself to do these things—because I thought that's what single people did. I wanted to earn back my boyfriend privileges. I wished everyone would stop calling me "a serial dater." When my brother jumped from relationship to relationship, everyone called him a "good guy" and a "relationship type." When I did it, I was a serial dater. Little did I know, being single didn't have to mean casual sex every Friday night—it could mean whatever I wanted it to.

My single stretch should have been about the fun nights and the kissing and the vodka lemonades, yes, but *also* about deriving affirmation and validation from within instead of from outside sources (men). I managed half the equation—the easy part. I drank a lot and spent a lot of time exploring the city with my friends and kept my schedule so busy I had no time to breathe. But I believed, deeply, that I was better off with someone than without. I believed, truly, that my worth was only if and when I was someone's accessory.

RULE
8

In September 2020, after six months of COVID-19 lockdown, I moved to New York City. I was going to Columbia University's Graduate School of Journalism. I set up my windowless bedroom in an Upper West Side four-story walk-up and listened to *The Daily* podcast every morning so I felt like a "real" journalist. I put on a new costume, played a new part, convinced that this serious, intelligent version of me would win someone's heart. Part of me always knew I'd end up in New York. There was a newness in the move—in walking up the endless flights of stairs to my first New York apartment, in lugging my laundry to the laundromat across the street, in ordering from Halal Guys late at night. There was an intoxication in that—writers had been penning love stories to New York for hundreds of years before I arrived. I wanted to know *that* New York. I wanted to write about that New York, I wanted to be as bright and as loud and as drunk and as careless. But me being me, I cared slightly too much.

I'd been single for a year at that point, and I decided I'd paid my dues. I was ready to find a boyfriend. I decided that since I hated being single, I was not going to force suffering anymore. I was no longer seeing my midwestern therapist, Heather, but if I had been, I guarantee she would've told me I hadn't made any progress on self-affirmation and validation. She would've been proud of me for recognizing that I hadn't taken the final leap—and then she would've urged me, for the last time, to leap.

My mother always used to tell me that insanity is doing the same thing over and over but expecting different results. I always ignored her because I knew she was right. This, though, was surely different. I wasn't focusing my sights on fraternity boys—I was an adult now. I was living in the greatest city in the world and I was an accomplished twenty-two-year-old woman.

I went on a reckless, Carrie Bradshaw-esque journey to find a boyfriend via Hinge and Bumble and mutual friends. I remember telling myself I was doing it "for content." (Bonus lesson: You cannot just write off your toxic behavior by claiming it is "for content.") For four months I expended all my energy and hair spray and lip gloss on some decent nights, many horrible dates, and a handful of short-lived "situationships" (see later Rules of "The Talking Stage" for a more complete explanation of this kind of relationship). It was fun, it was funny at some points, but it was also exhausting—I'd been channeling all my energy into dating for months and I'd still had no success. To be honest, reflecting on it now—how could I expect someone to want to get to know someone who didn't know herself? I would never want to be with someone who avoided being alone for fear that they'd have to understand themselves. Why did I expect that others would?

One day I was on the phone with my mother discussing another fizzled-out five-date-long rendezvous.

"What if you just took a break from actively dating for a little while?"

Silence.

"I'm not saying you should stay single if you meet an amazing guy, but what if you just stop trying, so desperately, to meet someone?"

I brushed it off but when we eventually hung up her question lingered with me.

What if you just took a break from actively dating for a little while?

What if?

What *would* happen if I just took a break?

I pondered this, sitting on the lip of my unmade bed, looking at myself in the mirror. The key word was *actively*. It wasn't mutually exclusive. It didn't have to be all or nothing.

I'd never taken a break from active dating. I ended a relationship on the phone once and downloaded Hinge while I listened to him sniffle on the other end. I'd never just had myself and no-body else. Ever. It felt pathetic, as a self-proclaimed feminist, to step outside myself and realize this hollow truth. And it suddenly sounded kind of nice anyway. It was late fall. I had a thesis to write and a year to close out. If I took a break from actively dating, just for a little while, I realized, nothing terrible would happen. All that would happen is that I wouldn't have any sex I didn't want to have or waste my time on strangers who I didn't even like.

Nobody had ever told me before that single could look like con-tentment. Nobody told me I could be happy alone. Maybe I was supposed to know this inherently. But the truth is I didn't. And suddenly, I wanted to.

Who are you? The familiar question clamored in my skull.

I'd been forcing myself into situations where I could meet the one—swiping on dating apps until my fingers hurt. I'd al-ways happened to life and I never let life happen to me. I was always the one seeking, obsessively searching for someone to make me feel valid. But what if I let these things come to me instead? What if I just lived my life? What if I focused on Eli, and let things happen how they were meant to happen? What if I let people come to me, and in the meanwhile, I could happen to myself?

Who are you?

For the first time, I wanted to know.

RULE
9

I came up with "the 10% rule"—only 10 percent of my brain space would be occupied by any romantic or sexual pros-pects or, in my girl-boss attitude vernacular, conquests. The rest would be dedicated to me. Whoever I was. Who-ever I'd be. Whoever I could become.

I forced myself to get to know who I was as though I were a stranger meeting me for the first time. It takes time and energy to get to know a stranger and make them a soulmate or a friend. I was intentional about the things I did and made sure I was doing them for *me*—I interrupted each thought to make sure I was doing what I wanted to be doing, not because I thought a man wanted me to do it, or wear it, or think it. The influence of the male gaze is something really fucking hard to turn off. My intense desire to be affirmed by men existed in part because I didn't think I was supposed to affirm myself and in part because I saw myself as a nobody and figured I'd aspire to be someone's wife.

I wanted to understand how I'd internalized the patriarchy's misogynistic messaging and unpack my need for partnership and, furthermore, validation. I wanted to lay it all out on my bedspread and say: Okay, what if I redefined success not as having a boyfriend, but as getting my stories published, or going for a great run, or having a fun weekend with friends? What if I redefined failure not as male rejection, or being single, but as doing things solely for others instead of for myself? With each breakthrough came the realization that male validation will never and could never start my engine and keep it running. Only I can do that.

As stated prior, being single doesn't look like one thing. There's no right way to do it. Being single can mean hibernating and ordering takeout and rewatching *Sex and the City*. It can mean deleting your dating app profiles and focusing on work or school or just the life you have now. The love you have now, which is as wonderful as the new love that you could stumble on one day soon. It can mean a new sexual partner every weekend. It can mean going out dancing with friends and ignoring advances and looking for nothing at all. It can mean scrolling dating apps and getting set up and going home alone. It can mean being excited or a little lonely or sad or happy. It can be two, three, or all these realities at once.

They say Rome wasn't built in a day. It actually took 1,229 years to build it until its historic collapse. Just like how it took me about six years to realize that being single doesn't look one way. That I had to unwire the internalized misogyny and patriarchy built into my psyche without being electrocuted. That I feared myself without a partner and I ran away from myself until, like a boomerang, I was forced to come back and answer some questions: What things do I like, alone? What do I want to do in this life? What are my goals? What do I want to wear? Who do I want to kiss and dance with and eat dinner with and make friends with?

That fall, I made a lengthy bucket list of things I'd never done before in my life and hung it up on my wall, slowly making my way through it, a personal, grown-up version of what Sadie and I made in college. I tried a lychee martini, went to a comedy show in a basement and met a person I grew so fond of, visited my friends in new cities and ran over all the bridges in the five boroughs of New York. I wrote a great fucking thesis, traversing all Brooklyn to meet my sources. I dated New York City, and my friends, and I made impulsive decisions and let random people buy me tequila sodas at the bar and owed them nothing. I tucked myself in at night. I realized I could do anything alone or with friends I could do with a partner. Including have sex. Seriously, just buy a vibrator and then tell me you need a partner. You don't. Bonus points if you get a body pillow too.

I focused on myself, and I finally felt sort of free.

The journey to self-love is lengthy and often difficult and

it plants little seeds inside of you along the way. I read books I wanted to read, I cried, I tried things I'd always wanted to try, and I only did things because I wanted or needed to do them. I didn't date anyone seriously. I walked foreign roads, and I attempted things that scared the shit out of me. I dressed for me, ran for me, cooked for me, and prominently posted fearlessly on social media not so that anyone else would perceive me, but so I could finally perceive myself. Eventually the seeds sprouted tiny buds and then I looked down at the garden after a few months and it was vibrant and colorful and healthy and it was, importantly, self-made. It was by Eli, for Eli. I realized it's okay to want to be desired. We all want to be loved and desired. What isn't okay is when the want to be desired is your *only* want.

I met a group of people who have become my best friends and support system. I babysit their puppies and they dance with me in my living room. We have dinner parties on Thursdays and we go on long-winded walks together. I jump-started my career and felt myself take control of the wheel for the first time. I was proud of myself. I learned to parallel park and collected vibrators and tucked away menus from restaurants I loved eating at. I could affirm myself without questioning whether or not I deserved that affirmation. I could look at myself in a mirror and say, *Wow, that is a beautiful, beautiful human being looking back at me.*

•

RULE
14

If I told you today that you'd meet your soulmate in a year, you'd spend the next year living for YOU. You'd go on meaningless and stress-free dates, just because you could. Have fun sex when you felt like it and make core memories with your friends. You'd travel and dress for yourself and cut your hair and be radically selfish. You'd live like you weren't worried.

I decided to start living like that, and the gates to a new reality opened. One where life was good.

For a former serial dater, being single was hard and uncomfortable. It was trial and error. But eventually it became strangely addicting—liking myself is a druglike high that doesn't have a comedown. The rosters and the seemingly endless nights and the connections to friends and the self-affirmation and the way I finally viewed myself became something I enjoyed.

Who the fuck are you?

You are one of a kind. Which is pretty fucking cool. When you've got nothing else, you have the knowledge that there's only one of your brain. One set of your fingerprints. You are an amalgamation of memories and hard days and great days and your favorite season and smell and that one linen dress. You are a work in progress, you are a Picasso, you are a national treasure, you are trying your best, you are so fucking interesting—and there are people out there who will get to know you one day, and call their mom and say, "she's just incredible." You are a fully formed and valid and hot and exciting and sad and sexy and lost human being all on your own. You've been equipped with everything you need to go through it all. You are whole, and any person entering your life— friend, lover, or otherwise, will only add to your overflowing cup. You have your goals, you have your cake and sometimes life gets so good you get to eat it, too. Light the candles and make a wish; it's someone's birthday every day, after all.

So look at yourself in the mirror. Live like I told you your soulmate is around the corner. Allow yourself to feel validated in your singleness. Being single is no greater and/or worse than having a partner. Have your single nights. Go crazy. Get in bed at nine p.m. Read and read and read; you'll never run out of things to read. Get to know yourself. Keep a long roster and play hard to get and buy a vibrator and make core memories with your friends. We all want to fast-forward to the good part, but the fact of the matter is, the right choice is to always take the bad news first. Bad news teaches us something. It makes us work for the good stuff. Good news is when we celebrate naked with champagne. And good news can come when you're all by yourself or on your wedding day or when you're in the shower or hungover in bed. Don't run from the hard part, from the work in getting to know who you are. The hard part is your becoming. Treat yourself right first. Shake hands with you. The rest of it will all fall into place.

Rules for Dating Apps

1. On a dating app profile, 90 percent of the photos should be of JUST you.

2. Get a dating app ghost writer. Have your friends help you.

3. Make your prompts on your profile approachable— give people an easy in.

4. If a date is not set within forty-eight hours of connecting on a dating app, it is time to move on.

5. HUMOR is a green flag, always.

6. NO. SNAPCHAT.

7. You are the captain now. It is not all about if THEY like YOU. It's also about if you like them!

8. The stakes are low, so keep them low—you're just trying this person on!

9. The ten-date theory.

WHEN I WAS in seventh grade my mom took my brothers, me, and a friend to Atlantic City for the weekend. We stayed in the Borgata Hotel and swam in the pool and ate at Hibachi. Though I can't remember why we were there, I do remember us traversing the corners of the casino area of the hotel wearing bathing suits and flip-flops at nine a.m., and my mom commenting that most of the bug-eyed gamblers sitting (or sleeping) next to half-drunk martinis in plastic cups had been there all night. She said people come to Atlantic City for the casinos (Why did she bring twelve-year-olds there then? Unclear).

The only time I ever felt like one of those bug-eyed gamblers was when I dipped a toe into the world of dating apps and realized that, much like gambling, swiping on a dating app could be, and was, incredibly addictive. And if you play your cards right, you *could* theoretically come out a big winner. But usually, as the gamble goes, you just lose and end up in bed with a pint of ice cream. Dating apps are a gamble—some people hate them, some people love them, some people travel all the way to Vegas just to see it all through.

Online dating is like roulette or blackjack or a Wheel of Fortune slot machine. Listen—I'm not proud to admit it, but I was addicted to dating apps. I would stay up late into the night, swiping until I could hardly make out the faces of the questionably eligible options illuminated in front of my face. I would bet on some and not on others—taking risks that sometimes ended in a win, and others that ended in a somewhat shattering loss.

If you're addicted to validation from potential romantic partners (guilty), you may be entitled to financial compensation—or a lifetime supply of Tums for the heartburn. Kidding, but you may also be addicted to dating apps because the gratification and validation are instant—you can open the app and get asked on dates, flirt, and laugh at shitty pickup lines all in the first five minutes. Anytime you want it. If I wanted a quick compliment, to blow off steam, or a chat with a handsome stranger, a dating app it was. It often felt like my dating app persona was the most fearless, the sexiest, the most elite version of myself I'd ever be. Sad that I felt I'd never be her in real life.

When I look up the words *Hinge* and *Bumble* in my phone contacts, this is what comes up:

Kevin Hinge

Kyle Hinge

Jake Hinge

Chris Bumble

Henry Bumble

Max Hinge

Sanjay Bumble

Paul Bumble

Noah Hinge

I was a Hinge addict, and I loved it. I loved the swiping, the gratification, the game, and the gamble of it all. The way it felt to move things from the app to texting or Instagram DM, or even a first date. I liked being anonymous to people—a stranger—someone who they had no previous knowledge or perception of. It made me feel like I could be whoever I wanted to be.

It made me feel like someone could fall for me.

Let me be honest: when I was single, I spent a lot of time on dating apps—I paid for premium features and had a ritual like an evening prayer where I swiped through New York City's most and least eligible bachelors searching for a perfect match. I competed with myself on a daily basis, seeing how many matches I could get before my eyes grew too heavy to stay open. As unhealthy as this behavior was—as I was relying on the apps for all my validation—I sort of mastered the art of the dating app.

The dating apps weren't even about the boys messaging me and swiping right—they were about *winning*. About coming out advantageous. About feeling desired because I never felt much desire anywhere else. I was using them often for the wrong reasons, and yet . . .

Human beings are wired to crave some sort of connection. Think of the way you feel when you see your crush from across the room: you start sweating, your heart races, you feel nervous or giddy. Not to get scientific on you, but that's chemical. Some form of love.

Dating apps were the exact cocktail I thought I needed—affirmation, validation, human connection, and the potential to find someone who knows *nothing* about you. I didn't want someone to know the real me, anyway; I wanted them to know my profile. And a dating app gave me that ability. There are both benefits and drawbacks to online dating. For me, a drawback was centering online dating as a way to derive confidence—based on the external comments of strangers.

In a world where an Instagram DM is more popular than a phone call, Twitter is where we get our news, and TikTok is the most socializing some of us do in a day, dating apps allow us to seek out that craved connection. Naturally, flirting today happens more often online than in bars or at work or in coffee shops. Not to mention dating apps reached their peak during the Covid-19 lockdown—even if the dates that came from our matches were socially distanced walks, or outdoor dining in the middle of January. And the proof, I suppose, is in the pudding. These days, almost half of heterosexual couples meet their partners online. More people meet their spouses online than through mutual friends. And those are facts—you can look it up.

Most of my friends met their partners on dating apps, and Hinge's infamous slogan is, after all, "designed to be deleted."

I always wondered, then, if so many people are doing it, and not only that, finding success on these apps, why does it feel so taboo? Why does it embarrass us? Why does it cause us shame? And furthermore, why do we all wish we could have that early 2000s, spill-my-coffee-on-your-suit-or-dress, awkward-but-sparks-flying subway meet-cute instead of using the internet, like we do for everything else in our lives?

I remember the distinct feeling of shame when I downloaded my first dating app, Tinder, in the fall of 2017, my sophomore year

of college. In 2017, dating apps were *embarrassing*. I made my profile in silence and in secret, feeling a sense of shame creep over me
as I silenced notifications so nobody would know. As my roommates slept, I felt the tingle of energy in swiping and matching
and chatting. But among the tingle, I felt desperate—like I couldn't
find someone out at a bar or a party or in class, so I had resolved to
swiping through manicured profiles to find someone in the internet stratosphere instead. I used the internet to make everything in
my life a little bit easier, but for some reason, I didn't want to make
dating or love feel a little bit easier. I didn't want that convenience.
I wanted it to be difficult—so it felt worth something.

   Due to this shame, my Tinder career was short-lived. One chilly
October night, after a party, I opened up the controversial app. I
pushed through throngs of my sweaty, perfumed peers, holding
red cups with glassy eyes and wide smiles, until I reached the front
door of the infamous University of Michigan theater party house
and slipped outside alone. On the porch, people I barely knew
shared a cigarette and otherwise ignored me, which was good,
because at that moment I wanted nothing more than the icy thrill
of being ignored. I wanted to be seen as my curated online profile, and not as my shivering, naive, baby-faced self. I wanted to
be an airbrushed manic pixie dream girl. No peach fuzz, clogged
pores, waxed upper lip, and too loud voice. I sat on the curb, my
flushed cheeks lit by the glow of my Tinder matches, who I tried
to imagine as people and not profiles, to no real avail. I'd never
met up with someone on a dating app before, especially not a
dating app that was mostly used for sex, at least so I thought. I
wondered if the drunk, swaying passersby, Uber drivers, and old
women walking their dogs knew I was on Tinder. The pickings
felt slim but my options were still options. They were better than
nothing. While I debated just heading back inside and rejoining
my friends, a message popped up. The culprit's location showed
him just .2 miles away and he was asking me to come over. I

typed in his first and last name on Instagram—a quick check to ensure we had enough mutual friends that it seemed like a fine idea to accept his offer. "On my way," I typed briskly and started the voyage to my first ever Tinder meetup. I texted my friends to let them know I'd left to meet up with a guy, sending along my location. (In retrospect, I'm not sure I'd recommend going over to a stranger's home for your first meeting.) At that moment, I wanted to feel empowered by my brazen ability to meet up with guys on the internet. I was a writer, and I wanted to have something to write about—good or bad. *How had I stooped low enough to pivot to Tinder?* I wondered, as I shuffled closer to his house. But I decided I'd rather be ashamed than alone. Almost instantly— the minute the guy came to the door, actually—I regretted my decision and wanted to delete the app, forget the night, and be at home, in bed with a pizza. He didn't do anything wrong. In fact, he was really kind. He had a goofy smile and lanky limbs. He offered me a glass of water, and we sat on his bed and talked about school, our friends, football season, and other stupid but well-intended topics. He kissed me one time, for five seconds, and I pulled away, feeling panicked.

"I am so sorry," I said. "I think I want to go home."

Wordlessly, I stood up, shifted my top, grabbed my bag, and walked out of his room, racing down his carpeted staircase and out the front door. Three blocks away, I unmatched him on Tinder and deleted my whole account before running all the way home. My hasty exit is the exact reason I don't remember this poor boy's name—luckily, we must've done a decent job avoiding each other, because I never saw him again. Nobody ever knew about this except me, and him, and whoever he told.

On my miserable trek home I longed for the ease of high school flirting—the way we all passed each other around for brief makeouts and flirtations like handles of warm liquor. Now, the pool had opened—the options endless, and it was overwhelming, especially when the weight of the world felt like it was resting on an iPhone app's shoulders.

The shame from losing my dating app virginity only lasted so long, because just weeks later, after realizing that I was not going to find the love of my life in the basement of Delta Tau Delta (and under the guise that I needed a boyfriend desperately), I downloaded Bumble.

What makes Bumble different from Tinder is that women are required to message first. I wasn't sure I liked it, but at least it gave me a shred of control.

From the same bunk bed one evening, as I secretly swiped, matched, and scrolled through Bumble's profiles of Michigan students and Ann Arbor locals, I received a text message from a girl who lived in my hall freshman year. I hadn't seen her in a while, but she told me her good friend and I had matched on Bumble and that he was "really into me"—he'd allegedly been looking for ways to approach me on campus for a few months and hadn't found the proper in.

It was easy and natural to message and chat with someone I already had mutual friends with. That was one of the first things I truly liked about dating apps—they allow you to reconnect to people you never would have reached out to romantically had you not matched with them. It cultivates an appropriate circumstance to approach a previously unaddressed attraction, one that may be more difficult to re-create in the real world—it lets both parties know they're mutually interested with ease. On a college campus, you scroll through a dating app and you'll stumble upon profiles of friends' ex-boyfriends, roommates, freshman-year hallmates, classmates, and people you met a handful of times through clubs and activities. Sometimes matching with them on the app, though you know them in real life, helps to spark a conversation romantically you wouldn't have had otherwise. Using Hinge in New York City was different, as the pool was more open to utter strangers—

but I still managed to match with people who had serendipitous connections to my life (more on that later).

Bumble Boy quickly became Luke. What started as a simple, playful back-and-forth conversation poking fun at each other on a dating app became a full-blown relationship. We fell in love. He was my first true love, and my second true heartbreak. So I found love in a hopeless place: the yellow abyss that is Bumble. I had a dating app success story. Get her a gold medal because she made the dream come true. But the catch: for some reason, it was still taboo. We agreed that we'd tell everyone our mutual friend introduced us. We didn't dare tell our parents, or anyone else, that we'd met on a dating app. It was as though it was illegal and strange for us to have connected online opposed to in person. It often struck me that the two of us likely never would have met had we not both secretly downloaded Bumble. I never would've found myself in the throngs of infatuation and heartbreak and love and heartache. We never would've ridden bikes in Washington, D.C., in the summer. Our breakfast dates, shared weekends, and mutually learned lessons would never have taken shape. And even if we no longer know each other, I don't want to unknow the unique feeling that is my first love. Bumble gave me the first human being I ever saw everything, and eventually nothing, in. Though I unlearned his cell phone number and Starbucks order, the experience still hangs in the gallery of my life and it isn't something I despise and it isn't something I miss, either. It just is. I want it to be this way.

I didn't start admitting that we met online until after we'd broken up. It wasn't the fairy-tale meet-cute I thought I needed, but having it any other way wouldn't have felt right.

So all this leads me to a question I've often pondered: What the fuck is so taboo about a dating app? Why couldn't we just say we met on Bumble?

It isn't cringe if everyone is doing it. It's cringe to do it secretly. It isn't cringe if you've had great sex or good dates or perhaps fallen in love and planned a wedding or rewired your whole life because of Hinge or Bumble or Tinder or anything of the sort. It isn't cringe if you have a wonderful experience or a hilarious story to tell. Embarrassment is a choice, and my ex-boyfriend and I chose embarrassment and stigma instead of choosing the truth. I choose the truth every day now. We met on Bumble, we fell in love, and falling out of love hurt worse than anything I'd experienced. I'm on the other side now.

Tip #1: What if we treated dating apps like we do when someone approaches us at the bar? Many wouldn't dare match with a guy under six foot on Hinge but would happily let the hilarious and adorable five-foot-nine guy at the bar buy them a drink and kiss them before the night was over. The apps make us picky. Of course, if there's a major red flag, I'm not suggesting you ignore it and move forward. But we need to start differentiating between our wants and our needs when it comes to a partner. So treat dating apps as though you're meeting in a real room, face-to-face, except that room is virtual for your first meetup. These days, we're used to things being virtual, like it or not.

My parents met at a bar in Spring Lake, New Jersey. My father had to ask my mother's friend (whom he knew) for her home phone number. When he called, my mom didn't even really remember who he was. She had no way to look at a photograph of him, she had no cell phone to text him or reach out to him on. He called her on her parents' *landline* to ask her on a date. They didn't communicate between the phone call and the first date at all—they had no way to.

If I haven't convinced you yet, what's more awkward: a dating app or having to ask my grandfather over the phone if my mom was home?

You don't have to love dating apps, and you don't have to hate them—but they are convenient and can be fun and interesting and you can even be wildly successful on them if you just reframe the way you look at them. The stakes are low, the point is simply to get to know other people—lower the stakes, lower your expectations. Dating apps are allowed to be sort of like a game. If you play your cards right, you could win.

.

When I first moved to New York, I was determined to conquer Hinge dating. I was feeling starved for human interaction and attention, and I wanted to try out the whole "dating in New York" thing with fresh, new prospects. Twentysomethings in New York tend to be like horny soldiers preparing for battle . . . and the battlefield is dive bars and romantic, smoky speakeasies lining the East Village among pillows of trash and graffiti markings. Writers have spent decades droning on about how absolutely dreadful and isolating it is to date in New York City. But to me, it was sort of exciting—no matter what, and no matter when, there'd be thousands and thousands of options, and besides that, there's always something to do when you go on a date. And I really fucking like people. And if New York is good for one thing, it's our people. We've got lots, and they all have a good story.

How to Set Up Your Profile for Success

RULE
1

Step one to mastering Hinge is making a profile that is both approachable and funny. It is hard to brag about yourself. But the people swiping on your profile want to date YOU, not your friends. Having all but one to two pictures on your profile that are just of you is the way to go.

It also appears confident, and confidence is sexy. If you don't have a ton of pictures of yourself, make it a mission among your friends to go out for a day and take a ton of photos of one another for your dating app profiles—make it a group effort. And pro tip—bring costume changes! You don't want to be in the same outfit in all your photos, even if you did stage a shoot and take them all at once.

RULE 2

Dating is much more fun if you're in it with your friends. Sit around one night and project your profiles onto your television screen and get wine drunk, give one another some honest feedback, dedicate time to making a profile you're proud of that's also a decent representation of who you are. Use one of your friends as a ghost writer. If you pretend to be someone you're not online, you'll never find success offline, convincing people to fall for someone you're not. You can even project potential matches on the screen as well, and get some input from the peanut gallery.

RULE 3

Your dating app profile is your blank canvas, and you, the artist. Make it a glimpse into your life. Show them exactly what they'd get if they spent a night or a week or a year with you. If you have hot takes or preferences, or if you eat SpaghettiO's for dinner every night—INCLUDE that. The reason we don't want to fabricate our profile is that eventually, if you start meeting your matches in real life, they'll see that you aren't who you said you were. Don't waste your own time. Don't waste anyone else's time either. If you're looking for something casual, be up-front. If you're looking for a partner, be up-front. Put out what you'd like to get back. You want transparency, you don't want your own time wasted. Your energy is your currency; don't go broke trying to be someone you're not so someone you'd never like or even love in the first place likes you.

I love the prompt features, because they allow you to share a little about yourself and also give people easy chances to slide in and start a conversation. Dating apps, in general, tend to be a little intimidating—so make it easier on everyone and create prompts that are "slide in-able."

Some ideas I love:

Ask a question with your prompt
Tell a crazy story
Two truths and a lie
My favorite hot take is . . .
How to ask me out . . .
My ideal date . . .
Fuck, Marry, Kill . . .
The craziest thing that's ever happened to me . . .

If I have one rule for dating apps, it's to remember that they're for *dating*—meaning whatever you want it to mean, but chiefly, meeting in person. So after thirty-six to seventy-two hours of chatting with someone, take it off the app and go to another medium (but never Snapchat) to make plans. If you're worried about safety, move it to Instagram DM—but remember, you're on the app to make plans, not to have a pen pal. Another rule: While the first thing we notice about someone's profile is whether or not we're attracted to them, and attraction is necessary, it isn't everything (unless you're looking to get that head, get that bread, and peace out). So if you're looking to get to know someone, make sure it seems you align on something other than the physical. I think a person's biggest strength is when they're more attractive in person than they are online, and they're equally funny online and in person. I used to have a personal rule that I'd never answer a dating app message that opened with the single word *hey*. You deserve

RULE
4

RULE
5

more than a hey. You want to go on a date with someone who has a sense of humor, who tries to make the dating app rapport a little less awkward. You can have sex with a "hey," and it can even be good sex, but don't you dare go out to dinner with a "hey."

Also, don't be a "hey" yourself. I know you're more creative. You don't have to open it up with "when's our wedding," but a reaction to one of their photos or prompts is more engaging than a pleasantry.

So remember, you can fuck a hey, you can't eat pasta with a hey, and you should never give another adult your Snapchat—grown people can send text messages.

Your mindset here is everything. Keep the stakes as low as you can—of course, you're going to be concerned as to whether or not people like you, but remember to ask yourself "Do I even like them?" It's hard for me to say "don't take it seriously!" when, for many people, dating IS serious, and at first, I took the apps way too seriously myself. I looked at every potential match as a future husband, and not as what they are—a stranger. Someone I don't know, who I may never meet, or who I may meet only once, or who I may see five or six times. But really, don't take it seriously—just have fun with it: go on a few dates, chat with a few people, decide what you like and don't like, experiment a little. Remember, everybody is in the same boat. The boat may be a life raft and you may be adrift, but you're in it together. Nobody is on a yacht docked in Capri. We're all on the fucking shitty little lifeboat reinforced with duct tape just trying to get to shore. Sometimes we find someone with a life jacket, sometimes we find someone to paddle with or paddle toward. Sometimes we make it to shore alone before deciding the water wasn't so bad at all or that we'd like to stay on land for a while.

A word of advice if you're dating and swiping in pursuit of a relationship: nothing is going to work out until something does. Every date, relationship, talking stage, and one-night stand is not going to work, until just one does. I put an unearthly amount of pressure on each message sent and received in the early days of my Hinge usage and it made each and every rejection a tougher pill to swallow. I didn't know what I didn't know back then, and my heart paid the price.

My first Hinge faux pas concerned a guy we'll dub Joe. We matched on Hinge and immediately hit it off. He was funny and charming and cute and I fell for all of it. Before we'd even met we had inside jokes, and I'll admit, I was nervous for our first date because the chemistry was electric via text. We ate quesadillas and talked for five hours and made out on the West Side Highway under a tree at the end of August. If a cop had passed us, we would've been arrested for public indecency—it was risqué, and late at night in the heat of summer and it was hot in general. I felt like Carrie Bradshaw. He used his hands well and made me laugh and I instantly felt drunk in his presence. Immediately I started to envision what it would be like if we dated. He had plans to move into Manhattan soon, and I could see us together into my future. My brain projected our happily ever after as I took a cab back up to the Upper West Side when we parted ways at two in the morning. The day after our first date, we went on a second one. We poured bottles of wine into our reusable water bottles (Sustainable Queens) and got drunk walking over the Brooklyn Bridge as the Manhattan skyline illuminated the dark sky at sunset. It was uniquely romantic for such a small blip. It happened in a nanosecond when I wanted it to linger. Standing on the bridge, breathing side by side, I spent five minutes wondering about the possibilities for us. It was then that Joe told me that he couldn't tell his parents about our budding romance (for reasons that are too convoluted to get into here). I continued seeing him anyway, deciding that it was worth it, and his parents were his problem. Visions of us growing together projected in my mind like a well-curated slideshow—we'd make the same stupid jokes at our wedding, always be laughing, always holding hands, always enamored. Yet, I had a gut feeling, which I ignored, that we couldn't keep seeing each other if we were going to be lying about it. So, eventually, consumed with guilt, I asked him to tell his family or end it. He chose to end it. Some days I wish I hadn't planned our wedding in my brain, because the rejection stung.

Eventually I reveled in the reality of this fast-burning fire, quickly extinguished: most things aren't going to work out. That's why it's all the more tantalizing when one thing does. Nothing is going to work out until something does. And we never know who or what or when that something will come.

I remedied the sting of rejection with more swiping, more matches, and more dates. I met a guy who asked me to go on a run through Central Park, who I never saw again, until he moved into my neighborhood and went viral on TikTok; now I run into him once a week or so. I met a thirty-year-old with shaggy brown hair on Bumble who made me a lot of amaretto sours; eventually he told me that four months prior he'd left his girlfriend of nine years and moved out of the apartment they shared. He pointed at the table where our Bondi sushi takeout sat and said, "She took everything but gave me this table." He told me they'd been in couple's therapy for months before he ended it. I met another thirty-year-old who ordered the most expensive wine on the menu and came on too strong for my liking. I met a guy in dental school I had nothing in common with, a guy I went to college with who was so sweet but wound up ghosting me. I swiped and swiped and swiped until I was matching and hanging out with guys who had the same name and I couldn't keep track. If you're dating more than two Maxes at once, you've maxed out. I needed a spreadsheet or an assistant or something. But all this dating app experience is how I developed my "ten-date theory," which I swear by religiously. The theory is as follows: If you go on ten dates with ten different men from a dating app, five of them are going to be one date and done, five of them are going to be viable. Of the five viable dates, one will ghost you, one will be a one-night-stand situation, one will not be looking for anything serious, and the final two will be potential matches. Of those two, one will fall through, leaving you with the last one: a potential partner.

I always, always try to make things simple, because otherwise, my brain tends to overcomplicate them. So when I look at online dating, I look at it in very simple terms. All you're doing is expediting the process of organically finding someone. All you're doing is getting to know someone to see if they could fit somewhere in your life. The worst-case scenario is that nothing comes of it. The best case: those chats are a domino, and one domino after another starts to fall. A few mediocre dates could oil my wheels and prepare me for the best date of my life. You never know what's waiting around the corner. You never know how one conversation could catapult you into the best version of your life.

My now boyfriend and I met after I matched with his friend on Hinge. The friend and I never met in person, but we exchanged a few messages and our social media handles. Months later, he had found love in another Hinge match and reached out to me, on a whim, asking me if I'd like to be set up with his friend. I said yes.

Two years later, sitting at an airport bar next to my boyfriend, drinking beers and waiting for our flight to his hometown to board, I pondered the funny way life shook out. Shit happens in very strange ways. If I hadn't matched with that friend, we wouldn't be sitting here with our knees angled toward each other, laughing into beer foam.

Dipping a toe in the water is easy when you realize the water is what you make it. I hardly doubt anyone's sitting around saying, "Dating apps are the best, I hope I meet the love of my life on Hinge and not because we somehow stumble into each other while living inside of a rom-com." It doesn't have to be great. It can be fine. It can be awkward. But it can also be a catalyst, a lightning bolt, a unique opportunity to just find out what you're looking for, what you don't want at all, or what you need from the world and from yourself.

What I'd wish I'd known is my now bible: nothing is marriage until it's marriage, and even then, it isn't marriage. Nothing is permanent. You're never stuck anywhere. You're only forced to commit to yourself. So you might as well swipe fucking right on you.

I'm an introvert, yet the type of person who craves the intimate ease of good, warm, dense human connection. Of meeting someone who has a soul so bright it illuminates your face through their T-shirt. I crave the empathy that comes with being in someone else's dazzling orbit. Dating apps can do that. A bike ride can lead to forever. A glass of wine can lead to good sex or an earth-shattering realization. A table for two can lead to something or everything, but it never leads to nothing. Even an ache is something. Hangovers, hickeys, emotional roller coasters—all inevitable and all feeling. And what a gift to feel.

Once I was on a plane next to Luke, my Bumble boyfriend, and it was about to take off. We'd just gotten into a fight about something real and relevant and parallel to the future happiness we'd desperately fought for.

"Do you want to be together?" he said.

The wheels of the plane started whirring and the engine started and the sound made my brain want to explode. I looked up at his eyes, before the plane took off. I wanted to say yes but nothing came out.

We both knew, I think, that my answer was yes, but we would fall apart anyway. But I don't regret matching with him on that app. Finding us and then losing us.

Swipe right, swipe left, match, miss, chat, meet, and keep the stakes just low enough that there's still a little fire lit under your ass. It just takes one swipe to rewire your life, be it through conversation, sex, or connection. But most prominently, none of this experience is just for finding love or partnership. It's about becoming someone you'd want to swipe right on yourself. It's about being a match for you—because if you wouldn't swipe right on yourself, nobody else will either. It's hard to be obsessed with yourself—it feels weird. But step outside yourself and be someone you'd want to swipe right on. Be that person on the screen and off. Be your own breath of fresh air, your own striking first impression, your own version of approachable and cool. Be bold enough to swipe right on you. Because even if you run out of matches or it just isn't working out, you'll never find it in you to unmatch yourself once you get bold enough to swipe right.

Rules for Flirting

1. Flirting is supposed to be fun.

2. Keep the Immature vs. Mature flirting breakdown in your back pocket at all times.

3. Make eyes with the person you fancy, hold it for three seconds, then look away. Do this three times.

4. Make sure that they do not have another person with them, that they appear single.

5. The most attractive thing you can be is confident. GO THRIVE. Touch your hair, smile, enjoy your friends. Your prerogative is having a good time.

6. Enter with a compliment. Everyone likes a compliment. Even if they reject you, they will still think fondly of the interaction.

7. Later, ask them to do a shot with you. Eye contact is king here.

8. Maneuver a DFMO (dance floor makeout) when the time is right.

9. Figure out their intentions yourself.

10. Flirting with your long-term partner is possible (and healthy).

MY FIRST COLLEGE class freshman year was called Introduction to Drama. It was located in a dark, windowless basement classroom in the drama building, and the vast majority of students in the class were theater majors. I was so nervous for the first class of my undergraduate education that I got up three hours early to get ready. I brushed through my long hair, haphazardly put on an eclectic mix of drugstore makeup, picked out my favorite jeans and white floral cropped blouse, and upon reflection, the ugliest J.Crew sandals I have ever owned. I had a purple backpack with a gray puffball keychain attached to it and a deep fear that nobody was going to like me.

I am, as some are, a sweaty person. Whenever I go anywhere, I require a five-minute buffer to find a bathroom, reapply deodorant, chug a water, and regulate my own body temperature. Despite this, I was the second person to arrive at the classroom, and I fiddled with my pen and notebook as I waited for the rest of the students to file in.

Ezra was a lanky sophomore with dark hair and glasses, wearing a T-shirt with his fraternity on it (red flag), which was a grouping of three words I'd grow all too familiar with in the coming year. He was a math student who did improv comedy (another red flag) and my first impression of him was nothing sensational. I will not pay many compliments to Ezra. However, I will give him this: he was excellent at flirting. I'll never forget noticing him looking at me from across the oval wooden table, the way it felt to have a stranger's eyes on me—the way it felt to feel wanted. But even still, for me, it wasn't love at first sight. It was just . . . first sight.

You know when someone utterly fucks you over and it's all the more frustrating because you never thought they were *that* attractive to begin with? After it all ends, you're sobbing in your bed to your best friend as she combs through your matted hair and you're, like, "Literally what the FUCK. I DIDN'T EVEN LIKE HIM AT FIRST. HE forced *ME* to like *HIM*."

Well . . . this was one of those.

As class was dismissed, I packed up my things and beelined to the elevator, too insecure to make small talk with my new classmates. As I waited for the elevator and pretended to be engrossed by something on my phone, I felt someone come up behind me.

It was the seemingly unremarkable improv comedy math major whose name had slipped me.

"You're Eli, right?" he asked. These three words were the beginning of the most disastrous, unorganized, clumsy relationship of my life.

He introduced himself and instantly began asking me questions, giving constant eye contact, and using future-leaning statements, suggesting I'd have to come by a fraternity party sometime, or that he looked forward to seeing me that Wednesday, at our next drama class.

Our short exchange of words, just that brief interaction, made me feel somehow special, like he'd lit a spark somewhere inside me. Like I was a candle and he was the only person in the world, or in Michigan, with a match. He looked at me when he spoke like he was anticipating my every word. He smiled in a way that seemed welcoming but mysterious. He'd boldly approached me, a stranger, and made me feel wanted.

Someone I'd felt no grand attraction to became someone I hoped to run into as often as I possibly could. I looked for him around campus. At the career fair, I purposefully wore a top that showed off my boobs and made sure I smelled like coconuts and marched up to his improv comedy club's table to pretend I was going to audition. He later told me that when I walked away (like I was the hottest woman at the career fair) his fellow improv members all gave him a knowing look—he was flirting with me, and I was, like a horny boomerang, sending it right back. He was a strong flirter. He had an A+ in flirting. A gold medal. He made me feel special but was simultaneously hard to attain or pin down. He was the perfect cocktail of effortless and casual, mysterious and cunning, coy and sweet.

Eventually, of course, we exchanged phone numbers and made out at two in the morning under a tree by the back door of my freshman-year dorm building. He gave me his high school cross-country windbreaker and it was so fucking ugly and smelled like stale beer, but I slept in it for a week.

But just because we started a little situationship didn't mean the flirting was over—it was just executed in advanced and more intricate ways.

I was so distracted by him in class that I nearly failed. I hardly paid attention, just watched as he wrote my name over and over and over in his notebook in curly handwriting. Being flirted with felt like someone poured ice cold water into my veins but I still couldn't quench my thirst. The thicker the pour, the more I craved it.

The "slow burn flirt" is genius when executed well, and it makes your prospect hang on every syllable. I was a puppy, and he was a tennis ball. As he hurled himself to the other side of the world, I followed in glee. Being flirted with in this way was a master class on how to flirt myself. They say you can't outdo the doer, but in fact you can, if you just become smarter and hotter than the doer. Flirting with him was ecstasy.

Intro to Drama, otherwise known as Intro to Flirting, made me an expert on the subject. I am a flirting savant. A flirting wizard. I can tell you what someone wants with you based on how they're flirting, and how to get what you want based on how you flirt.

The cardinal rule of flirting: it is supposed to be fun. This isn't supposed to be anxiety inducing or stressful, and if it is, you have to change your mindset around it.

The stakes are incredibly low when we flirt: either someone is going to think you're trying to let them know you're interested, or they're going to think you're super nice and friendly, because when we flirt in waves, we ensure that we don't embarrass ourselves. We allow the other person to give us the cues, even when we're instigating the flirting (more on that later).

Flirting is FLATTERING. Getting hit on is an ego boost. The worst-case scenario of a flirt-gone-wrong is that the object of your affections doesn't reciprocate in the moment. That could be for any number of reasons: they're not interested in a relationship right now, they have a partner, they're out with their friends and don't feel like incorporating other people in the mix, and so on. Really, it's not that deep. Typically, if we're hit on (in a respectful, noninvasive, and nonthreatening way) even if we're not interested, we walk away feeling flattered or slightly inflated—because someone had found us attractive enough to shoot their shot. And that feels good.

So now that we have that out of the way, I'm going to give you a rundown of the five types of flirting: immature flirting, online flirting, mature flirting, relationship flirting, and friend flirting. A couple of notes before we dive in: The baseline with all types of flirting is respect. Take cues from the person you're flirting with to ensure that they're comfortable. Don't come on too overtly sexual, too invasive, or too presumptuous. Especially with a stranger, or someone you're meeting for the first time, as you don't know their boundaries or comfort levels. Dip a toe in. And don't put up with someone making you uncomfortable because you think it's better than being alone. It isn't.

Immature flirting is the type of flirting we do with the goal of getting physical with the person we're flirting with. We're looking to go home with them, make out with them, and/or start a very casual hookup relationship with them. Immature flirting most commonly takes place at night—at parties, bars, clubs, and other places where one would find alcohol and the song "Closing Time."

Immature flirting is two things: easy and fun. It requires a good deal of confidence and a short-term end goal. Keep your eyes on the prize, but if you have to close one eye to focus on calling your Uber, stop while you're ahead, and go order a pizza. Though immature flirting is typically seen in party-adjacent settings, it can still be executed soberly or in our waking hours as well.

It's January 2020—I'm wearing black jeans, black booties, and a black tube top. It is 12°F outside but I do not wear a jacket. My chin-length hair is glossy and pin straight, and I have my token redhead on my arm to navigate us through crowds of our drunk, sweaty peers in a bar called Skeeps. The bar is a little like a panopticon—it has tiers, allowing those on higher floors to look down to the lower ones. You never know who could be watching you. We gracefully elbow our way up to the top floor and secure two pitchers of tequila soda with extra lime.

That night I'd entered with a plan: I was going to immature flirt (successfully, to completion) with a six-foot-four Gemini in glasses. Naturally Sadie and I had a rule: we ended our evening with boys or a pizza. And we had to be on the same page. That night was a boy night, thank goodness, because I had a thorough scheme plotted out in my brain.

Once I spotted him, I kept myself in his line of sight and waited for him to spot me. Being that we knew each other vaguely, if he was interested, there was a chance he'd approach me if I gave him the classic, quick, three-second eye contact hold, inviting him over with my gaze. Once we locked eyes, he approached me, and a little bell went off in my head: let the games begin. This was all meant to be fun, and because I had no concern about being rejected (rejection is simply redirection, embarrassment is a choice), I was ready.

RULE
3

RULE
4

> Eye contact is a great way to signal to someone across the bar that you're interested. It's low stakes, and if they're interested back, they'll likely come approach you. Three seconds, three times. Foolproof. But back off if you see them with someone else out of courtesy. You wouldn't want someone flirting with your partner across the bar, would you?

Immature flirting requires confidence. Confidence is the ultimate outfit-completing accessory. Looking around, I knew I was more annoying and less conventionally attractive than other girls in the bar (by some arbitrary standard), but I was more confident than anyone in the room, more willing to put myself out there, and less inclined to care if someone said no. Those three things combined made my odds of succeeding higher than if I was just standing around waiting for someone to approach me. Furthermore, I was looking to flirt not because I wanted validation from the guy (though it never hurt), but because I wanted to have a little fun, and this was how I was going to do it.

RULE
5

The key to success in flirting is always confidence. We are like magnets—we gravitate toward the energy we put out ourselves. So to attract a confident, fun, exciting person on a night out, you have to be exuding that same energy.

Once you have the object of your affection engaged in conversation, it's time to launch into the four waves of immature flirting.

Wave one: a subtle (consensual) touch
Wave two: a compliment

Wave three: an inside joke
Wave four: leaning in

Wave one—the number one way to tell someone "I'd like for you to take me straight out of this bar and into your bed"—is to ask them to compare hand sizes with you. I actually think Jesus Christ made this one up because it is, truly, my scripture. I'll let you know why: it is an excellent excuse to touch someone consensually, it is an excellent excuse to make someone feel like you think they are sexy, and it is an excellent gauge of how someone's feeling about you. If they compare hand sizes with you and quickly retract the physical touch or try to reroute the conversation, yellow light. If they refuse to compare hand sizes with you, red light. If they lean into it, squeeze your hand, hold it, or find an excuse to linger, green means go baby.

If you've passed by wave one with flying colors, it's time for wave two. That's when you're going to pay them a compliment. Compliments are currency when it comes to flirting, because everyone likes to be complimented. So even if the person isn't interested in you, they'll be flattered.

"You have such nice eyes, I like your glasses," is what I said, because people hardly ever compliment straight men on their eyes. He thanked me, locked eyes with me, and told me mine were more beautiful. The reciprocation was another green light, signaling that it's time we move on to wave three.

At this point, I know he's at least interested in something about me, because he hasn't found an out to walk away from me, has given in to all my little tactics, and we've developed a good rhythm, a nice rapport, and we were surrounded by our peers, meaning if he wanted to walk away, he could've.

Wave three is just about finding absolutely anything to make a little joke over with this person—and luckily at a bar, there's decent enough people-watching so you should be able to latch on to something.

My easy-in was poking fun at him for sliding into my DMs earlier that night. But get creative—poke fun at their T-shirt, whatever they're drinking, or the way they dance. And if you have absolutely nothing else to work with, ask them to take a shot with you.

If you've successfully immature flirted your way through the first three waves, it's time to lean in: DFMO time.

The moment before you start making out with someone in a bar is the most incredible three seconds of your life. Around you, it feels like the world turns so fast that everyone else is just a color. Just a blur. Even if the person on the other side of your lips is an utter stranger, it is one of the most romantic and tantalizing of all human experiences. And hot take: I love the taste of cold beer on someone's mouth while everyone else watches.

Now that you've learned how to immature flirt correctly, let's set the record straight: If someone is immature flirting with you, you can almost guarantee they're looking for something casual or fleeting. And that is TOTALLY okay. But if you're not looking for something casual, I wouldn't attempt to immature flirt your way into a relationship. You will be wasting your precious time and energy on someone with different priorities.

We can often tell what someone is looking for with us based on how they flirt with us. It might sting to realize someone you're interested in dating is immature flirting with you. But here's the truth of the matter: by telling you the inside scoop, I just saved you a lot of hurt and a lot of time. Why would you ever want to *beg* someone to fall in love with you? Here's the truth: no matter how much you like someone, you don't want to do that. You deserve someone who WANTS to be with you, not someone you have to convince to be with you. The right person would never put you in a position where you find yourself begging.

I cannot describe to you how much I wished for guys who were immature flirting with me to fall in love with me. And it wasn't their fault that they didn't. I was interpreting their signals how I wished, instead of facing the facts. Immature flirting probably won't lead to an engagement ring and a family of five. It'll lead to potentially really great sex and his picture frame falling off the wall and giving you a black eye, which will then lead to you with a bag of frozen peas on your bruised face in his bed, killing the moment but making for an excellent memory (clearly).

I was the girl on the couch with my roommates, sipping iced coffees, braiding my hair, listening to the original *Call Her Daddy* podcast serve us a shoddy bible of how the fuck we were supposed to flirt. But what that podcast, and everyone else, failed to tell us—we don't have to wait for someone to give us a cue, or give us the time of day. We don't have to wait for someone to come up to us. We don't have to dress and act so that someone will approach us. We're allowed to give our own cues. We're allowed to give someone else the time of day. We're all in the driver's seat of our very own car.

When the world smelled like the strong aroma of college: perfume, hormones, sticky basement floors, vodka and beer—immature flirting was a golden ticket. It was all we knew how to do. It was how we interacted when we were twenty years old and a little stupid. And it was fun.

•

Now let's talk about online flirting. When I say online flirting, I mean flirting on social media, mostly. I mean the coveted, the cringe, the insanely wonderful type of message that is best known as "sliding into the DMs." I mean the late-night Snapchat, the direct message on Instagram, the dating app pickup line, and the LinkedIn message (if you are to be so bold).

I think, personally, that in this digital age, a DM slide is our most effective way to tell someone "I'm interested in you" and just cut to the chase. First of all, many times, we develop crushes on local baristas, friends of friends, classmates, acquaintances, and people we met one time, for five minutes—how else are we going to get in contact with that person, other than hope serendipity may have us run in to each other again? Using Instagram to connect or reconnect to that person is a really simple way to, for lack of a better phrase, shoot your shot.

When I was nineteen years old, I was having my very first original play produced through a student organization at Michigan. My friend, who was a junior at the time—and a member of an improv group, of course—was directing it.

Her good friend, and fellow improv group member, stopped by our audition room one day to say hi. He was also a junior, a phenomenal actor, and really hot. I'm not sure I've ever had my ego inflated more than when he texted her, later that night, "Eli the bat is hot." He meant BTA (bachelor theater art), which was my major in the theater program, but being a bat was fine by me.

At this point, back in the same drafty drama building basement, I wanted to put the flirting techniques I had learned in Introduction to Drama to work. So, I did the most low-stakes thing I could do and followed him on Instagram. Following someone on a social media app is an action with absolutely no connotation attached to it—but it can dissolve into an incredibly flirtatious move. Before I could calculate my next steps, he followed my lead and slid into my DMs. Had he not, I likely would've slid into his, or gone back in his photo archive and liked a really old photo, just for fun.

He sent me a picture I'd posted earlier in the evening, holding a coffee cup from beloved Michigan student coffee spot Espresso Royale. His DM read something to the effect of, Are you an Espresso Royale fan?—and it was the perfect segue for him to ask me to get coffee sometime.

If I was going to instruct you on the best way to slide into someone's DMs, I'd say take the easy way out and swipe up on a story they put up. If you're nervous about sliding into the DMs, remember that you could always mask your message as a genuine question or a compliment—gauge where their head is at and if you don't want to follow through, then you head back to the bench and try again next time.

If there isn't a story for you to respond to, I say just go for it anyway. The thing is, if you're sliding into the DMs, it's obvious what you're doing, and you may as well just own up to it. A simple "Hey! It was great to meet you at xyz party on Saturday, just wanted to say hi and let you know I think you're really cute" works just fine.

What I want you to do after you send said DM is delete the message from your Instagram chats—that way you cannot check if they've viewed the message. The only way you'll know if they open it is if they respond. Out of sight, out of mind.

And besides, what's the worst-case scenario if you send a DM? They don't respond.

A lack of response may mean a variety of things, but it doesn't make you undesirable, or weird, or unworthy. It just means that the person at the receiving end of your DM didn't want to respond, and you wouldn't want to be with someone who wouldn't have the decency to even like the message.

The key to online flirting is intentionality. Be intentional. If you want something casual, use Snapchat, or be explicitly casual. If someone asks you to dinner but you're thinking more of a Netflix and chill situation, say that. If you want something a little more serious, if you're looking for something more—suggest that. If you slide into the DMs and the person suggests a movie night at theirs, ask if they'd rather get lunch or coffee.

The ball is in everybody's court. If you are intentional, nobody gets hurt feelings. If you are up-front about what you're looking for when you're flirting, you stay on the same page as the other person, and set the precedent that honesty is key when navigating the rough terrain that is flirting.

•

There is a way, of course, to flirt in pursuit of a relationship—and we call this methodology mature flirting.

Mature flirting is a method of flirting that can be executed romantically and platonically, which I think makes it all the more necessary to master. Mature flirting is most commonly executed on dates, in meet-cute settings, with new friends, and romantically between individuals who are dating in the pursuit of a relationship.

When we mature flirt, we're focusing on getting to know someone. We're looking at longevity, an opportunity to widen your circle to this person and let them in—and not just one night, or several (depending on how long your sneaky link or acquaintance may last).

I was a nervous wreck on my first date with Nate, whom I dated for a few months in the summer and fall of 2019. I'd had a crush on him for the longest time and thought he was enigmatic and sexy. I couldn't believe he was interested in going on a date with me. I started with online flirting: I sent him a DM about a book he posted on his story. Then one night, under the guise of a little liquid courage, I sent a message.

"I want you to know that I think you're really cute and would love to go on a date with you in New York City this summer."

He didn't respond that night. But the next morning, he sent me a message.

"I wanted to wait until you were sober to respond to make sure you still felt that way this morning," he said.

"I do," I replied.

"I'm glad," he said.

And then another message: "I think you're really cute too. When do you get home? Let's go out for drinks."

Instead of showing up to said drinks and saying, "I hope we fall madly in love," I brought him a book of poems. We bonded a lot over books. It's how our friendship began. We were at the Jimmy, a rooftop bar with a pool on top of a hotel. I used a fake ID to get in. He was twenty-three. I was twenty. It was embarrassing but so was everything back then.

We sat on a bench lining the pool and drank a cocktail with julienned cucumbers in it.

When I told him I thought it was funny that there were julienned cucumbers in a cocktail, he said, "Who's Julianne?"

We laughed about it.

Then I pulled out the book and said it was one of my favorites, and I thought he might like to read it. It was my way of saying: *I want you to think about me while you read these poems and then I want you to call me on the phone and tell me everything you thought about all of them. I want to know the words you paused on, the way you felt when you set it down. I want to know if you read the book on the subway, or in bed at night. I don't ever want you to give it back to me.*

It helped that the collection of poems I gave him were erotic poems. I'm nothing if not bold.

He took the book from my hands and told me he had a new standard, that he'd never go on another date if the girl didn't bring a book with her. And then he kissed me. It was fucking insane. I was on top of the world, or a SoHo hotel, but you get it. We made out for two hours and all I could think about was how he knew exactly what I was trying to say, without saying it. And his kiss told me that he wanted to think about me when he read the poems. And that he did. Cover to cover.

Mature flirting isn't done in waves, because we already know both parties are on board—we've moved past immature flirting.

The first step to successfully mature flirt: show interest in your differences. If I'm on a date with someone who's never heard of Patti LuPone, but he figures out he should ask me what my favorite musical is, that's a huge green flag.

The second step to successful mature flirting: recall facts about the person they mentioned previously. If this is a first date, and their Hinge profile said they've watched *The Office* series nineteen times, ask them for their hottest hot take. Pam and Jim: toxic or true love? It's flattering when someone remembers an intimate or small detail about us. If you're meeting up with a girl you met in your elevator for drinks, and she had a dog with her on your first meeting . . . ask her about her dog. If it's a second date, and on the first they mentioned their twin sister had a big interview that day, ask them how it went for her the next time you see them.

Another great way to send the "I like you" signal when flirting—speak in future tense or bring up future events. If you've been on five dates with this person, and it's your birthday the following week, you can say, "Should we do something to celebrate?" If they bring up an artist you both love, and you know they're having a concert in a few weeks, mention that and see if they want to go together.

If you bring up your favorite restaurant, and they say they've never been before, you have a perfect entry point to say, "We should go sometime soon!"

Obviously, on the first date, if they bring up their grandmother's lake house, it isn't the appropriate time to say, "I can't wait to see it sometime!" Conversely, if they try to make plans to jet off to Europe with you on the first date, you need to be cautious of love bombing.

Tread lightly with how you're speaking about the future, but, if it feels right, you can reference the future to subliminally say, "I'd love to continue to see you, or, I'd love to do this or experience that with you."

Finding an opportunity to brush someone's hand or arm, or

finding your way into holding their hand, is inherently intimate and flirtatious. I would not hold hands with a man I was trying to have a one-night stand with. I would not hold hands with a man I made plans with via Snapchat. That's called boundaries. But holding someone's hand, brushing their arm, asking them interesting and important questions about the things that matter to them—is exactly how you say, "I really like spending time with you."

We spend most of our lives trying to say something without saying it. Everything would be a hell of a lot easier if you could walk up to a perfect stranger standing in the bar looking gorgeous and say, "Should we go home together right now?" Everything would be so much simpler if we could, on a first date, say, "I really want to fall in love with you." But the vast majority of us are looking at easing ourselves into what we want, because jumping off the high dive is scary and sometimes the impact can hurt. So we go after what we want without explicitly saying what we want—and that, my friends, is flirting.

·

Flirting, of course, isn't just used as a tactic to get someone to be a part of your life—it is used to maintain those relationships as well.

RULE
10

If you *do* mature flirt your way into a relationship, and if you do flirt your way into love—the flirting doesn't end there, either. I'm a firm believer that some goals limit us because they curb our potential. If your goal is to get into a relationship with a person, and you make it there, you can't just stop flirting because your goal has been met. Every relationship needs a dash of flirting to keep it alive and well.

A relationship runs on flirting. It is the gas it needs to go the distance. The flirting will look different, because you're no longer trying to say things coquettishly without saying them outright—and you pee with the door open and they hold you while you have your weekly mental breakdown—but it'll still be flirting, and you're allowed to still be flirting even when someone has seen you at your lowest point.

Sometimes we forget that we should be flirting with our partner, and being actively in love with them—in a much different way than when we first met, but special nonetheless. Just because they sleep beside us in bed every night doesn't mean the goal has been met or we arrived at the destination. It just means we decided to get in the car together, and we take turns driving and the goals change as we do.

Now, the goal is to keep our relationship alive. And flirting is one of those solvents that help keep relationships sexy and bright.

Just because you've been dating your partner for two years doesn't mean you can't say, "You look so hot tonight" or whisper in their ear when you're in a crowded room, "I can't wait to take you home"—even if home has become a place you share.

Even when you've grown comfortable with your partner to the point that they feel sort of like an appendage of you, you can instigate a quickie on a hotel bathroom countertop, risking missing your flight, or tell them you're madly in love with them or slap their butt on their way to the bathroom.

You can fuck and flirt and fool around like you just met, even if you've been together for ten years. It sometimes takes a little more effort, because we grow comfortable with someone, and comfort can bring complacency. But be intentional with everything you do—if your partner looks really great while they're cooking dinner, squeeze their hand, hug them around their neck, say, "You look really good tonight."

Let your boyfriend pull you into the kitchen when his friends are ten feet away watching sports and surreptitiously push you against the frosted glass, telling you how pretty you are.

Let your girlfriend say spicy things in the bedroom, even if the bedroom is a place you've frequented together for five years.

Let your partner be silly and competitive with you while playing mini golf. Let them be playful with you. Of course being playful and silly may take more effort than it once did, but as a cherry on top to a great foundation, flirting makes for a perfect ice cream sundae.

•

Next up: friend flirting.

Friend love, to me, is when you meet someone in a platonic setting and instantly have a fiery, deep connection and deeply entrenched understanding of each other. Your souls see each other. It is the exact feeling of romantic love, only you're not interested in taking their clothes off. You just want to watch TV with them and go on walks with them and talk to them about how their day went. Because you care.

Friend love is one of the most important types of love we can ever have. I wish I could bottle up the feeling of friend love and put it in my pocket. In my life, I know I'd be okay if I never experienced romantic love in any sort of long-term capacity—because I have enough platonic love to keep me afloat forever. One thing I constantly remind myself of whenever I'm experiencing heartbreak, in any of its forms, is that my friends will always love me. I'll always have them. Sometimes, I'd ask myself what I'd do if everything else—my passions and my career and everything—went wrong in my life. And then I'd remind myself, I have my brothers and I have my friends. I have their shoulders. Their words of wisdom. Their sparkly eyes and doses of tough and gentle love.

Platonic love, especially when it comes to female friendship, is a currency akin to gold.

One of my best friends, Daphne, peppered on the friend flirting heavily the first time we met, which apropos, was at drama club my senior year of high school.

On the first day of rehearsal, during the brutally mortifying walk around the high school, I felt a tap on my shoulder. Daphne came up and met my stride, looked at me, and said, "I know we're going to be best friends."

Forward? Yes. Has she been wrong since? No.

After rehearsal, I gave her a ride home for the first time of thousands. We like to drive together. Our time spent together is so often spent doing nothing at all, but more valued than the time I spend anywhere else. She's a person I trust more than I trust myself. I am in forever friend love with her.

Daphne's audacity that first day of rehearsal also taught me that it would never be weird to approach someone you think you'd like to get to know or be friends with and say, "Hi, I'm Eli, what's your name?" or "I always see you in these Pilates classes and you have the best workout sets; I just had to tell you." It would never be seen as weird or off-putting to turn to the person next to you in class or the girl in the elevator with you in your building and just say, "Hey, I'm Eli, what's your name?" Nobody ever thought being friendly was weird.

My personal favorite trick is saying, "Oh my god, you look so familiar, do I know you from somewhere?" Drop in to your big acting career, you can do it. I know you can.

What I'm trying to say is, you can flirt with a friend. Flirting can be platonic. If there's a really cool girl or person in one of your classes you really want to be friends with, you can approach them like you would someone you were interested in at the bar. You can ask them questions about themselves, ask for their number, say you should hang out or grab coffee sometime. You can slide up on their stories and develop a rapport—and you can do all this platonically, with the end goal of having a friend.

Sometimes, I like to say it all comes back to sex—but not everything, I suppose, is about sex after all.

At the end of the night, or the other end of a phone call, or the end of the bar—flirting is supposed to be an uncomplicated, human, and universal signal of attraction. It's not that deep, and even when it is deep—it's still the way we start digging into someone's psyche. It isn't the trenches of their being, their late-night thoughts and all the baggage. It's playful and sweet and sentimental and just good. Just like dating apps are only cringe if we decide they're cringe, if we rid ourselves of the fear of rejection, flirting can just be fun.

And the truth is there are plenty of ways to say let's bang without saying let's bang. There are plenty of ways to instigate something. Sometimes we fear the flirting, we fear the rejection or the embarrassment.

If we view embarrassment as a choice, then we don't give ourselves the runway to fail. If flirting was easy and convenient, it wouldn't be so damn good. Everything that ends really well starts really cringe. Look it up, it's a Bible verse.

It is cliché to bring someone a book of erotic poems on a first date. But with the right person, it works. So here's the whole truth: decenter embarrassment from your life. YOU DON'T KNOW HER. Risking being rejected is nothing if you don't fear rejection. You're in control here.

So next time you see the object of your affection across a crowded room, or posting an Instagram story, or at a coffee shop or a restaurant or in an elevator, ask yourself: *Do I want this more than I fear it?*

If the answer is yes, well, I think I just told you what you need to do next.

Rules for Flings, Things, and No-Strings

(otherwise known as manifestation and manipulation)

1. Do a three- to four-day ghosting session after you hear from them after the first date, and then slide back in with a cryptic message—a meme, a TikTok, a simple "hey."

2. Leave your underwear somewhere and make them find it.

3. Borrow their clothes when you leave and then return them drenched in your hair products.

4. Sleep over for the first time but then get up and leave at six a.m.

5. Have a great fucking roster.

6. Let them have space to think about how amazing you are.

7. Go on a PHENOMENAL first date and then immediately become mysterious afterward.

8. Use your eyes as a weapon. Look them dead in the eyes. Bat your eyelashes, be a major tease.

9. The pepper rule: You're going to pepper in some of their favorite things randomly as though you had no idea it's their favorite thing.

10. Do something crazy with them—this way they associate adrenaline with you.

IF PLAYING GAMES was an Olympic sport, I'd be the coach of the US Women's team. I don't always condone playing games—but I know the sport and I know the sport well.

> **Games are reserved for flings, things, and no-strings attached.**
>
> **They are not for the person you're hoping to fall in love with or hoping to build a relationship with.**

Now that I've given you the disclosure, we can move on, and you're not allowed to sue me if you play a game and it backfires (fabulously, but still).

If you want to know how to play the game to get the guy to come home with you, to get that person to hang on your every word, to get your hookup to reach out and ask you what you're up to—I have the nuclear code and in good faith, I'm going to share it with you.

Let us never pretend we're above anything, because we're not. And frankly, if we look at all types of relationships on an utterly even playing field—romantic, casual, serious, platonic—then a casual fling is no greater than a wedding ring if it's serving you in the way you need at a specific moment in your life. Playing your cards right, when something is casual, and you're both happy with it being casual, is integral to your success. When it comes to games, happiness is key—it's just supposed to be fun.

There are many different kinds of games: flirty games, competitive games, games of the manifestation style—and we're going to play them all, and you're going to become the coach of an award-winning varsity team. In casual relationships, everyone's playing games, and if everyone is playing them, you have to outplay the player.

•

Likely, the first "game" that comes to mind when I say the term "playing games" is the tried and true: playing hard to get.

We hear it from EVERYONE. Time and time and time again. My best friends, and even my mother, would pretty consistently remind me that the only way to get what I want, the only way to get someone to be utterly obsessed with me, is by playing hard to get.

I was sitting at my desk in my attic bedroom senior year of college in front of my mirror, plucking every single tiny hair off my upper lip and from the edges of my eyebrows as Halsey played from a speaker resting on top of my minifridge. Sadie sat on my futon, sipping a mixed drink from a plastic red cup and scrolling through Instagram on her phone.

"What's the update with the new guy?" she asked as I stared at all my pores in the mirror, imagining how much easier life could be if I was a little prettier.

"I don't know. He didn't answer my Snapchat from earlier, which is weird because he asked ME what I was doing tonight and I replied."

Before I could suggest the plan I'd already mapped out in my head—that I would wait until we were pregaming and then text or snapchat him again under the guise of liquid courage to avoid the inevitable burn that would accompany possible rejection—she cut me off.

"Don't double snapchat him," Sadie said. And she was a Sagittarius, so it was easy for her to follow her own advice. And her advice worked. She hardly answered any guy she was casually involved with, ever, and when she did, it was often in jest—she played the game perfectly, and every single person in her life constantly hung on her every word. She was also never the one going to them; they came to her. She played a perfect game of hard to get and they just kept begging for more. The best part about Sadie was that she very rarely cared much about the attention. She was independent and fearless and everything I always wanted to be. She said the same of my empathy and sensitivities. I guess we both gave the other what we felt we lacked ourselves.

For me, playing hard to get was a whole different set of challenges. In my brain, if he didn't answer me, he must've been busy, and if I didn't remind him of my presence, he may forget about me altogether, and never reach out again. I wish someone had told me that a guy isn't worth my time if he decides he's over me because I didn't reply to him once or twice. A friend would never unfriend you due to your lack of reply to one text.

This was the reason that I never played hard to get. I was worried that playing hard to get would give off the impression that I wasn't interested. I was worried they'd move on to someone else. I wish someone would've told me that if they did do that, they weren't worth it. I wish someone had told me that during the most casual of college hookups—nobody owed me a reply.

Playing hard to get is reserved for situations wherein you're both single, have a roster of eligible candidates you flirt with, and are looking for late-night hookups and fun nights out. My worry that someone would get the impression I wasn't interested was silly, because it didn't matter—we were never really going to date. I shouldn't have been even considering playing games in the first place if I had true, sober feelings for the person on the other end of the phone.

It took me until I was playing hard to get *unintentionally* to realize how right everyone really was about its efficacy. Not only just that, but there's also SCIENCE surrounding "playing hard to get" that confirms my findings to be, in fact, correct (thank you, women in STEM).

When I was a senior in college and I took my pledge of singlehood and then hit the dating apps, I wanted to become the world's biggest flirt. I wanted a stacked roster, nights that ended at three a.m., and a camera roll full of half-blurry, half-remembered photos. I wanted that quintessential college single experience—and I was ready to go out and get it. Everyone needs to have their early 2000s Y2K party girl Paris Hilton era—and my first step was developing a decent roster so I had a team to lead.

I matched on Tinder with a transfer student who happened to be in the play I was producing (never mix work and pleasure) and decided he was a wonderful prospect. He was also in an improv group (notice a pattern?)—he was goofy and a little anxious and tall, and it was good enough for me.

I was a senior graduating in May. It was October. I decided to give something casual with the transfer boy a whirl, add him to the roster, and just have fun. He fit the casual fling mold perfectly—a little more than friends, a little less than anything serious. I didn't like him enough to ever want to date him, so my feelings were under control and I enjoyed his company. This was my utter sweet spot. The gray space didn't feel so bad for once, and I prayed we could be on the same page.

Transfer Boy deserved a bit of transparency, as everyone does, so I told him early enough on that I was planning to stay single for my entire senior year and would maybe consider exclusivity down the line, but for now I wanted to be casual. I told him I'd be down to spend time with him, hang out, and enjoy each other's company, but if he was looking for a relationship, we should just stay friends, because I knew I didn't want that with anyone and didn't want to see him hurt. Communicating what you want and what you hope to gain from someone is the only way to truly avoid wasting everyone's time.

He told me that it worked for him, so we went for it. We'd go to the diner after a theater school function and eat Hippie Hash some nights. We sat up at night drinking wine and chatting, went to a concert together, and walked to class some days. Every time I worried that he might be getting invested, I reminded him of my boundary. I was happy being single, happy casually dating and playing the field, and for once, it all felt really good. He seemed content. And when we spoke about the state of our relationship, he never once seemed on another page. Little did I know, he was being agreeable so I'd stick around, while secretly hoping to convince me I wanted something more (something I'd done too many times, after figuring I could change someone's mind about how they felt).

Eventually, someone else drifted into my life as well, and I kept myself open to anything coming my way. Transfer Boy had mentioned he was okay with that, so I figured it was fine. Unintentionally, throughout the time I spent with Transfer Boy, I was playing a little hard to get—I wasn't always available, didn't have enough time or attention to devote to answering every message, and I wasn't putting all my attention toward him or all my eggs in his basket. I hadn't intentionally opted into playing the game. The busier I grew, the more interested he became. The less I replied, the more he reached out. The more I kept my prospects open, the more he narrowed his.

I was frank with him, and we both knew it would never turn into anything, but when someone plays hard to get with us, and we can't have them in the palm of our hand, we want them even more. We always want what we can't have. We grow hungrier for them. We lust after them harder.

Eventually I had to end things with Transfer Boy, because we just weren't on the same page. Sometimes you have to see something for yourself to believe it to be true—but I realized that, for the first time, I knew how it felt to be on the other side. To not be the one waiting for a text back, overthinking each and every reply down to their punctuation. I wasn't the one left thinking deeply about what they must be doing on a night when we weren't together.

So the truth is playing hard to get works. And the other truth is that if you plan to try to change someone's mind about you, I urge you not to waste your own time—your time is precious.

Remember—if you're looking for a relationship, don't play games. You cannot build a healthy foundation for a relationship on a bunch of games. Second, if you are interested in more than something casual, and the other person's actions or lack of actions is causing you distress and anxiety, or if you've been avidly combing through their sneaky social media giveaways, like Snap Score or Snap Maps location or Venmo transactions—they're playing games with you, they're not interested in you as anything more than casual, and you deserve more respect than that from someone you're interested in pursuing a relationship with.

Tough love, I know, but I don't want to mislead you. And I simultaneously don't want you to be misled. To know how to play games is one thing, but to know how to spot them is something entirely different. If someone is consistently not texting you first, if they're opening your Snapchats and not responding, checking your stories but not replying to DMs—they might be busy, but they also might be playing a game with you. Stay alert, remind your friends when it seems like they're being toyed with, and outplay the player.

•

Flash forward to the second semester of my senior year, when I met Gemini Boy. I truly liked him and actually wanted something serious with him, though he never wanted that with me—and I just couldn't face that truth, because it came with a lot of disappointment. Eventually, I decided that I was fine being something casual to him, because at least it meant I was something.

I wish I'd held myself to a higher standard, but I'm telling you the story as it happened. And this is what happened. I wanted to be around him so badly that I decided I was okay being shelved as casual. I tried to push aside the feelings of want and desire and emotion, as I watched him do just that to his feelings for me. After all, if it weren't for the emotional dredging we both did and the complicated production it was to pretend that there was nothing there, we probably wouldn't have both cried when it all ended.

All that said, Gemini Boy played games wonderfully. He never gave too much away. I never knew much about what he was up to. I never knew how he felt. He left my Snapchats on opened just often enough that it put me on edge; he would text me nice, cute messages and then proceed to not respond. He didn't owe me anything. He was doing exactly what I did with Transfer Boy. Keeping options open, being casual with me, and he was always pretty direct about what he wanted; he was just out there living his life.

And I wanted him more and more and more in spite of it.

So I decided to play the game back. When he didn't know where I was, when I pulled away, offered less, and acted busy—he was suddenly all consumed with me.

> RULE
> 1
>
> Go ahead and take a few days and don't respond or reach out. You don't owe this person anything, especially if you hang out with them late at night or just meet up at parties—three days without a message isn't going to change things irrevocably, and it's easy to slide back in with a simple tweet or funny TikTok or just "hey."

Once, I left a pair of underwear at someone's place. Tale as old as time, of course. But the true trick is that when they ask "Are these yours?" and send you a picture of said undies, you don't reply. They know the trick if you reply and say "omg sooo sorry, those are mine lol!"—but if you flip it on its head, and you don't reply to them, it leaves them thinking of you.

I stole that same person's favorite sweatshirt. Wait, stole is a harsh term . . . I *leased* it out for a bit. He claimed he needed it back, because it was his favorite one, though it was salmon pink and from Zara. He was six four and the sweatshirt came down past my knees. I wore it to Chipotle, hungover one Sunday morning. After I washed it, I returned it smelling of my hair product. Most people will recommend you spray a bit of perfume on someone's clothes before returning them—but unfortunately, this trick has become too widely known to not seem intentional. Hair products are a bit sneakier, because if you've ever slept in someone's bed, the smell of your hair has lingered on their bedsheets long after you've gone.

I played the games so well it was suddenly Salmon Sweatshirt inviting me over, instead of me asking if I could come. I'd find him at the shitty college bar we went to on Saturday nights, crowded and sticky and perfumed with an array of vodka and sprite and the white noise of people calling each other's names. Once he was eating chicken fingers and french fries near the front door. I ran into him on my way to stand in the interminably long bathroom line.

He asked if I'd just like to leave.

Maybe we weren't in love, or even in *like*. We weren't much of anything, but we had the same priorities. We'd walk through the snow back to his house. It would be empty because everyone stayed out much later than us. We'd watch YouTube videos and talk about our college admissions counselors in high school. He once explained to me that his favorite cereal was Weetabix. What a weird, geriatric cereal to like so much at the age of twenty-one. I remember those tiny little things. I don't remember what it felt like to lie there or what it felt like to get up and leave.

I'd stay over, but often we stayed up all night. Staring at the ceiling. Swapping stories. Sometimes I figured he just wanted someone to listen, but I'd be lying if I told you it wasn't the same for me.

Sometimes it's just a night, or just a string of them. It's comforting to have someone to fall asleep next to, to talk to about the shit you don't really tell your friends. It feels nice to not sleep alone.

But the bubble burst when the sun came back up, and it was time for me to go. Sometimes I wished I could laminate what it was at night and protect it into dawn. I was smart enough to know that it wasn't the same during the day. I suppose that's why they say that true ignorance is bliss. To avoid the awkward dance of—when do I leave, how do I leave, and what do I wear when I leave—I would try my best to not sleep over at someone's place unless we were in a relationship. But even a rule maker breaks her own rules, and with certain people (Salmon Sweatshirt included), I wanted to spend the night, or I was too tipsy or tired or it was too bone cold to find my way back home.

In the cases where I did spend the night, I'd get up around 5:30 a.m. or, latest, 6:00 a.m. to the quietest alarm I could find, trying not to wake him while I tiptoed around for my boots and socks and something warm to wear on my trek home. It might be surprising for him when he woke up and found I was gone, but it helped me to create a boundary for myself, to keep myself in check, and to remind myself that he wasn't going to take me on the breakfast date, and eventually would have just kicked me out anyway. I might as well play the hard-to-get game and leave on my own terms. I knew that the disappointment would come when he woke up and it wasn't the lazy, romantic Sunday morning we hear about couples sharing together. It would be an awkward hour of us lying there half awake, wondering who would decide to get their day started first.

One particularly hungover February morning (after I'd left my friends at the bar around 12:30 a.m. to head back to Salmon Sweatshirt's house), my eyes peeled open at 5:15 a.m. It was Valentine's Day. I had heart-shaped pasties on my chest. We'd only slept for maybe two hours, and the night before, while we were watching TV and eating double-stuffed Oreos, the framed picture hanging above his bed fell off the wall and hit me in the eye. He'd given me a bag of frozen peas and apologized relentlessly. I was intoxicated and giddy enough that it didn't hurt that badly.

When I mentioned it was Valentine's Day, at two in the morning, he didn't say much of anything.

Now I had a splitting headache and a black eye and I wanted nothing more than to be clean and in my own bed. I quietly got up, holding my breath at the creaks of the floorboard and the ruffle of the sheets. I grabbed a sweater from the floor and pulled it over my sheer black tank top, picked my shoes up from the carpeted floor, and headed out to the living room to pull them on. I was warm and sweaty, in need of a shower and a glass of orange juice to silence the rattling in my brain.

I stepped outside and fat, wet flakes of snow fell on my hair and my red cheeks. It actually felt pretty good. Three inches of fresh snow was piled on the sidewalks, and our sweet college town was absolutely silent. As I dug through my jeans pockets for my keys, I realized I didn't have them. Either I'd left them in Salmon Sweatshirt's room, or I hadn't brought them out to begin with. If need be, I could go back, but it would 100 percent require waking him up. Sometimes my roommates left our front door unlocked, and I hoped, selfishly, this was one of those nights.

As I trudged farther along toward Greenwood Avenue, I saw a shadow coming from the opposite direction. The shadow was female, dressed in black. She had strawberry-blond hair and the way she moved seemed familiar. As though heaven's gates had opened and directly planted a miracle at my feet, the figure coming toward me was Sadie—who, thank god, had her keys. At 5:15 a.m. in the middle of a silent, snowy street, I found my Valentine.

I am lucky that when situationships were confusing and crushes were literally heart-wrenching, I had my true soulmate—a shadowy redheaded figure trudging toward me in the snow—all along.

The Roster

To distract myself from Gemini Boy while simultaneously prohibiting myself from developing an emotional attachment to someone who had made it clear that he would never develop that feeling himself, I also kept a roster going. The roster kept me invested in just enough people that I didn't have the time or energy to give away to just one guy.

When I think of a roster, I think of somewhere between five and seven people who you have in a flirtatious rotation. One person needs to be your all-star, midfield player (for me, this was Gemini Boy). Then you need two strong alternates, and these should be people you do hang out with one-on-one, but not as often as you do with the all-star player. To round it off, you need a great benchwarmer (old reliable, someone who will always pull through for you) and you should always be trying out one more player for the team, just in the event that someone else quits or they aren't playing up to standard. A roster is allowed to be whatever you'd like it to be. You can sleep with the people on your roster, you can go on dates with some of them, you can keep it PG-13—rosters are individual and personal, and as the coach, you get to choose.

When you're in a single era or feeling like pursuing casual relationships and not getting too involved, the roster is the perfect way to keep your prospects organized and compartmentalized. Keeping yourself busy is the best way to keep your mind from drifting to just one person.

I met Salmon Sweatshirt because his roommate was hooking up with my roommate pretty consistently, and he'd seen a photo of me on her Instagram. He followed me and slid into my DMs. The rest of my roster was composed of two strong alternates (a guy I met in one of my classes, and an MBA student I matched with on Bumble), a great benchwarmer (a guy I'd been involved with freshman year who I knew was always at the ready if and when I needed him), and another guy from one of my classes who I'd been flirting with a little but had never actually gone out with.

The best way to develop a roster is to pull from different places—flirt a little in class, ask your friends for setups, go out to bars and parties, use dating apps, and join clubs. You cannot have a roster of seven people from the same Greek life chapter, school group, or friend group—I mean, you can, but then you're going to need a reality TV series because we need to see some confessionals.

Ultimately, a roster is crucial to every fling, thing, or no-strings situation. Without one, we run the risk of catching feelings, which is an incurable illness that, when in a single era, we cannot afford to come down with. Trust me, I know because I've fallen victim before, and it took me months to recover.

The most important thing about roster development is ensuring that everyone knows what you're looking for and the role they fill in your life. You don't owe someone an explanation the first time you spend time with them, but eventually if you're seeing someone consistently, they deserve to know where your head is at, just as you'd like to know where their head is at. Be honest and open, be intentional about what you're looking for so nobody gets hurt.

There are, of course, mature ways to play games as well—which we'll call dating tactics. As you've learned by this point, we can't rely on games to build a relationship—but I want to share some healthy tactics you can use to simply place the relationship odds in your favor.

In my own observations, men and women develop emotions, lust, and love differently—men fall in love through time spent apart from someone, when they're able to think about them. Women fall in love through deep conversations, and sex. With that in mind, I recommend giving someone the space to think about you. If they're the right person, chances are, they're going to let their mind wander to you. They're going to think of you. This is a more mature way to play the same game we just discussed above.

My first date with Noah was a freezing January Thursday night. He came right from work, I came straight from a two-hour-long first-date preritual. It was the greatest first date I've ever been on. He asked all the right questions, ordered all the right things for us to share. My lips tasted like espresso martini and my hair looked really nice.

It was so perfect that I didn't feel nervous. It was also imperfect in terms of first-date standards. We sat outside in freezing weather, we didn't kiss goodbye, we overordered. But that just became us, eventually. Unexpected, silly, untraditional. And the truth was a good one. I didn't overthink every word I said. I didn't overanalyze the way he laughed or the questions he asked. I felt like I was sitting with someone I already knew my whole entire life. Someone I wanted to know for longer. But the best part was, it was only the beginning and everything lay right ahead.

After our date he invited me over to his apartment for a drink and to see the view of the Empire State Building. I wanted to go, but I also knew I was going to see him again on Sunday. For once I wanted this to go slow because I already knew where it was

Friends with Benefits

I'd be remiss if I didn't mention the deadliest of all the sins—friends with benefits—which is an excellent idea in theory and an absolutely horrific idea in practice.

On occasion, if every detail and circumstance is exactly right, a friends-with-benefits situation can work for a while. When I say "friends with benefits" I effectively mean you decide to enter into a sexual relationship with someone you were formerly friends with, and the purpose of that relationship is sexual and physical fulfillment, in tandem with your friendship.

The issue is how it ends, and when you think about it, there is no truly good way to end a friends-with-benefits situation.

Option one: One person develops feelings that the other person doesn't reciprocate, things grow awkward, the friends-with-benefits situation ends, but you're also no longer really friends.

Option two: One party decides they'd like to date someone else or they meet someone they'd rather hook up with or spend time with, hurting the other person.

Option three: One party decides they no longer want to be friends with benefits, and it's difficult to go back to being just friends.

I'm not saying it's impossible to end a friends-with-benefits situation amicably, but the odds are not in your favor. If you've seen your friend naked numerous times in a sexual setting, you probably aren't going to ease right back into the friendzone.

Alternatively, if you accidentally wake up in a friend's bed *one* time, and you both are mature enough to not make it awkward and embarrassing, then you can proceed as normal. Embarrassment is a choice—it is not a feeling someone else can thrust onto us; it is an emotion that we fall into ourselves. A feeling we can turn off if we just decide it wasn't that embarrassing, or it isn't that awkward. I'm not suggesting you ignore what happened, but you do have the potential to proceed as normal in your friendship if you both make the choice to do so.

But as you can see, friends-with-benefits situations can and will be very messy, and for that reason, I recommend steering clear.

headed. I didn't want to speed up the good part. I didn't want to fast forward over the fumbling of newness or the freshness of a beginning. I wanted it to be drawn out and syrupy and long-winded. I was so obsessed with being on the precipice of falling, and I wanted it to last just a few more minutes.

And, in a practical sense, I knew that while prolonging the date wouldn't change much, it would take away that immediate aftermath he would otherwise spend thinking of me. It wouldn't give him the subway ride recalling details about me, or the way I made him feel. He wouldn't climb into bed planning out the date he asked me to on Sunday. If I was there, I'd be a bit too tangible. We'd know each other so deeply soon enough; I wished for a little time when we were strangers to each other. A little more time to wonder about the details before they arrived on our doorstep.

RULE 7

It wasn't a game as much as an intentional tactic—a way to keep the flame hot and me in control. Three days later, I went to his apartment for the first time for cheese and wine, and the distance I allowed to sit between us, albeit brief, conjured up a higher degree of excitement as I stood in the elevator, seconds away from seeing him again.

It's not so much about playing games, but more so about dating smart and dating sharp. It may seem simple, but our body language is almost more important than our words (without us even realizing it) on a first date. So make good, intentional eye contact. It's coquettish and a little awkward but sometimes even steamier than a makeout session under low bar lighting. Likewise, hold on to the tiny details they share about themselves. People are flattered when you remember something they told you they love or a small memory that may have not seemed memorable to them. Last, adrenaline is an emotion we all lust after, and if you can find some way to link adrenaline to the memory of your date—in some small way, this person grows excited and jittery at the sheer thought of you.

When we're deploying these tactics in our dating lives, it's important to strike a balance and find a good mix of high hopes and realistic expectations. We all deserve romance and the happy ending, but typically we find both when we pursue dating with our eyes peeled and our rearview mirrors clean. It's important not to send mixed messages or lead someone on—and the best way to prevent this is to just be clear about what you're looking for. If you're on a dating app, letting someone know that you're not looking for something serious before you've met up is really integral to not wasting anyone's time. If you meet someone at a bar, or in a class, or from a mutual friend, it's respectful to let them know: "I'd love to keep spending time with you but I need to be transparent that I'm not looking for something serious right now."

I know it can be nerve-racking to open yourself up to someone saying, "Thanks for letting me know, I think we should just be friends then"—but it would serve neither of you to continue something sexual, romantic, or flirtatious if you're not on the same page. The last thing you ever want to do is lead someone on.

We all know how much that stings.

·

There's a world in which someone is playing games with you when you don't want to play games at all. With Ezra, it was relentless. After we demoted our relationship status from dating to nonexclusive friends with benefits meets exes hooking up meets situationship, he played endless games with me while I plotted to try and get him back.

One weekend we'd be back together, the next he'd end it, the next he reconsidered. I'm very serious when I say I lived eight months waking up not knowing if he loved me or loved me not.

I would never get him back, because he didn't want to be with me, and he was playing games to let me know without explicitly saying so. I was letting him play these games because I figured that if he spent more time close to me, he'd realize it was all a mistake. He'd take it back, and we'd have our happily ever after.

What I wish now is that I could've recognized that I don't want to have to beg someone to be with me. I don't have to put up with all the manipulation and hot and cold games and negging and love bombing and bread crumbing. Because those games weren't ones I'd signed up for—and the playful nature of the casual situationship games couldn't quite exist when I was being ruthlessly mentally manipulated.

My friends tried to warn me—they pleaded with me in crowded bars and at Starbucks tables and as we walked to our classes—to just give up. To block him. To let him go. But there are some things we have to learn for ourselves. Even if they were right, and even if it would've been the right thing to stand up for myself and block his phone number and move on, I needed to let him break me. It was perhaps sadly the only way I was going to be able to rebuild myself again.

I don't regret withstanding the way he treated me for so long because eventually I learned what to look for in a person before choosing to fall for them blindly. I learned to be cautious with my heart but liberal with my love once someone proved worthy of it. I learned how to identify a love bomber and to pick a good guy out of a field of guys that would lead me on and break my heart.

And perhaps I do wish I hadn't spent so many nights up in my lofted dorm room bed, wishing he'd send me a text—knowing if he had, it meant he probably struck out with anyone else. Maybe I do wish my friends hadn't had to watch me walk into the fire and come out burned after ignoring everything they begged me to see. Maybe I do wish I hadn't wasted so much time on someone who was never in my corner to begin with.

And I could call myself weak and codependent and antifeminist and depressed and shitty for that behavior. And I did. The self-loathing ate me alive like mosquitoes on the hottest August night.

But in all that disaster and in all that anger, there was a tiny shred of hope. I saw in myself someone who wanted to see the good, but who needed to learn how to keep an eye out for the red flags or the stop signs. I saw in myself someone who wanted to believe someone. Who wanted to take them at their word. I saw in myself someone who could find a lovely quality in almost anyone, who wanted, more than anything, to give the person she loves every ounce of love she could muster.

I saw empathy. And it was brilliant and bright and it almost blew away all the hurt. But some still remained, because in some ways it always would. Being manipulated and subsequently hurt by the games he played with me taught me about how I valued myself and how I valued others and how I wished, one day, that I'd believe I deserved to be treated well.

Now I know to be careful and stingy with my heart in the beginning but an overachiever when someone deserves it. I know how to protect myself through the casual flings and how to separate out the casual from the potentially serious. I know how to use my voice and how to make someone find you even more attractive than they already did before.

It's all just trial and error, I guess. You have to try and then fail to finally find what feels right—not because you've manufactured a reason why it's right, but because it truly is.

Rules for a First Date

1. Do a check-in. Text a friend or your mother a thumbs-up in the bathroom if it's going well, and a thumbs-down if you need help.

2. Pregame every first date with one and a half glasses of wine while listening to Ariana Grande.

3. The Outfit: 1. Canadian tuxedo, 2. Eff Me sweater.

4. Your first-date personality is your real personality but tame, just slightly toned down.

5. You tell a SINGLE comedic trauma story as a gateway into your relationship personality.

6. Order a spicy sexy margarita.

7. Share things if you're eating because it's less awkward.

8. Split nachos with them. This is an important key decider in whether or not someone is worth your single girl time.

9. You've never seen a check in your life when the bill comes. You can thank them after (if they paid).

10. Discuss the second date on the first date if it's going really well.

11. Don't add phone numbers into your phone until the third date. They don't need to be taking up property in your phone until they're worth it.

12. Make tentative plans for after so you have a decent out if it's going terribly.

I CANCELED ON our first date twice because I have anxiety and strong gut instincts. It was a setup, anyway, and a setup made me feel somewhat out of control. I didn't choose him. I was doing it half out of spite. I was worried that it would be a waste of time, and I was in an era of my life that was meant for being selfish and wasting no time on men.

For a week we conversed over text and tried our hand at flirting with each other through messages. When he sent me text messages one night as I half paid attention to an episode of *The Bachelor*, though we'd never met in person, I felt the anticipation of falling deep in my gut. I wasn't sure if I wanted that.

It was January and cold. Joe Biden had just been inaugurated, my hair was blond and short, and my bedroom had no windows. My roommate always had *SVU* on in the background.

I couldn't tell what was stopping me from going on the date. Part of me thought it was because I just didn't want to go on a date with anyone. I was enjoying my nights spent drinking white wine out of a mug, mulling over my grad school work, and watching the lights in the apartment across the street flicker on and off. I liked hearing about Sadie's boyfriend and I liked developing pointless crushes on Broadway performers and always sleeping in my own bed. Though I was content, most of me knew the real reason was that deep down, the universe was telling me that if I did open the door to the opportunity, it was going to work out. And nobody talks about this, but something working out is frankly more terrifying than something not working out at all.

When you go on a first date and it doesn't work out, you risk wasting a face of makeup, a bruise to your dignity, and losing $20 on an Uber, but you tuck yourself in and your heart stays intact. If it goes well—you have no choice but to be brave.

One morning he sent me a video of himself putting a pinch of salt in his Dunkin' Donuts iced coffee because he'd seen me do it on TikTok. His glasses rested on the bridge of his nose and he wore a gray sweatshirt.

I asked him, impulsively, if he was free Thursday, and he was.

We went to a restaurant in the West Village called Sveta. We had dinner and tequila shots and we didn't even kiss goodbye. We didn't need to. I didn't want to. I knew we'd be kissing a lot in the future, and the rush, for once, wasn't top of mind.

Either way, my gut instinct was right. The boy I canceled on twice turned out to be Noah, who would become my boyfriend not long after.

The great thing about a first date is that there's two plausible outcomes: either you walk away with a story to tell your friends or a second date. When you look at it like that, it's a win-win situation. You can't lose on a first date. If faced with the choice, I'd rather be rejected or ghosted after a first date than strung along by the wrong person for months. I'd rather dedicate three hours than three weeks or three months to someone who didn't end up sticking around. The stakes, then, are pretty low.

My therapist has told me I do a very good job with silver linings. Not everything has one, she says, but you manage to find a way to say everything could.

But just because there's a silver lining doesn't mean you don't have to stop in a Starbucks public bathroom on your way to the bar for the first date to avoid shitting yourself out of anxiety. I've always been a nervous person. And my nervousness was planted, and grows, in a soil of perception. I fear being perceived—fear the perception others may have of me. The idea of anyone having an opinion about me makes heat crawl up my neck.

The reality is, nobody is perceiving you with the intensity you think they might be. I promise you, we are all thinking of ourselves approximately one thousand times more than other people are thinking of us. We are selfish beings. You're not thinking of the person who believes you're thinking of them, and vice versa.

We also cannot allow the perception others MAY have of us to skew or obfuscate our perception of ourselves. Because the truth is the majority of people aren't viewing us the way we fear they are. We must perceive ourselves, with the truth we know and hold close.

Whenever I grow concerned about what someone, specifically in a romantic setting, may think of me, I remind myself of what I know to be true. Someone who met me once for a span of three hours and their opinions of me hold no candle to what I know of myself after spending twenty-five years getting to know who I am and who I'd like to be. And all that matters, truly, is not what other people think about me, but what I know about myself.

I've often placed so much weight and pressure on what a date thinks of me that I've forgotten to wonder what I think of my date. For most of my adult life, I viewed dating in a very heteronormative and scripted way, and I have society and tunnel vision to blame for that. In my mind, dating was a simple formula: boy meets girl, boy asks girl on date, boy decides if he likes girl, and then you proceed accordingly.

When I moved to New York after I graduated from college, I went on approximately fifty first dates, with fifty different guys, who all wore glasses. Five of them were named Max. My weeks were packed with first dates. My hair was always done right. I spent hours rifling through my closet for the perfect top. I had a date planned the night Joe Biden officially won the election, and I watched his acceptance speech through two hedges on a television mounted above my date's head. I'd spent the hours leading up to it drinking champagne and dancing on my Upper West Side apartment rooftop, overlooking the chaos in the street below. I never saw him again.

Somewhere toward the end of the fifty first dates, I realized that I didn't need to approach a first date waiting to see how the other person felt about me. Instead of placing the other person on a pedestal—as though I was waiting to see if I'd made it to the next round—I could view us on equal footing. Because the fact of the matter is, even if the person you're going on a first date with has a six-pack or a cool job, you're going on a first date TOGETHER. They're not taking you on a date, you're not taking them on a date, you're going on a date—together. And why would you ever want to be with someone who sees you as inferior?

In the same way that you're a little nervous, they're probably a little nervous, too. They're sitting there asking themselves, "Do they like me?" Just like you are. While you stood in front of your mirror and applied a body spray of choice so you smell really great before the date, they were doing the same thing.

This person is going to go home and ask themselves: "Did I like them?" and "Would I like to see them again?" So I task you with doing the same. Shift your postdate inner monologue from "Did I say the right things?" "Do they want to see me again?" "Did they have a good time?" to "Did I like them?" "Would I like to see them again?" and "Did I have a good time?"

A first date is just as much about you as it is the other person. It is just as much about what you're looking for, how you're feeling, and what you're experiencing as it is for the other person. On a first date there is absolutely nothing on the line. There's no real major risk. It is either a good story or a second date.

Before I go on, I do want to caution you to always be safe on a first date: go on a date in public, share your location with your friends before you go, make sure someone knows where you are, and look into the person before you go on the date. Because when I say the only risk is a good story or a second date, I want to make sure you know that I mean that this is the only risk when we're in a safe situation, looking out for ourselves. Take the precautions you need to so that you can look out for yourself. I hate that I have to remind you of this, and split from our fun to say "stranger danger," but it's too important to go unsaid.

My mom always asks me to send her a thumbs-up emoji from the bathroom if I'm safe and the date is going well—this way she knows I'm okay without having to take up much of my time. Set up a system like this with your friends, your roommates, whoever you feel comfortable with because, unfortunately, stranger danger is still real.

RULE
1

I used to prepare for dates like I was getting ready for the Met Gala. Once a date was neatly recorded into my Google calendar, I forced myself to view the event like I was trying to convince this person, who I likely had never met, to be my future husband. In reality, a first date is just a few drinks. It's just getting to know someone for the first time and asking yourself: "Is this someone I'd like in my life? Platonically, romantically, or not at all?"

When you view a first date like you're going into a business negotiation, begging someone to invest in your business, you're not going to get the investment you need. This isn't about one person's investment in the other, it's about partnership. I put so much pressure on myself and on the situation and on the other person and on us working out before we'd even met that I drove myself crazy. But it does no good to decide how you feel about someone, or what you'd like to become with them, before you've even met them.

On a first date I went on with a guy who had curly brown hair and goofy humor and a degree from Brown University, I planned to try to convince him to fall in love with me before we even met face-to-face. I liked our banter over Bumble messages and thought he checked all the boxes, so I would have to ensure that I checked all the boxes for him. I'd squeeze myself into a mold that I didn't necessarily conform to for him. I'd discard pieces of myself to be the right fit for him. He felt perfect for me over the hazy glow of iMessage, so I'd make sure I was perfect too.

I hadn't even heard the sound of this man's voice, and I had decided that I wanted us to fall in love. This mindset was a problem. Instead of setting yourself up to be pleasantly surprised, you set yourself up for it not to work out—and when we've inflated something ourselves, we'll end up out of breath, gasping for air as we watch it deflate. But nothing is going to work out until something does. If you go on ten first dates, only one of those COULD be a love of your life, or someone you spend a good amount of time with. Meaning 90 percent of the time, it isn't going to work out.

Nothing is going to work out until something does.

I was stuck in a mindset that each date was required to work out, and it would be surprising if it didn't. Now I recognize that it's surprising if it does. That's what makes it so exciting. If you go on ten dates, and you end up with the tenth person, the first nine are going to end somehow—maybe in some dramatic way or maybe in no response one morning.

If you have trouble with viewing every first date you go on as very casual and not very serious, I implore you to pretend like you are going to have dinner or drinks or coffee with your friend. On that date, you might realize you'd like to get into bed with your friend, or that you'd like to see your friend again because you kissed before you got into the cab and the kiss was electric. You might say, "I really like spending time with my friend, but I can't really tell if I'm sexually attracted to them or if I just want to have them around as a friend." You might realize your friend isn't serving you in your life, and you don't want to see them again.

Whatever you decide, you're not forced to make a decision about a first date in that moment. Nothing is black and white. Even the starkest white and the darkest black are just shades of gray. It would be ludicrous to expect you to have a fully formed opinion on someone, or to know you'd like to spend every single day for the rest of your life with them, after spending two hours enjoying two Aperol spritzes with them on a Thursday night.

Dating is one step in front of the other. The first step is the hardest step. Your legs will stop shaking once you realize no matter what, the ground under you is solid. A romantic partner would be an addition to an already sunshine-filled life.

•

The anticipation of anything is more troubling than it actually occurring. Hence, we're typically more anxious before a date than we are when we're actually on the date. The morning of a first date, we'll sip our coffee and run through the myriad scenarios that could play out in our mind. We create catastrophes, convince ourselves of embarrassment and failure. Anytime I feel overwhelmed, out of control, or anxious, I typically counter those feelings with something stable—and a ritual is always stabilizing. A ritual or a tradition tends to take the edge off, because routine is control, which helps us to balance the unexpected nature of going out on a first date. So maybe your predate ritual doesn't include exactly one and a half glasses of pinot noir and a playlist consisting specifically of Ariana Grande songs—and it doesn't have to. But having a ritual makes things feel more in your own control and makes them a little less consequential. First dates are going to be a little uncomfortable, and we all need to get on the same page there—do what you have to do to take the edge off a little. The act of putting on makeup while listening to Ariana Grande while your roommate lounges on the couch while you split a half bottle of red wine is comforting, especially if you consistently behave this way before a first date.

Abiding by your own rules before a first date makes it feel a little bit more like a game you're navigating and less like a life-or-death situation. My ritual of wearing a Canadian tuxedo (denim on denim) or what I call the Eff Me sweater (the perfectly sexy yet mature, soft sweater) on a first date gives me a much needed dose of confidence and comfort—both are outfits I feel good in, ones that I wear consistently on first dates and give me stability when the outcome of the date is uncertain.

The outfit is never about appealing to the person at the other end of the high-top table. It's about making myself feel sexy, because the way we treat ourselves is the way others will subsequently treat us. The Canadian tuxedo was born of a college fling who went behind my back, slept with my friend, and obfuscated the trust I thought we'd built in one of those unspoken ways. For once, instead of throwing myself a pity party, I threw myself a pregame. It was a Friday night, wintertime, and I planned to make myself feel really good by looking really good, and then I planned to go out and dance.

Before I did, though, I, perhaps immaturely, posted on Instagram just so he'd see it and, theoretically, feel worse for losing me. The photo was in our sorority house hallway, and I was wearing a tiny black tube top, jeans that accentuated my waist and butt, and an oversize jean jacket. He messaged me saying he regretted everything five minutes after liking the photo, and I never responded. The Canadian tuxedo became my confidence uniform, and I've never looked back. The energy it gave off reminded me to never accept less than I deserved, and even if it took me a little longer to fully grasp and incorporate that lesson into my life, that night was when it was first introduced.

The Eff Me sweater is a simple story. I sat on the couch sipping a glass of pinot noir while my roommate got ready for a first date on a winter evening, trying on different outfits and modeling them for me. Eventually, she settled on a red sweater. It was soft, hugged her in the right places, and complemented her pretty dark hair. There was no need to try too hard or overaccentuate any particular feature. It just felt good.

I don't believe in the taboo. I say whatever is on my mind, and my favorite thing to do, in the world, is stay home on a weekend night and watch Broadway videos on YouTube. If that doesn't sound fun to you? Oh well. When I go on a first date, I don't give the person 100 percent of my personality, because frankly, my full personality is a hot ticket, and it comes with the price of three dates. On the first date, you get Eli-lite. I'm still being me, just ever so slightly more reserved. It wouldn't be called "getting to know someone" if you got to know me all the way in the first three hours. Our first-date personalities are our relationship personalities without stories about explosive diarrhea, queefing, and childhood trauma. You have to edge your date (emotionally, not sexually)—give them almost everything, but leave a little bit to the imagination so they have no choice but to hear the rest of that story, or what happened next, five days later when they take you out again.

On a first date in the heat of September with someone from college, we ate cacio e pepe pasta and drank big glasses of wine. I ordered pasta because it was what I wanted, not because I thought there was something I was supposed to order to appear a certain way. He was sweet and charming and really hot and I felt fine smiling with my teeth and talking about my theater degree in a way I formerly felt ashamed of. We moved from dinner to a dive bar he said he frequented after work (he worked at JP Morgan—again, we had nothing in common). The dive bar had picnic tables outside and we sat on the same side of the picnic table and looked each other in the eyes when we spoke.

When we kissed, he tasted like beer and sweat. It was September but it was still warm out. He asked me to come home with him and I told him I didn't sleep with people on the first date. He said he didn't mind either way. I didn't feel inclined to do anything

I didn't want to do. I felt like I was making decisions I wanted to make, for myself, and because I was being true to myself, the guy on the other side of the table was genuinely interested and attracted to me. It was a different kind of euphoria to be sexy to someone when I was being myself, and not playing a part.

Am I suggesting you get drunk before a first date? Absolutely not. I'm suggesting that you simply don't hold back. Dress how you like to dress. Speak about the things that matter to you. Order your favorite food on the menu. Drink what you'd drink if you were across the table from your best friend. Don't be concerned if your favorite movie or hobby or way to spend a Saturday is lame or weird, because the truth is, why would you want to go on a second date with someone who thinks your way of life is lame or weird, when there's someone out there spending their life in the same way? Don't be concerned if there's someone else—and if that person is "better" than you. There's no such thing as one person being better than another—you can be better for someone, just like someone will be better for you.

Being ourselves avoids wasted time. It avoids a clock running out. It avoids heartbreak, among other things.

•

Once I was pregaming a first date with my uncle. We were drinking some red wine at the bar of one of my family's restaurants, taking turns pressing pieces of bread into a plate of olive oil. Don't ask me why I was pregaming a first date with my uncle, but he had just finished telling me about a time he ate shrooms on a pizza and went to a concert, and I asked him a very important question.

"What do I order on a date to seem sexy and sophisticated?"

The guy I was trying to convince was older than me by a few years. In my mind, he was going on dates with twenty-five-year-old models and not twenty-year-old theater kids, but I digress.

"Blanco muddled with lime and jalapeño, shaken, on the rocks, with a salt rim."

I tried to practice this so I wouldn't forget it, because it's sexy to know what you're talking about when you order a drink at a bar, but it seemed overcomplicated and too anxiety-inducing to remember, so I settled with the spicy skinny margarita. Having a go-to drink is part of your ritual—you feel confident ordering it, you're still in control.

I got to the date and the cocktail menu was expansive and after a few drinks we saw one of the menu drinks had cotton candy on it and we thought that was funny so we ordered it to share. Our relationship felt like a sugar rush the entire time. I think we set the precedent by just being ourselves. I didn't trip over my words once, trying to say what I thought he wanted me to.

I always recommend a first date including a beverage. I think coffee or drinks are the most ideal options for a few reasons. First of all, you have something to do with your hands, because you have a beverage in front of you. Nobody discusses how we actually have no idea what to do with our hands ever. Nobody does. If you don't drink or you don't like to drink on a first date, that's totally fine—alcohol is not required, and sobriety is perfectly normal. Have a coffee or a Diet Coke or a mocktail instead.

Second, doing an activity on a first date with someone you've never met impedes conversation. Playing mini golf or going bowling is fun, but if it isn't preceded or followed up by drinks or dinner, you won't really get to know who they are as a person. A first date is a time to play twenty questions, find out if you enjoy sitting at a table and conversing with them—which is the first step in knowing if you'd actually like to commit to spending time with them.

I think we all fear an awkward silence on a first date as well—a moment where neither person knows what to say next. I recommend having three back-pocket topics to bring up if this happens. We all hate an SOS conversation (meaning one that tries to prohibit the entire date from tanking), but sometimes you need to use them, and that's not necessarily a bad thing. These SOS topics might range from pop culture news, favorite movies or albums, something crazy that happened to you in the past week, or favorite restaurants in the area. Sometimes reaching for an SOS topic, because conversation has lulled, is a good way to spark seamless dialogue.

When walking away from a first date, I believe you can have a steadfast opinion on seeing them again—you might know for sure you'd like to, or for sure that'll be your first and also last date. But always remember that attraction can grow, and just because the first date was a little awkward, it doesn't mean the second one has to be. Hypothetically speaking, if you never see this person again, that's fine. Which is why first dates are allowed to be utterly hilarious. The concept, anyway, is weird and unseen in any other life setting: you meet up with someone you don't or hardly know, get drinks, dinner, or coffee, ask questions like "Where did you grow up?" and "Do you have roommates?" and use your own deceptive reasoning to decide if you'd like to have sexual intercourse with them, see them again for another date, or never see them again. We joke about our best friends showing up in disguise at the bar where we have a first date, because first dates are a weird concept that we all wish we had moral support for.

One night in college, Sadie and I decided we would both go on dates on the same night. Sadie's date ended before mine, and we had plans to meet up after the date. She has my location on Find My Friends, so she literally showed up at the bar we were at. My date, a future dentist named Fred, and I had nothing in common. He liked hiking, backpacking, climbing up mountains, surfing, and walking; I like handbags, lip gloss, Broadway shows, and cheese boards. So after about an hour of pretending to be fascinated by rare leaves Fred found in Costa Rica, and after he literally told me I'm "not his usual type," Sadie's undercover arrival to the bar was a welcome one.

Sadie told the bartender that she was here to meet me, and that I was on a date that wasn't going well. Out of the corner of my eye, I could see her, at the end of the bar, waiting with two drinks, scrolling through Instagram. A few times, we locked eyes and I almost choked on my frozen margarita. Eventually, I told Fred I had somewhere to go and we walked outside of the bar, hugged goodbye, and I waited for him to turn the corner before I reentered said bar and met Sadie.

We laughed about it for weeks.

For both Fred and me, our date was an icebreaker to the many other dates we'd both go on before deciding to fuck around with someone for a few months or years. It was practice. And I treated every first date I went on following that one like practice, too. Telling myself it was all a dress rehearsal made it a little less scary when a first date eventually led to a tenth date, which led to me falling in love, and I realized it was opening night all along.

·

I prefer a nonmeal first date. It's hard to talk and eat dinner simultaneously, and the point of a first date is to get to know the other person. If you date me, you can almost guarantee that when we're eating dinner, we're silent, because I like to focus on my food without distractions. If for some reason, a meal is unavoidable, I think you should always recommend a place where sharing plates is the norm.

I went on a first date on a frigid November evening and we had no choice but to sit outside in the first pandemic winter. I recommended a Mexican restaurant, because he said he was going to be hungry, as he was coming from a paddle tennis match. (In addition to improv comedy boys, I highly recommend NOT ever sleeping with a man who plays a racket sport.)

RULE
8

Ordering nachos on a first date is, additionally, the best way to decide if someone is worth your time. Not to be an investigative journalist, but watch the way someone splits a plate of nachos with you, and then decide if you'd like to sleep with them.

If a person leaves all the best nachos with all the best toppings on your side of the plate, instead of hogging every nacho bite that includes a ratio of cheese, beans, meat, and guacamole, they're going to go down on you without you having to ask. If they're a selfish nacho eater, they're selfish in bed.

Not only did Mr. Racket Sports order us nachos to split, he also got hypothermia and his fingers turned purple so he couldn't even pick up a nacho and I got to eat all of them. He earned an invite up to my apartment to warm up when he didn't hog the nachos, even if the whole reason was he couldn't physically pick them up. It ended up working out for a period of time despite the fact that he froze to death and I ate all the food.

RULE
9

Perhaps the question you have for me is not what to order or what to talk about, but what the fuck to do when the bill comes or it's time to pay. When I go on a first date with a cis-het male, I typically expect him to pay. If I'm expected to fall into specific gender roles and scripts, if I'm going to be making less to his dollar, and if I'm going to be stripped of my rights by a patriarchal society and misogynistic line of thought, I'll reap the benefits of these gender scripts when I can get a free dinner out of it. Thank them once they've paid, and leave it at that.

Now the bill has been paid, and the nerves that dissipated during the actual date return with a vengeance the minute it's time to decide:

Do we part ways? Do we change locations? Do we go home together? It's like our anxiety takes a three-hour break as we drown it in tequila drinks or caffeinated beverages or nachos but reenters through the back door when it's time to decide what happens at the end.

We all know that the anxiety of actually going on a second date is preceded by none other than the post-first-date waiting period, a time when three days feels like three years. You start pacing around your living room and choosing to clean as a hobby to distract yourself from your phone. You go to spin class so your phone is locked in a locker for forty-five minutes, under the guise of "a watched pot never boils." You have exactly two near-severe DIY haircut ideas that are shot down by concerned roommates.

Make a decision about whether you want a second date before you leave the first one. Avoid the awkward post-first-date dance. Maybe that means making plans for the next date before you've left the first. If you enjoyed spending time with someone, and they enjoyed that time, too—great, why don't you let them know? Maybe that means reading between the lines of what the other person is communicating as you part ways.

Perhaps they say, "Text me when you get home safely"—a perfect excuse for you to send a message that says "I had a lot of fun tonight, I just got home. LMK if you want to do it again sometime!"

Maybe they say (and you can say this, too), "This was a lot of fun, I'll text you."

Maybe it'll be "Tonight was a lot of fun"—and this is a great excuse to say, "We should do it again sometime, text me!"

Let's say you don't hear from them at all. That's when you start vacuuming your apartment floor to ceiling as a distraction. When this happens, know you're allowed to text them first. Sending a text can and will not change their mind about you. They already know how they feel, as do you. Either they're interested or they're not. You texting them does not change this.

If you're not interested in texting them first, I recommend you wait a few days or until the following weekend before concluding their disinterest.

It's common these days for people to prefer silence over letting someone down easy, but after a first date, things can be a little awkward, so I understand. I do operate under the assumption that you don't owe anyone anything, especially someone you met one time. I recommend not adding someone's contact into your phone until the third date, so there's nothing lingering to delete. If you've made the decision not to follow up with them after the first date, and they do text you, my recommendation is to send a message letting them down. Ghosting is disrespectful and immature and frankly leads to bad karma.

A good message you can send:

> **Hey! I had a great time on Friday too. If I'm being honest with you, I don't see a romantic future for us, but I think you're really awesome and I wish you all the best.**

My cardinal rule about a letdown text is don't lie. If you don't want to be friends with the person, do not say "let's stay friends." If it isn't great to hear from them, maybe don't open the message with "good to hear from you." Instead, be polite and brief. Be respectful. Be kind. And do the right thing.

If you're the person waiting for the text, I caution you about idealism. It is always good to be hopeful. Hope is one of the only things we have to hang on to. But making excuses after being ghosted for ten days—like they're studying, or they're busy, or they have a packed week, and that's why they haven't texted me—will only cause you more agony. Face the thing head-on. It's easier to get past it when you're looking at something dead in the eye.

Cold hard truth time: nobody is ever too damn busy to send a text. People can certainly be too busy to have a text conversation, or to open the door to a dialogue. People can forget, can think they said something or pressed send when they didn't, can be dealing with something and not have the bandwidth to reply. I don't answer anyone's texts that are not urgent or timely until I have the capacity to reply at 100 percent, which is sometimes twenty-four to forty-eight hours. But if something is timely, regards someone's feelings, is urgent, or is necessary to converse about now, then I will ALWAYS reply, or ALWAYS let the person know I'm busy right now but will get back to them ASAP. Unless I am in a really dark place, I respond. Even at my busiest, I can let someone know I am not ignoring them but will touch base when things slow down.

It's good to have a mix of idealism and realism when we're dating. It's good to hope for romance, to revel in the exciting magic of something about to work out—but it's good to also be realistic. If you haven't heard from someone after a first date, and it's been a week since said first date, don't make an excuse for this person. Be brave enough to say: this person does not deserve my energy, as they've decided I am not worth a bit of theirs. The stakes are still so low. And you will heal the scrape of rejection with a bit of Neosporin and a distraction.

I've gone down every possible post-first-date avenue—I've headed to a second bar, gone home with them, had one-night stands, left without even kissing, and kissed goodbye but still gone separate ways and wound up at home in bed.

Here's the truth: if you're on a first date with the right person, nothing will stand in the way of a second date. If you have sex with the right person on the first date, it isn't going to change their mind about pursuing a relationship with you. If you say you'd like to go home but would love to see them again, ending the night early won't change their mind about pursuing a relationship with you. This is why you should always do what you WANT to do, and not what you think they want you to do. With the right person, you doing what you want to do is the sexiest choice you can make.

Just like how I have a predate warmup, I have a postdate

cooldown. Maybe I don't get to cool down in the same way after every first date, but I'd like to if I can.

RULE 12

One of my favorite rituals is making tentative plans with friends after the date, so you have a built-in out, if you need it. Going to drinks at seven p.m. on a Thursday and saying you have to get to a birthday pregame at ten p.m. puts a cap on the night. Even if you do enjoy their company and hope to see them again, the lingering final moments of the date are more comfortable. And if the date is awful, having somewhere to go after is a welcome palette cleanse. I've never been one to enjoy spending more than four hours with someone I don't know very well, anyway. My social battery drains, my judgment gets clouded, and I start to interpret situations differently than I would if I was with someone I know very well.

Above all, my first-date experience has enabled me to get to know myself better. I've found what works for me: drinks with plans after so I have an out. I've deduced what doesn't: drinking too much or going home with a person I don't know well. And I've learned about my own desires, confidence, and boundaries. A first date can open a window to a house with exposed brick walls and a kitchen with stocked cabinets. You can climb through the window together, find the linen closet, light a candle, and make the beds. You can unlock the front door from the inside. Together this will be your emotional real estate. A house you design to your liking. A place where your relationship can live.

I tend to believe in signs. Because I don't know what else to believe in some days. Signs can come on first dates, and in my mind, they're signs from the universe—be it good or bad omens. I try to look out for the ways the universe could be quietly telling me something.

Six weeks after a brutal breakup, I went on a four-hour first date in New York City. The conversation flowed brightly and with enthusiasm—we had a lot in common, we brushed hands and I felt a little spark of energy between us. And above all, I felt like that night wouldn't be one where I cried myself to sleep. Because that night, I saw a world where I could proceed. I could move forward. I could be okay. I felt pretty and giddy and alone. I had braced for impact and somehow moved forward. He went to the bathroom and I took the moment to open up my phone camera and reapply my lip gloss.

That first date was great. It reinflated my heart ever so slightly. It felt sort of like a rebirth because I felt myself settling sweetly in my own next chapter. One categorized by a stronger sense of self. It was also a sign. Maybe the good guy I went on the date with wasn't my good guy. But he wasn't supposed to be my good guy. He was a sign—it was the first page of a new beginning.

There will be good first dates, bad first dates, ones that change your life and ones you will entirely forget about. If you dose yourself when it comes to love and like and affection, only allowing yourself to accept the amount of love you believe you're worth, you'll miss out on what it feels like to have everything. You deserve it all. A great first date. A free dinner. Good sex. Wonderful conversation. You deserve for things to work out. You deserve to casually date if that's what you want. You deserve for first dates to be fun and funny and some kind of a lesson. So next time you're prepping for a first date—be it romantic or platonic or anything else—remember that. Remember that you're worth it. That you're interesting and sexy and cool.

No, I can't see your underwear lines. Yes, you should order the pasta if you want the pasta. No, it isn't always going to work out; nine times out of ten it won't. But you'll realize why when it finally does work out.

You might walk away with a story, a hickey, a hangover, a second date, a great kiss, or the motivation to try again—but notice one thing—you'll never end up with nothing. Be a person you'd want to sit across from a table from first. Even just the spark to keep going is something. And that something is enough.

Rules for a Second Date

1. Take a temperature check on longevity.

2. Low expectations, open mind, open heart. Remember, it's not that deep yet. Take it for what it is: trying each other on. This is still, and always will be, FUN.

3. A second date should take place no more than a week after the first.

4. Wear a chill outfit: great jeans, cute sneakers, a really cute top, and more relaxed makeup.

5. Pregame with a walk or a run and a superstrong coffee.

6. Follow on Instagram but NOT anywhere else.

7. At this point you should still have a roster; you don't need to be concretely seeing a ton of other people, but do NOT cut anyone off until there's a full exclusive label.

8. The soft launch of caring: recall details about their family, their background, make them feel desired.

9. Share something intimate with them! Tell STORIES. Start developing inside jokes.

OUR SECOND DATE was on a Monday. We couldn't wait more than forty-eight hours before seeing each other again. In the interim, I moved from my parents' house to an apartment on Staten Island, where I lived that summer. I had a new internship, a freshly broken heart, and no curtains. That Monday morning the sunrise trespassed through my windows at five a.m.—this early wake-up would become his favorite part about spending the night at my place. We spent the hours between our first and second date talking about how we wished to sleep together—and the way two writers sext is very interesting. It's almost like we were competing over who could say "please sleep with me" in a more poetic way—and unfortunately he always won.

On our first date I told Nate about a bookstore in Chelsea Market. It's called Posman Books. "I've loved it since I was a little girl," I told him.

He wanted to see it for himself, so we planned to meet outside Chelsea Market Monday after work—the first day of my internship—for our second date. I liked the urgency, the desire to see each other with haste after our first. It showed that our excitement boiled over like hot water in a saucepan: impossible to contain, dangerous to touch. You should never prioritize a man over your own career aspirations, but I wasn't even nervous for my first day of work. I was overcome with coquettish giddiness, like a child who knew she'd see her crush that day on the school bus. The minutes ticked by as I waited for five p.m.

As I approached the market, the sky opened up and poured down. I love the rain and I hate umbrellas. Sadie tells me this is her favorite thing about me—I never brace for the storm, but when it comes, I'm fine to exist within it. I don't really feel the need to take cover. While everyone else runs, I am strangely at ease—even with mascara running down my cheeks and my hair clinging to my neck in strands.

"You'll always dry," I often say when someone asks where my umbrella is. Practical? No. Romantic? Yes.

Luckily for me, this Monday rainstorm was unexpected. Neither of us had an umbrella. Nate was wearing a white T-shirt. Simple. We spent an hour in the bookstore, pulling books off the shelves, making recommendations to each other, reading poems quietly to the other's side profile, stealing brief moments of eye contact. I recommended *M Train* by Patti Smith and two others. He bought all three of the books I told him I loved and nothing else. He didn't even glance at the back cover or request a synopsis. He made a midwestern brand of polite small talk with the cashier while I stood beside him trying not to seem too excited. I remember thinking there couldn't possibly be something more romantic than someone buying a book on your recommendation alone.

We stood on the sidewalk, our arms brushing. The rain persisted. The sky was gray, the taxi drivers were aggravated, the New York traffic was swallowing the street whole. We were hungry and happy. I told him about how I love the rain. He told me about this one time in Michigan. I traded in his story for one of my own. Nate spoke about his little sister and his mom and his guitar. I loved it all. He pressed me up against brick apartment buildings and held my face in his hands. Rainwater dripped from his hair to the bridge of his freckled nose. He stopped at every street corner to kiss me while cars skidded on the slick streets. I did what I thought I was supposed to do to appear more creative and interesting and sexy. I made the mistake of believing that chemistry was the same as potential for longevity, emotional connection, or realism. I made the mistake of believing that chemistry alone meant we could build something together.

How could you not, I guess, when an artist is pushing you up against brick buildings in the middle of a Monday rainstorm?

But truthfully, there is no real way, on a second date, to gauge what you as a couple could become down the line. There is no way to know if you'll last forever, or even if you're right for each other. You can hope and wish but you can't know. On two dates alone, there's not enough substance to decide whether you could spend forever together. I wished for that, of course, but I also was trying my best not to get too ahead of myself. I had become an expert at being so far ahead of myself I ended up lost.

Chemistry, specifically intimate and sexual chemistry, is 20 percent of the equation when it comes to a relationship. Chemistry is an essential ingredient to a great relationship, but it isn't the concrete foundation for a sturdy home. On a second date, we can decide, with certainty, whether or not there's chemistry—but not compatibility. So often, early on in a relationship with someone, we try to decide that there's a potential for longevity. A potential for love. And sometimes there is. But it's pretty impossible to diagnose a relationship until you've known the person for more than a mere handful of dates. A relationship is not something that simply exists between two people. It is something that is built. So our biggest downfall is mistaking sparks of early chemistry for being the start of something incredible, which can sometimes lead to great disappointment. Sometimes, of course, it does work out. Sometimes it *is* the start of something incredible. I just caution you about getting your hopes up too high on a second date. I'm a perfect example of a person who did.

Kissing in the rain and seeing the outline of his body through his wet T-shirt and racing each other down MacDougal Street were all indicators of chemistry. We knew we'd have great sex. It was a given. I watched his hands as he paid the bill and wished for them to trace my silhouette. When I spoke, sometimes his eyes flickered to my lips. We knew it would be good, great even. But we didn't know if we would one day buy a home together and have two kids and a dog. We couldn't know that. But in my brain, lights went off and a symphony played. If there was chemistry, the love would come . . . right? All I could think was "he's the one," when the only thing I really *did* know was that he was going to be an incredible lay. I wish I had checked my pulse. Stopped to breathe. Reminded myself that the pace was sexy and fun and cool but it didn't mean we'd be together forever. It would have been impossible for me to know then. I think I would've avoided a lot of gray space had I just realized that chemistry does not mean love is around the bend. Sometimes it means sex is around the bend, and that can be perfectly fine too.

After the bookshop, we went to the Mermaid Oyster Bar in Greenwich Village. We sat at a high-top table. The restaurant was poorly lit and our table had a little candle that illuminated our faces like an old film. We were rain-soaked and giggly. He had red wine, I had prosecco. That's how it went for the rest of the summer. Whoever got to the bar first knew what to order. One glass of red, one glass of prosecco.

We stayed in the restaurant for so long the night edged to Tuesday. He held my hands, told me a story that I felt like he didn't tell just anyone. The waitstaff mopped the floors around our feet, and eventually asked us to leave. The restaurant had closed and we failed to notice we were the last ones there. This was the beginning of another tradition: we lingered everywhere, long after the main event had packed its things.

Our waiter gave us these red paper fish, called a "miracle fish fortune teller." They kind of look like Swedish Fish but made of translucent paper. You were meant to place the fish in your hand, and let it unfurl, and it would tell you how you feel, akin to a mood ring. Our fish told us we were in love. We looked up at each other with candy eyes, sugary, anticipating the shoes we would fill of two people destined to be in love. We played our parts for an entire summer. We were full of idealism and wine and M&Ms, romanticizing the shit out of a partnership that'd never truly be. We did things people in books did—we wanted to be a real love story. In another life it might've worked. Sometimes I think our second date was the best one we ever had. We got high on the chemistry and tried to survive on that alone. For a while, it worked. Eventually, we couldn't sustain ourselves.

On a second date all you really know is (1) Would I like to see this person again? and (2) Am I attracted to this person? Both of those answers were yes for Nate and me. We both internalized that and decided that because we were perfect for each other on paper, we'd be perfect for each other in real life. And on paper it felt like he could've been the one. In the flesh, he was a good guy. Just not my good guy. Someone else's. I hope he finds them. Maybe he already has.

·

Second dates can be a lot of things. They can turn into happy endings, be the very last time you ever see someone, or be neither great or bad—just fine. I find second dates to be slightly more complicated and stress-inducing than a first. Imagine you were on *The Bachelor* or *American Idol*. It would be much easier to be eliminated in the first round than a later one. It would also, as a judge, be much simpler to eliminate someone on the first round than the ones to follow. The more time that passes, the more one gets invested emotionally, the more difficult it becomes to untangle two lives, the more skin you have in the game.

With this in mind, the pressure is naturally elevated on a second date. You've mutually decided you'd like to continue seeing each other—but it doesn't mean we have to crack under its weight, or even bear its weight at all. We get to make the choice. Something that seems daunting or heavy gets to be carefree and simple.

On a second date, we often continue to fear much of what we feared on the first date, only this time, we fear it on a deeper level. I would never bullshit with you, so I'm not going to paint a happy picture of a carefree, stress-free second-date experience and tell you that's how it always felt for me. It takes work to let go of the preconceived notion that dating is scary and anxiety inducing and shitty and unfun. Usually, you're a little fucking scared. And I am not here to say, "Don't be a little fucking scaredy-cat, girl boss! You've got this!" I'm here to say, "I too am a little fucking scared. Let's talk about how we can alleviate some of that fear, and make a second date simple."

Step one: choose you. Like yourself. Enjoy your company. You're pretty cool. I like the way you wear your hair and the way your eyes light up when you talk about your favorite episode of TV or your mom. You're uniquely pretty, innately unique. And I love the sound of your voice. All we can do for ourselves is choose us, because not everyone is going to like *us*. And that's okay. Sometimes you'll meet someone and you'll have a personality conflict, or you just won't get along. It's human. It's not a bad reflection of you, or them, if you just don't get along—sometimes, it just happens. And if this phenomenon is inherent, then we don't want to be paying any mind or giving any energy to someone who effectively doesn't want or deserve it. What I'm trying to say is you have a great personality. He might, she might, they might go on a date with someone else right after yours and fall for them—that has nothing to do with you. They weren't your right person. You are no worse than whoever they chose. You are different. You're funny and cool and interesting. Not everyone will love you, and you won't love everybody either. So just be yourself; avoid the effort of pretending. This way you can find out after two dates and not two months that you're just not compatible with someone, whether this is a mutual or one-sided decision.

RULE
2

The biggest problem I found myself encountering on early dates with a person is that I would start falling for the *idea* of someone in my head, instead of getting to know them and letting myself fall naturally if that's what my heart chose to do. I pride myself on being hopeful and positive, but I would often view someone

I'd been on a few dates with as the person I *wanted* them to be. I'd start creating a future life for us in my mind, molding them into the character that would fit the partner in my dream life perfectly. And then when they didn't turn out that way, and instead of my fictitious prince, they were just a regular person from a regular place who liked art and music and food and taking showers together, I was disappointed. And it wasn't his fault, ever, that he was a human being and not a Prince Charming. It wasn't really my fault, either, for being overzealous when it came to a potential new flame, but I can't help but wonder if I ruined our chances of ever being something because I didn't view the person across the table as a human being. I try to pause before seeing someone as more than they are, because I wouldn't want someone to see me as an inflated version of myself that they created in their mind either. I'd want someone to see me as me. For me. For everything I am and everything I am not, for the way I get nervous before boarding an airplane and the way I get excited and teary-eyed when my favorite song comes on. All we can ask on a second date is to try to see each other at that uniquely human level, where we're willing to say, "It's cool that you are human and so am I—it makes us nuanced and interesting and troubled. It makes me want to know the folds of you more."

It is a beautiful thing to see someone as human and choose to love them exactly as they are. And when you meet someone and you're on a second date with them, and you're meeting them right where they are, and they're doing the same, you avoid disappointment, and open the door to something wonderful. Because let's face the facts. Your person might have childhood trauma. He might have a thyroid problem. She might have fears. They might have depression. They will have insecurities and anxieties and fixations and favorite foods. So do you. The beauty is unpacking all that with someone who says, "I think you're even sexier now that I know."

I wish I would've known that. Sometimes I'd pull back and realize I wasn't trying to get to know the person at the other side of the dinner table. I was trying to get to know someone I'd created. Someone who didn't exist. Someone I'd resent because they were breathing the same air as me and not just an idea. Don't waste your time on someone who is inflating you in their mind. Don't waste your time on inflating someone else in yours.

Time is currency, and it is precious. Don't waste it. I want you to be intentional about how you're spending it. Don't beg someone to be with you when you could be giving your time instead to your deepest friendships and brightest passions.

A truth I wish I'd known sooner: there's no real way to increase your chances with someone. You are either going to be a yes, I'll see them again, or a no, I'm not interested, and vice versa. That doesn't mean you're not good enough, or not worthy enough for them. It just means you're not compatible long term. Not to dissolve something so nuanced to a simple yes or no, but effectively, this is what dating is. We succumb to the idea that the way we craft a text message or the outfit we wear or the perfume we spray could change our fate with someone and garner a second date. But no carefully worded sentence, or what you said or what you withheld, what you wore, what you posted, or what you ordered can swap your spot from yes to no in someone's mind. Especially if you're being yourself. If they're right for you, they're going to like the outfit you wore because you like it, and they're going to like that you ordered your favorite food and spoke adamantly about your favorite movie.

Recognizing this is a form of freedom. Frankly, the time I wasted on my notes app, typing and retyping different versions of the message "Hey! We still on for Thursday? Where do you want to go?," could've been spent doing just about anything else.

Allow me to illuminate this stupidity. (I'm allowed to say it's stupid because I did it too.)

Can you imagine any of these messages truly changing your opinion of someone? Truly changing their chances of being with you?

1. Hey! We still on for Thursday? Where do you want to go?

2. Hiiii . . . still on for Thurs?

3. Hey, do you still want to go out on Thursday?

4. Hi! Where should I meet you Thursday?

5. Still good for Thursday?

6. Would love to see you Thursday if you're still free!

7. Still down for dinner tomorrow?

Those are seven versions of the same exact idea, getting the same message across—the way you word something will not alter your chances of being with them and will change absolutely nothing about how they feel about you.

Furthermore, texting someone first will not change your chances with that person either. As I said earlier, if someone wants to pursue you and is interested in seeing your relationship through, you sending a text first will not change that. If the person isn't interested in being with you, sending a text won't change that either. So if you want to text someone first, just do it. Besides, you'd never want to be with someone who found it annoying that you texted them. You'd never want to be with someone who made you feel anxious about reaching out.

•

After a good first date of drinks and dinner, followed by a wonderful couch makeout and tipsy goodbye, I was looking forward to my second date with a guy named Cam. I knew we'd have one, because he told me he wanted to see me again as soon as possible. He was goofy and lanky and smart and he texted me in a way that felt like the banter was just ours.

Cam wasn't big on giving away how he felt, and he was also several years older than me, so I was trying to play it cool by not asking. I decided his desire to see me again as soon as possible could mean many things. It could mean he wanted to see me again as soon as possible because he saw potential for a real relationship. On the other hand, he could have been one of those guys who takes a woman on a first date to be polite and respectful, with the intention of only pursuing something casual thereafter. That is, the first date will be the final date, and all other time spent together will be less holding hands in public, and more takeout, Netflix and chill, late-night hookup, or sneaky link.

It's not necessarily anyone's fault if one person is looking for a more casual connection and the other isn't—oftentimes the blame is to be placed on a mutual lack of communication. It is disrespectful if someone leads you to believe they want a relationship with you when all along it was about something casual—but we can chalk it up to a lapse in communication when one person wants a relationship, the other wants something respectful but casual, and no one ever speaks up, leaving everyone confused.

If time is our currency, and we treat it as such, we have to get familiar with letting someone know, right off the bat, what we're looking for. If you're looking to be in a relationship, you don't have to say exactly that. It's plenty to say, "I'm looking to see where things go, and I'm not looking for something casual." Conversely, if you are looking for something casual, you'd say, "Just so you know, I'm looking for something casual, let me know if that's okay." If you're using a dating app, be honest on your profile and put down what kind of relationship you're swiping for.

A lot of times we fear being plainspoken about what we're looking for because we worry it could stifle our chances with this person. Our egos tell us all the time that we have the power to change someone's mind about us. We don't. And you know this, because when you decide you're not interested in going on another date with someone, them begging you or being persistent about it changes nothing; you're just not interested in a second date and you're not going to change your mind in that instant. When you tell someone that you're interested in strictly casual sex, and they try to change your mind, you'll likely feel as though this person doesn't think you can make a strong decision for yourself and stick to it. Even if that's not true, and they're just hopeful you'd come around. Ultimately, nothing is impossible—but typically it's good to be on the same page early on.

If we choose not to share our wants early on, we run the risk of being disappointed. Nobody is a mind reader. Not even my boyfriend after asking me "Where do you want to eat?," unfortunately. Human beings are human beings are human beings. Treat them how you want to be treated—with direct, gentle honesty.

The age gap with Cam intimidated me. He didn't do anything, I just wanted him to think of me as casual and chill and I also figured that I could change his mind about being with me in a serious way. In light of that, I didn't let him know I was looking for something a bit more serious, which I thought wouldn't be very casual and chill of me. Eventually, around seven or eight dates in, he told me he was looking for something casual, and I was disappointed. I wasn't dating to have a boyfriend instantly, but I also wasn't looking for a hookup.

There were signs, even before he flat-out said he was looking for something casual, that this is how he felt. After our first date, we never went *out* on a date again. I'd go to his apartment, we'd order sushi and open wine, or make cocktails and watch music videos on TV. It felt more mature than a college Netflix and chill or a late-night hookup, but it had the same ethos—hanging out, enjoying each other's company, hooking up casually. The difference was he was thirty and not twenty-one, so his casual relations included amaretto sours and fancy takeout sushi, not microwave popcorn and a Hulu documentary.

I enjoyed his company so much I wanted to convince myself that the second date—takeout and wine at his apartment—was still a date equivalent to going out to do something. It wasn't the kind of at-home date that felt like a date: a planned movie night, or cooking together. It was the kind of at-home date that was a hidden message, an intentional but unspoken decision, made by him alone, that this was never going anywhere, so we needed to keep things behind closed doors. Keeping it in his apartment let us exist in a perfect bubble. As long as all you ever do is stay in, eat takeout, and hook up on the couch, the relationship is never tested in real life, and you'll never actually know the other person or how you as a couple move through the world.

.

Now that I've broken your hearts about twelve times, we're going to discuss what happens when you get to that second date. What are our sacred rituals? Do we have sex? Do we wear underwear? Do we panic beforehand and break down on the phone to our emotional-support long-distance best friend?

We do a whole lot of . . . some of that.

Here's the thing about dating for partnership and not dating to date. To me, there's a little haste. A little need for motion. And maybe, for you, there's not—maybe you're casually dating and enjoying that, and you don't feel a need for haste. But I believe if you're dating looking for a relationship, you're not going to want to be stuck in a waiting room. The first three dates—for me at least—must all land in the span of a month. That way if things don't work out, I can gracefully move on to something else.

RULE
3

So let's break down the logistics: unless either party has a major conflict, I prefer that the second date land somewhere seven to ten days after the first. If the first date goes really well, there should be a spark behind seeing that person again. I don't mean you need to be head over heels in love with the person, but being excited to see each other again, and your plans reflecting that, is a really great sign.

A second date is a great time to do something during the day, if you already haven't. Do the opposite of whatever you did on the first date. If the first date was coffee, go to dinner. If the first date was drinks, go mini golfing, grab lunch, or have a picnic. Getting to know someone in one environment at one time of the day can give us a false idea of them as a person. Get to know someone truly and wholly, in the daylight and the nighttime and with coffee and with wine. We all deserve to be known wholly.

There's no one way to go on a second date or even a first one. Sometimes you'll both decide you want to have sex on the second date or the first date or the fifth date. Sometimes you'll decide to save your first kiss together, and do that on the second date. Sometimes you'll spend the night, other times you won't. The right person is going to make you feel comfortable and at ease, and all the impulses you both have will feel natural. There is no wrong time if the moment is right for it.

And when you're on the way to that second date, remember to keep asking yourself the questions you need answers to. Do I enjoy time with them? How do they make me feel? Do they make me laugh? Do they make me nervous? Because the truth is, sometimes butterflies aren't all that.

He gives me butterflies, I'd tell myself all too often, as the taxi rounded the corner and pulled up to his apartment complex and my heart plummeted through my asshole, through the stained cab back seat, and into the city's smoky, hot asphalt. I'd be dripping sweat but simultaneously promising anyone who would listen that he gave me *butterflies*. Not anxiety, but butterflies, instead of facing the awkward fact that he actually made me feel a little uncomfortable and his hard-to-read feelings and thoughts made me anxious.

Cam's lack of consistent communication and his unclear feelings about me did give me anxiety—not butterflies. His unwillingness to express his emotions, or tell me where he saw me in his life, made me want to shit myself and constantly made me feel like I was on trial. Those weren't butterflies. This was just the wrong person.

Three days after my first date with Noah, I remember how I felt getting ready for our second date. It was deep winter in Manhattan, we'd both just been vaccinated, and outdoor dining was the only option at the time, so he suggested a wine and charcuterie night at his apartment.

I wore the soft pink sweater (remember the Eff Me sweater?) I almost always wore that winter. It was formerly my mother's; wearing it feels like a hug from her. As I got ready, I kept things simple—my favorite jeans, makeup that makes me feel good, a great pair of sneakers. I drank a hot coffee and curled my hair, watching snow swirl outside my Upper West Side living room window.

We'd recently followed each other on Instagram, but I still didn't have his number saved in my phone. I'll never add a man's phone number into my contacts until four dates. It's a rule I have to avoid attachment, which is difficult for someone with an anxious attachment style.

I was a little nervous, because socializing in general makes me nervous, but I had no butterflies. It was an adjustment from any other second-date experiences, but I'd walked away from our first date feeling comforted and comfortable, and that was pretty much all I felt. I didn't feel head over heels in love. I didn't feel like signing the marriage papers tomorrow. I didn't feel like he was this great prince. I felt like this person was really interesting and I wanted, badly, to see him again. I felt like I'd enjoy continuing to know him—I was intrigued but not infatuated. And I think that allowing myself to collect my thoughts about him after a few dates instead of prematurely deciding how I felt was the reason I felt so great. Not being crazy about him when I hardly knew him was actually a good thing.

The date was scheduled for five p.m. I remember scrolling Bumble and Hinge idly on my way over—trying to maintain a semblance of a roster in case this didn't work out. I try not to get my hopes up until my hopes elevate themselves. All I needed before knocking on the apartment door was three deep breaths, otherwise I felt like, no matter what, this would just be fun. And it was supposed to be fun. He had a cutting board set up with all the cheeses, jams, and charcuterie I had mentioned I liked on our first date. He had a bottle of wine split between two glasses, and I had another in my bag. I had made tentative plans with friends at eight p.m. in case something went wrong, but on the contrary, I ended up staying for hours. It was just fun. It was silly and a little sexy and sweet. We sat at his kitchen table eating grapes and drinking wine when he looked at me, and I knew he was about to kiss me for the first time. It wasn't the best kiss I'd ever had in my life—but it was all just good. And good was enough. He did a magic trick for me once we were pretty drunk, and I thought it was the dorkiest thing I'd ever seen in the best way. His roommates emerged to watch some sort of playoff game, and I was invited to stay. We went on a walk to find ingredients for espresso martinis and gluten-free Oreos (they'd just hit the market). We made the

RULE
9

martinis and kissed in the kitchen. Two years later, to the date, his roommates reminded me I needed to make them espresso martinis for the anniversary of me becoming their honorary roommate.

What I'm trying to tell you is that not every first kiss is a fireworks display. Not every second date is red fish telling you that you'll fall in love. Sometimes it's cheese and Two-Buck Chuck and a good kiss in a kitchen and walking the aisles of Rite Aid. And sometimes that's better than the running through the rain, imagining each other in bed, butterflies, and high-stakes second dates of my past. Sometimes something just feels safe. And it gradually becomes more than safe. It grows into something wonderful and strong. It becomes a real-life magic trick. Something that makes you cry if you think about it too much and too fully.

I wish I'd known I'd much rather have a slow crescendo to the loudest point than an immediate symphony.

Attraction grows. So does love. That's why I believe that butterflies can be a bad sign. Chemistry does not equal the potential for a relationship to develop. It usually indicates we'd like to get to know someone or sleep with them. Sometimes it's better if things start slowly. If there isn't crazy, intense, manic desire. Of course, attraction and desire can become wedding bells or a forever or just a really long, really great time. But for me that kiss didn't tell me that I'd like to spend a very long time with him. It told me that I would like to kiss him again, and that's all I needed to know in that moment. What suggested that I'd want to spend a while into the future with him was everything that came after that first kiss—the conversations and storytelling and time spent one-on-one.

But that second date was comforting. It was comfortable. I left after the football game because I wasn't invited to stay and also, I didn't want to. The way things were going, the pace, it all felt natural. Staccato. Rhythmic. I didn't want the music to come to a screeching halt or for the music to crescendo and be at its loudest too fast. So we didn't sleep together. Not because we didn't want to. I'm sure he did. I was open to the idea but wasn't immediately enthralled by it. So instead he walked me downstairs. Down the stairs (thirty-two floors) to wait for the Uber he called to take me back home to the Upper West Side. I remember quietly sneaking into my apartment, a little tipsy, telling myself: *That finally felt right*.

•

But for every second date that goes really, really well, that amounts to a third, there are others that don't make it past a second, or don't go as well as you wished. At the point of a second date, all you owe each other is respect. Just because there's a second date doesn't mean there's going to be a third, and that for me was often a tough pill to swallow.

Many times we use a second date to decide if we are interested in pursuing something with this person. I generally don't think a first date (unless it's a FUCK NO) is an accurate amount of time to decide whether or not you're interested. If it isn't a fuck no, and you're not 100 percent sure, I say always go on a second for that temperature check.

But second dates are still in that first-three-date cohort—a time when both people are still trying each other on. The stakes are still incredibly low. You don't know the other person in an intimate way yet, you're not in so deep that conversations about pursuing a relationship or choosing not to are hours long. So it's important, with this in mind, that you make the choice to not be passive, but rather, to be an active participant in the early stages.

Don't wait for someone to say, "Let's go on a third date." If you're enjoying yourself on the second date, on your way out, be brave enough to ask, "When do I get to see you again?" Choosing passivity means we put emphasis on the other person's decision in a way we don't on our own. Let yourself make the choice. Continue to ask yourself thorough questions, to check in with yourself:

Do I share values with this person? Are they attractive to me? How do I feel when I'm with them? Would I like to see them again?

We so often forget to tell women that it's better to be single than in a relationship just to be in one, or in a relationship that doesn't serve you. Don't settle on a yes because someone is interested, or because you worry you won't find another yes. If we're rejecting passivity on a second date, we're deciding that we will make a choice about how we feel, and what we want, just like the other person is going to make that choice.

If we're rejected after a second date, or ghosted, or the relationship doesn't progress further, the stakes are still low enough that the house won't burn down. It can be a bummer. It can suck. And it's allowed to. But when we make the conscious effort to think in terms of the present and not predict the future of our life with this person, we'll either be pleasantly surprised or slightly disappointed with the outcome.

We'll get to go home to our friends, or call them on FaceTime, and we'll realize we have so much good love in our life already, in so many different ways, in so many different veins, pulsing to the heart—that the person we went on two dates with who told us they didn't see a future with us doesn't really matter. There is always so much more love to be had.

•

I often remind myself that I know nothing when I think I know everything. I know nothing about this date or its outcome. I know nothing about this person. I know nothing about the night ahead. All I know is I am enjoying myself, and I'd like to continue to enjoy myself. I'm proud of myself for being vulnerable and intimate and brave enough to share something with someone else, or to open my door to the possibility. All I know is I am showing up as I am, welcoming the possibility of a something.

That is the energy I bring with me on a second date. My intention is always just to continue to try this person on. Reject passivity. Remember everything in the rearview mirror, but keep your eyes on the horizon.

For every time it didn't work out, there'd be a time, down the line, when it did. And I choose to hope for that. I choose to fill my cup with the love of my female friends, because dating is tough. It's tricky and sticky and anxiety inducing. It can also be sexy and cool and fulfilling. Everything can be anything. Anything can become everything. We can take the edge off ourselves, with a glass of wine or an affirmation or a smile at yourself in the bathroom mirror— you're in the driver's seat, and you have your eyes straight ahead. The view is going to be sunny one day, once again.

Part
2

Rules for a Third, Fourth, and Fifth Date

1. It's okay not to have butterflies or nerves!

2. Decisions, decisions: Are they a yes or a no?

3. Categorize where it's going.

4. Roommate check 👀—if you've met their roommates or friends, it's a good sign.

5. Inside jokes are a good sign.

6. Go on an out-of-the-box date.

7. Relationship personality is a go!

8. Wear your regular day-to-day hair and makeup.

9. Do a collaborative activity.

10. It's time for a soft launch of caring part 2.

THERE WAS NOTHING wrong with our first two dates. We went to dinner near the beach for the first one. It was a nice night until it started to pour rain and we ran back to his car and got soaking wet. In the right circumstances, this would've been romantic. Idyllic almost.

I think I had salmon. I know I wore a jean skirt. It felt sexy and cool and mature for someone to pick me up for a date, even if it was in his beat-up silver Toyota Camry. He was from my hometown, but we'd never met, nor had we gone to the same school. He became Hometown Boy. It felt straight out of a Nicholas Sparks film. I imagined a white picket fence. A dog. Three kids with blond hair. Things I didn't even think I wanted, but figured I'd settle for if it meant I could be loved.

I thought the absence of romantic love meant there was no love to be had. But there was plenty of love, plenty of people to love, plenty of ways to be loved. I wish someone would've told me that. The people and things I thought would furnish the vacant rooms inside of me would merely decide that type of a burden was too much work. The things I didn't give enough attention to were always clamoring to fill me whole.

Throughout my first two dates with Hometown Boy there weren't any red flags. No glaring discomfort. We kissed and it was fine. It was almost good, even. He was a good conversationalist. Seemed ambitious, driven. He was tall and had shaggy dirty blond hair. He complimented me. I could tell he was one of those kids that adults would've called a "good kid" when he was twelve years old.

On our second date we went to a Trader Joe's and bought a bunch of snacks and sat on a picnic blanket in a park and talked. Then he took me to meet his dog. As I stood in Hometown Boy's kitchen, my phone buzzed with Snapchat notifications from a person I had fallen for a few months before. The boy on my phone didn't have any plans to fall for me, and I knew this, but with each flash of his name on my home screen, my heart twirled with suspicion and longing in my chest. Hometown Boy didn't make me feel that way, and I wished he did. If I'd spent the same day with the other boy, I would've been in heaven. But being with Hometown Boy just didn't feel right. Life would be much easier if every good person, every person we go out on a great date with, was the right person for us. But unfortunately, that's just not how it works.

We can control a lot of things. Our heart isn't really one of them. Hearts are stubborn. We can't crate train them or discipline them or scold them—though we try. It's why we fall in love with people who hurt us or why we cannot seem to let go of the people who don't deserve us. Because to discipline our heart—to tell it that it's time to pack our things and go—utterly shatters us. It's the very reason that while a perfectly wonderful person stood in front of me with a goofy smile and all the boxes checked, my mind was floating off to Michigan—where the boy on my phone probably sat watching YouTube videos and making cookies and smoking weed from a bong.

My heart is excitable. At the anticipation of romance, she races around in my chest, stimulated by the thought of new beginnings. She's overeager, premature, constantly bouncing from one spot to the next. She'll run a marathon and never feel out of breath. She'll get into bed with you and give you everything—the whole pie— and ask for just a crumb back. I've always been proud of the way I love. My heart is definitely a bit of a bitch, too. She's stubborn and the word *no* isn't in her daily vernacular—she's a girl who knows what she wants. She is my favorite blessing and my biggest curse. When my heart decides she wants to rest, or isn't interested, or just wants to stay put, good luck ever convincing her to budge. When she's in, she's all in. So all this is to say, sometimes someone checked every box for me, and it was endlessly frustrating that the only thing that wasn't right was my heart.

Even though my heart is a stubborn bitch, I trust her endlessly, because she's always trying to steer me in the right direction. It's up to me to listen. And sometimes I don't—sometimes her plans seem a little unformed. But I let her blindfold me anyway. The heart is your leader—it'll take you into every battle, and always win. It'll guide you down a dark corridor like it knows what's around the corner. It'll force you to face life's biggest lessons and biggest joys and biggest disappointments. It can break and mend over and over and over, no matter who comes along to borrow or break it.

I compromised with my heart and decided to use the third date to make a decision about Hometown Boy. I could tell he liked me, and it would be unfair to string him along simply because I *wanted* to like him, or because I enjoyed his company. Wanting to like him and actually liking him are two vastly different things.

We went out to brunch at a place I always used to go with my cousins when we were little. I set my intention before he picked me up: I was going to decide if I wanted to continue seeing him, and I was going to hope for the best, whatever the outcome. The sun was in my eyes and we sat outside. While Hometown Boy told me funny stories about his friends, my mind slipped down the street and toward the ocean. I tried to stay present. Tried to ask myself how I really felt—sitting there with him, eating eggs, drinking coffee, laughing. And I felt fine. But I didn't feel like I wanted to see him again. I didn't feel the urge to kiss him good-bye. I wasn't going to lie up in bed imagining the next time I'd see him.

And I wasn't looking for a spark. Because, as the great Logan Ury (director of relationship science at Hinge, dating coach) says, "F*ck the spark." I don't even know what the right kind of a spark feels like. But I did know what the opposite felt like (dreadful butterflies, awkward tightness in my chest). And that's what I was facing. I was just looking for something: a nugget of feeling, a semblance of a future, a tiny moment that released oxytocin through my veins. But instead he was just a great guy I didn't really want to know. And the guilt that accompanied that consumed me as we got into his car after brunch.

While he drove me back to my house, it started to rain again. He had CDs in his car and let me choose one to play. We sat in mostly silence as we drove down slick roads, listening to the Fray (don't ask me why I chose that one). When he pulled down my driveway and put the car in park, we looked at each other, and he brushed his hand up against mine.

"Thanks for brunch again," I said, my stomach somersaulting in tandem with my racing heart.

"Anytime." He tried to lean in but I leaned away, feeling my fingers shake. I opened my mouth and my mind clouded with a thousand questions: *How could you end things with a good guy? What if there's no other good guys? What if nobody ever checks your boxes? What if he's the one and you're throwing him to the curb? What if he's right for you and you just can't realize it? Why the fuck can't you ever be attracted to the good person standing right in front of you?*

I pushed the thoughts aside. Don't disqualify your own gut instincts. Don't minimize your feelings. Maximize them. It's how you feel. It's no joke.

"I think you're great," I said.

"I think you're great too," he added. I smiled, looked down, and then remembered to try my best to maintain eye contact, because Hometown Boy deserved that.

"But I really think we'd be better just as friends. I don't want to lead you on." I paused. "I just don't see a romantic future for us right now, but maybe we could revisit things down the line?"

As I said that, I wished I hadn't. My number one rule when you're letting someone down: don't lie to them. Tell them the truth. The truth stings, but it's much better than the deep pain of being led on or lied to.

"Oh," he said. "I understand. Thanks for letting me know."

I awkwardly unbuckled my seat belt.

"Let me know if you change your mind," he said, and I figured that was my cue to open the car door and leave Hometown Boy behind.

"For sure."

I got out of the car and dipped into the house, watching him reverse out of the driveway for likely the last time. Though it's difficult to let someone down, to hurt someone's feelings, I was proud of myself for speaking up, though equally frustrated that I'd be going to bed alone that night and couldn't come around to the good guy right in front of my face. It was the right thing to do, because I'd never want to sit at the other end of the table, having brunch with someone who was convincing themselves to like me. I'd rather them set me free while it was still early enough to walk away unscathed.

This is the advice I wish someone had told me sooner: it's better to go to bed alone, laptop on my stomach, watching *Glee*, than with someone just to be with someone. I'd rather read my books and make my breakfast and take my walks than spend time with someone just because they're not bad. I'd rather go to bed alone than be with someone who wasn't right for me. This wasn't the first time I'd tried to convince myself to keep seeing someone because he was a good person, even if I wasn't interested in him at all.

Behind my facade of independence and self-reliance, I feared, painfully, that I wasn't worth love and that I'd spend my entire life alone.

I don't subscribe to the idea that we each have one "soulmate." I think you grow into being someone's soulmate—when you build a healthy relationship with them. I think your soulmate can be your closest friend or even yourself. This single story, limiting us to only having one soulmate who we're meant to go out into the world with, puts pressure on each new romantic and/or sexual encounter we have. You can have many soulmates. You can be your own.

I wished someone would've said to me, "What's the worst-case scenario?"

And when I'd say, "I wind up alone, I die alone," they'd shake their heads, take a sip of their coffee, and find my eyes avoiding theirs.

"Let us just say that came true. Let's say you didn't find one great romantic love of your life. What do you have? You have a family you are deeply close to. You have a career that fills your heart. You have a deep love for writing, for creating, for your friends, for all the romantic loves that came and went throughout your life. Look at what you do have."

Look at what you do have.

I was letting everything I did have go out with the tide, and I was sitting on the beach all alone, searching for what I felt I lacked, and what kept coming back to me was everything I took for granted. I gave myself emotional whiplash, placing romantic love on a shiny pedestal and kicking everything else—familial love, friendship, love for myself, my career—to the curb. I reminded myself that once I found that devoted, everlasting romantic love, I would no longer feel so much discomfort. But trust me, you must heal the parts of yourself you see as unlovable or desolate. No one else can heal you.

I remember being angry with my heart, as though we were opponents and not teammates. Up in my room, taking off my makeup, listening to Lorde, wondering why I could never seem to feel right with a good person, and only ever felt right when my adrenaline was coursing through my blood at a mile a minute. A third date like the one with Hometown Boy made me feel, truly, as though I would never find a good guy. My heart only seemed to want to make herself at home in the lives of people who didn't give a shit about me or vice versa.

My brain conflated good guys with a lack of passion and chemistry. And subsequently, it associated the dangerous, all-consuming, toxic guys with love—when really all they were giving me was spikes in adrenaline, fantastic sex, and chemistry. There was a road somewhere on the map of my life that I'd never traveled, marked "believing you deserve something good." One day I got lost and found myself there, and the leaves were really green and the sky was really blue. It felt warm and it felt right.

•

I view a third date as a gauge date. Especially if you've asked yourself all the right questions, reflected on the first two dates, and feel like you still live in the "maybe" camp and not the "fuck yes" or the "fuck no" camp. The "maybe" camp is a troubling place to pitch your tent. But when you're not completely sure how you feel about a person, a third date is the right time to make that executive decision. Sometimes we want to be drawn to someone, because they seem to check all our boxes, but we just can't. And it isn't fair to anyone involved to continue a relationship where you feel you're forcing yourself to desire them.

When I was sitting at brunch with Hometown Boy, I was living in the moment and enjoying our date—but I was also being intentional about my thoughts. I was asking myself: *Am I enjoying this? Is this someone I'd like to continue to get to know? Am I reacting genuinely? Would I feel comfortable telling him details about my life? Am I attracted to him?*

And it hurt to be honest with myself. Because my answers were words I didn't want to hear. I wanted to love the good guy. It hurt me to come to the conclusion that someone charming and lovely and handsome might just not be that person for me. But I had to free him to free myself. So often we get back from a date and we've mentally blacked out—and we don't even know how we felt or where our feelings lie in regard to the other person.

Even if you have to take a quick bathroom break and write it all out in your phone notes—be intentional when you're gauging where you stand with that person.

My anxiety likes to take scope of the many ways something

may work out. And so I decided that every third date has one of
four outcomes.

1. You're not interested in the same way that they are.

2. They're not interested in the same way that you are.

3. You're both interested.

4. Neither is interested.

The first outcome can often be troubling because, oftentimes, if
we've experienced a toxic or emotionally damaging relationship in
the past, we feel that any decent person coming our way is one we
should just settle on. I remember telling myself I was ungrateful,
and telling myself that my lack of gratitude or desire for a good
guy meant that I should just be alone. That I didn't deserve anything good. I felt like I should force myself to like the good guy,
because I'd been with bad guys before. If the universe was going to
bring on a good guy, my heart was probably wrong, as was my gut
instinct, and I should just ignore both instead of facing the truth—
not every good guy automatically has to be my good guy.

Let me remind you of something I often have to remind myself:
for every bad person, there is a good person. For every person who
doesn't care for your feelings or treat you as you should be treated,
there is someone who will do the exact opposite. So, the first good
person to land in your lap doesn't need to be the good person you
choose to seriously date. There is no shortage of good people; we
just hear about the bad ones with the most appalling volume.

The second option is often troubling in a very different way—
when you're interested, but the other person isn't. And nothing
I say will truly remedy the sting of someone saying, "I just don't
think we're right for each other," when you thought you could be.
Or "I just don't know if I see us as anything more than friends"
when you see something else.

Don't disqualify your feelings because someone doesn't recipro-cate them or feel them at the same level or in the same way. Don't say those feelings are stupid or invalid or unwarranted. You had these feelings. We cannot choose our feelings. We only choose how to react to our feelings. The person letting you down didn't choose their feelings either. I hope they do their best to express them gently.

To feel, to open your heart to someone, is vulnerable and brave. Don't tell yourself the story we all jump to when someone says, "I'm just not that interested"—a story where we're pathetic or ugly or uninteresting or uncool. You could check someone's boxes and not be their person. Maybe their heart is being stubborn. Maybe they're frustrated that they don't feel the way they think they should about you. Empathy is really sexy and really human. Tap into it. So, tell yourself a story about fate. About hope. Tell yourself the story about what you deserve. Tell yourself the story where that great potential is out there. Tell yourself that the rejection you faced is allowed to sting. Tell yourself you're brave. Tell yourself a story where you deserve good things. Tell yourself the story where you're all right alone. You appreciate every little thing. Tell yourself that the universe doesn't want you to waste time with the wrong good person, or the wrong person, because the right one could be waiting for you around the corner. And when they come around that corner, you wouldn't want to be distracted. You wouldn't want to miss them.

•

A handful of dates in with a thirty-year-old I was seeing, we were sitting in his bed drinking mulled wine. He traced a finger on my spine and we looked at the New York City skyline. His bed was pressed against a floor-to-ceiling window and the view was of the World Trade Center. It was two o'clock in the morning, and the world seemed like it was holding its breath.

The mug scorched my hand and the wine had too much cinnamon. He had been working on his recipe and I joked that it needed more work. We watched a series of music videos and he told me some stories about his friends. They seemed mature and cool, probably because they were. One of them was a big-shot journalist. The other was madly in love with her. I wanted my life to be like *New Girl*, and this seemed like a decent plotline.

I was infatuated by how adult he was. How well he knew himself. He had, after all, spent eight more years on the planet than I had, and he must've filled in some blanks that were still empty for me during that time period.

"I have to be up-front with you," he said. "I've never dated someone so young."

Everything came crashing down and I tried not to wince. I was twenty-two years old, and that was old enough—to me at least. I hated the word *young*. Who cares if I was twenty-two! I'd tried butt stuff! I'd dyed my hair blond! I'd smoked a joint! I was in GRADUATE school! That was plenty mature for a guy with an established career and a penthouse in Gramercy.

"I really like spending time with you, but I can't promise you anything. I'm not sure if I want anything with you. Maybe just keep doing what we're doing. Keep it here."

"Me either," I said, throwing in a laugh to make it seem more convincing. He seemed a little surprised, so I decided to dig myself an even larger grave so that I had room to bury myself with my collection of pink-heeled shoes.

"I just like spending time with you. I'm not looking for anything either. Plus, like, I have school and I'm busy, so it wouldn't even make sense, us, right now . . ." I trailed off, fixating on the cinnamon stick floating in the mug of wine.

"Great, well, then it's settled," he said, and he moved my chin so that my eyes met his, and he kissed me.

Fuck you, I wanted to say, but instead, I kissed him back.

I think we all know where I went wrong here. When he said he wasn't looking for anything serious, I could've said, "I totally understand and really like spending time with you, too. Does that mean you're not looking for a relationship right now?" Because truthfully, I didn't want to continue doing what we were doing— movie nights, takeout, hookups. I wanted to be called someone's girlfriend. I wanted to hold hands on the sidewalk on a sticky Saturday. I wanted to travel to each other's hometowns with someone and have them say, "That's the gas station where I used to steal candy bars when I was in sixth grade" and "This is the car I first learned to drive in."

My act of self-preservation was to lie. It was Cam all over again. To lie through my teeth—even when he could tell I was lying. Even when I had known, all along, that he didn't want anything serious. When we made plans, he took forever to follow up about them. He'd make plans with me and stand me up, or text me at ten p.m., or forget entirely. Instead of facing that truth, I decided to dedicate my time to changing his mind. But his mind was made up. It was foolish of me to believe I had the power to change a stranger's mind, especially because I wouldn't let a stranger change my own.

On dates three to six—it's important to try to categorize where you see the relationship going. When I headed home that night, I had to be honest with myself. I started telling myself the truth and it became clear enough: he hadn't given me any signals that he was looking for anything serious. If I wanted a consistent, casual hookup, he was a perfectly good option. But our desires didn't align, and that's okay. It served me best to pack up my things before it became too late, and shut the door behind me on the way out.

On the subway home the morning after he broke the news that he wanted nothing serious with me, I listened to the *New York Times* podcast *The Daily*. That was my subway-of-shame tradition back then. I forced myself to answer questions I didn't want to answer:

What do I want?
Am I disappointed in what he wants?
Why am I disappointed?
Am I okay being something casual to him?
Am I confident that I want something casual with him?

What I wanted was love. I wanted it desperately. I wanted the movie credits to roll and the audience to sob because the film was so beautiful. I wanted to star in that romance film—me with soft hair and someone who loved me. I didn't want to eat sushi and look at the view of the World Trade Center and watch music videos and talk about how we were just casual. It wasn't that to me, and I honestly wish I'd gotten out sooner.

I was disappointed that he wanted that. But it's his right to want that. He did the mature thing, the right thing, by communicating his expectations early on so I had the opportunity to get out before I caught on fire. And I was disappointed because deep in my gut I knew that it could feel really fucking good to spend a night with someone—to feel their hands on your waist, to get up and sneak out before dawn while they're still asleep. But it wouldn't last. The minute you step back onto Fifteenth Street and the wind and the smell of cigarettes smacks you in the face, the feelings dissipate. You feel more alone, a bigger ache than you did when you arrived twelve hours before.

So when faced with someone who said, "I'm not looking to commit to anything with you," I became brave enough to say, "Thanks for telling me, I appreciate it. I am looking for something a little more concrete, so I think it's best if we stop while we're ahead." This older guy I was seeing didn't deserve for me to assume that he doesn't know what he wants. And I didn't deserve to waste my energy begging for him to be with me. I didn't want my love story to start with me on my knees (for any reason, begging or otherwise). I wanted it to start while I felt grounded, at ease, firm on my feet. I wanted it to start when I looked in the mirror and said *You look really nice today* to myself.

There are many ways to gauge or categorize where the relationship is going on the third date. The bluntest is to simply ask, "Out of curiosity, what are you looking for dating-wise right now?"—the answer to this question clearly pertains to you, but it isn't about you, which takes a bit of the pressure off.

When asked that question myself, I tell the truth, but softly.

I say, "I'm really open to anything! I've been casually dating for a while, so I'm open to something more if it feels right." Or the converse, "I just got out of something and I'm looking to keep it casual," or even, "I'm not interested in anything serious right now, just trying to have fun."

If you're not big into the blunt ask, there are other ways to gauge where the relationship is going. Pay attention to the way this person acts around you, and how they refer to you.

Have you met their roommates on purpose (meaning not just when you were running to the bathroom to pee after sex)? Have you met their friends or mentioned meeting each other's friends on purpose? Have you developed inside jokes on the first two dates that you recall on the third and fourth? Have you made plans into the future at all (meaning the next few weeks)? Have you diversified your dates and tried something out of the box (not just drinks, dinner, movie nights)?

On a third date, and a subsequent fourth, we're still pretty early on in the relationship, but the third date is a decision-making date. So go get the clarity you deserve. You'd want the same.

•

The third outcome of a third date is both parties being equally interested in the other—both parties looking for the same thing.

Getting ready for my third date with Noah, I felt differently than I had previously. Of course, our first-date personalities can't last forever, and eventually someone has to see all of us to truly know us. A third date is a good time to roll out the relationship personality. Maybe it's not time to start unpacking all your childhood trauma, but you shouldn't be so intentional about holding back, you shouldn't worry about coming on too strong. This is a decision date—to make a decision about someone, you should know a bit more about who they are. Your best foot should be forward, but wear some shoes that you like, not just shoes you think they'd like.

With this in mind, I let Noah, who was early to pick me up for our third date, up to my apartment and got ready while he sat in the kitchen chatting about what had happened since we'd last seen each other. For this date, we decided to do an activity—something a bit more active—during the day. We decided to walk from the top of Central Park West down to his apartment in Kips Bay, stopping for coffees along the way.

I put my hair up in a ponytail (he'd only seen it curled and done) and I got ready like we were heading out for a long walk, and not like we were heading to a Saturday night dinner. If he was only impressed with me when I was done up and evening ready, we weren't right for each other.

When I go on dates, I like the process of getting ready—doing my makeup and hair, making myself feel pretty for me—because confidence is an outfit-completing accessory. But in my day-to-day, I typically don't wear a ton of makeup; I like comfortable workout clothes and having my hair up. So it was important for me that he saw all the many versions of me, and not just the ones on Instagram stories or nights out.

If we were going to make a decision to keep seeing each other, I wanted him to be making the decision about me. Eli. I talk too much and am a little too loud and tend to be pretty messy. I love musical theater, have a history of disordered eating and anxiety.

I didn't want to convince him otherwise. I'd never want to fall in love with someone and realize they weren't who they'd convinced me they were. I'd never want someone to fall in love with a person when they'd pretended to be someone else.

On the morning of the date, I remember feeling on the edge of great possibility. I wasn't wrought with nerves, because he'd done an amazing job at communicating in a way that made me feel validated. I wasn't worried that the wedding I'd planned for us in my mind would never happen, because there was no ring. I was just thinking as far as that afternoon. We'd been texting and it was coquettish and sweet and our conversations were crowded with heart emojis. I still hadn't saved his phone number but was ready to put it in writing and give him a temporary space in my contacts after the date (if all went well).

The stakes were significantly higher. I couldn't help but be girlishly excited. I had a crush. He was kind to me and sweet and was a good guy that my heart was intrigued by. But they weren't as high as they could be, or would ever be. As he sat in my kitchen and I searched for my keys in my bedroom, I decided to let go of resistance, and my heart did her thing and got involved.

The stakes are almost always elevated when a heart gets involved.

We got coffee before heading into the park, and then we took turns telling each other stories the whole way. I talked about my nannying job, because it was something that brought me joy. I wanted to show him my joy. I wanted him to show me his. He told me about the dogs his family owned throughout his life, the many bachelorette parties he encountered going to school in Nashville, his twenty-first birthday in Las Vegas and the unique loneliness he experienced moving to New York City that fall, a four-hour plane ride from home, amid the pandemic. I don't remember what else I told him. I tend to remember the tiny details and let the big picture get a little blurry. We stopped to pet a French bulldog. I said it was my favorite kind of dog, and he said same. I remember when we rounded the corner in the park and saw all of Columbus Circle and we stopped and just looked ahead. There was so much ahead of us still.

When we made it back to his apartment, he told me he bought a bottle of champagne and that we should pop it.

"What are we celebrating?" I asked.

"We finished our walk!"

I never wanted someone to be my good guy so badly.

I added his number into my phone contacts. He popped the champagne. We looked out of his window at the view of the Empire State Building. I had let someone else pour me a drink, silently gazing at the view out their window, before. Noah put his free hand on my back. We touched our glasses together and brought them to our lips. I'd lived moments like this before but this one felt strikingly different. I felt sort of like I could say anything and he'd listen. It was a walk through the park. A glass of champagne. It was perfectly sunny out and I couldn't wait to see him again before it was even over.

Especially if your first few dates took place at bars or restaurants, it's good to change your pace for the next few. Try something during the day, or an activity—try them on in different settings. Mini golf, bowling, paint and pour, cooking together, a game night—all excellent options.

I also like the long walk (destination in mind) because it's a good time to tell stories—and telling stories is a great way to get to know someone on a bit deeper level. What was their childhood like? Where did they spend their most recent birthday? Are they close with siblings? What did they like to do in college? In high school? What kind of music do they listen to? Have they been to many concerts? What was the best day of their life? The most embarrassing?

And just like anything can begin at any time, anything can end at any time. I like to suck the life out of it before it does—to try to remind myself that this isn't supposed to be arduous or time-consuming or awful. It's supposed to be fun. It's a third date. I'm supposed to be enjoying myself, no matter what comes next. The moment is what is so important. I want to truly live it.

A third date is the precipice of a something. Once we get into fourth- or fifth-date territories, we move toward talking stages, "What are we?" floating in our brains, involvement that could lead to commitment. A third date is the edge, the just before, the breath before the music begins.

It would be terrifying to fall—not knowing what could be below. It would feel exhilarating to choose to jump—the adrenaline pumping through you as you brace for an epic crash or for someone to catch you below. It might hurt to turn back and walk down the way you came. But if you walk down the way you came, you're returning exactly the way you arrived—you've not lost anything that you had before. You're exactly where you were when you began. And where you were before is a perfectly good place to be.

Every ending is also a new beginning. Every new beginning is also, in some ways, an ending. Birth comes with death and death comes with birth. Love comes with loss, and loss comes with love. Once we accept that the good never exists without the bad, the bad starts to look less bad.

These early stages of dating, at the end of the day, are about curiosity. We're curious about a person, about a potential. Every first kiss at age thirteen at a playground under a tree is born of curiosity. Every text to a person late at night is born of curiosity. With curiosity comes education—learning—lessons we leave with. I wasted so many early dates—so many third and fourth dates—without gratitude for curiosity, without a focus on fun, without the belief that I deserved to be happy. I spent years telling myself: *When I find love, I'll be happy.* I did this about everything. I did it all the time. This self-made scripture added an immense amount of pressure to every dating venture.

I told myself:

When I win a writing award, I'll be a good writer.
When I get an internship, I'll believe I can succeed.
When I get someone to love me, I'll realize I'm worthy
of love.

But each time I attained these goals, I didn't feel worthy or successful or good. I felt the same. It was never about reaching the goal, it was about believing I deserved to. I ruined myself with the excessive pressure. The weight cracked me whole. Every time I was on the precipice and chose to walk back to where I came, or was forced to head down the mountain, I saw my life as a run-on sentence, now with a period, finite, at the end of it. Failure. Undeserving. I didn't think I could start over. I couldn't view an ending like the beginning it had the potential to be.

After a few failed third dates one winter, I sat on the dirty rooftop of my Upper West Side walk-up by myself. I felt hollow. Swiping through Hinge matches, messaging with high school crushes, reliving moments from dates I wish I could redo to be more appealing. I stared at spots on the roof where I'd made out with people I used to know, listened to Bruce Springsteen, and played beer games with friends. I watched the grocery store lights flicker, the mothers tugging their children along, swaddled in puffy coats and winter boots. I wondered what it would be like to redefine success—to redefine failure. What would it be like to believe that every time I put myself out there, every time I got curious enough to see someone again—I let that be a success, even if it ended in the mutual decision that we'd be better off alone than in each other's company? What would it be like to decide that failure is the belief that I don't deserve love? What would it be like to decide failure is self-loathing? What would it be like to decide success is simply the impetus to try?

I was drinking prosecco from a mason jar, thinking about all these things, when I realized that the only person to whom success connotes everyone liking you and falling in love with you was me. And just as I'd defined these things for myself, in my own personal dictionary, I could go back and redefine them. The thing about your dictionary—you can always go back and erase and rewrite. You can always learn.

Failure was sitting at the third date bullying myself for my inability to feel something for the wonderful person across the table. Failure was playing tug-of-war with my heart. Failure was skipping lunch so he'd think I was thinner later on. It was assuming that most people were bad people, and if I found a good one, they must've been the only one out there.

Success was learning something about myself, being brave enough to say what I'm looking for with the confidence of someone who likes the sound of her own voice. Success was the way a seemingly banal walk became our first shared bottle of champagne.

I wanted to choose success on the third date. I wanted to choose the occasional storm cloud but the persistent sunshine.

I wanted things to feel good even when they didn't end in "you may kiss the bride." It was okay for the stakes to feel high, it was okay to let my heart get involved. It was okay for it to end after three or four great dates. It was a gift to have the ability to feel all the highs and all the lows. And so, on the next third date I went on, I decided to choose to feel—in whatever way the feelings may come.

Rules for "The Talking Stage"

1. Decide WTF you want.

2. There are no wrongs if it is right.

3. There are no rules about how much you can text this person.

4. Consider when to end a roster.

5. An exclusive talking stage of longer than two months without a label is a red flag.

6. Categorize the talking stage: Is it progressive? Moving toward something? Or stagnant and staying the same?

7. Tease and retreat.

8. The one-month rule (it takes four weeks to know for sure).

IT WAS NOON in Ann Arbor, Michigan, and I was lying on my bed wearing an oversize Columbia Journalism School sweatshirt. I found out that I'd been accepted a few days before and overnighted the sweatshirt out of pure excitement. Gemini Boy—guy I'd been seeing—asked me to come over and bake chocolate chip cookies with him. I was so elated that he wanted to spend time with me during the day that I decided to not remind him that I was allergic to gluten.

We were seniors in college. In those first couple weeks of spring, Michigan had ever so slightly warmed. We didn't talk much about our future plans (or in my case, before the grad school acceptance, lack thereof); we spoke about the upcoming weekend, the catering for graduation in May, the boys living in the lopsided house across the street. People often said they'd never apply to the University of Michigan because of how cold it was in the winter, which always led me to assume they must've never experienced a Michigan spring. Michigan in the spring is a spoonful of nirvana: purple skies, beers with wedges of orange, the greenest grass and bluest skies. I always felt freshly energized come March.

By March 15, 2020, a cloud hung low over our sweet college town where that kinetic energy should've been. The first cases of COVID-19 in Michigan had just been recorded on the tenth. Our classes had been made virtual through the end of the semester. Our graduation ceremony had been canceled. They didn't tell us much else because nobody knew much else. Forthcoming was a series of emails from our university president urging and then begging us to head home if we were able. The phrasing of these emails made the assumption that for all of us, home wasn't Ann Arbor. That the feeling of security, of solitude, of safety could be easily ripped out from under us like a magician performing a trick with a tablecloth. Except the trick was unsuccessful—the glass shattered and the audience fell silent.

Without guidance, we tried to maintain normalcy while it felt like everyone else held their breath. I lived with five other girls, and we decided to stay in Ann Arbor, see our lease through, ride it out—we were operating under the assumption that in the span of two months, or less, everything would be back to normal. News was breaking by the hour, numbers were being recalculated, rules were being re-formed. Life was changing quickly, and so, subsequently, would our minds.

I stood next to Gemini Boy in his kitchen. His roommates played video games on the couch. They were pretty familiar to me, as I'd been frequenting their apartment on sporadic evenings since January. Gemini Boy loved to cook. When we got home from the bar at 1:30 a.m. on a Sunday morning, he'd make four grilled cheese sandwiches with one hand, and smoke from a bong with the other. He was always using artisan cheeses. He was your typical frat boy, but with quirks that I was infatuated by—one of them being the cooking. Call it fucked-up that I found it charming that a college-age boy cooked grilled cheese sandwiches, but I did. Allegedly, his homemade cookie recipe was incredible, and he made them often for his roommates.

We took turns forming the cookie dough into circular balls. He congratulated me on my admittance to grad school—bare minimum behavior, but I was charmed. I'd been over at his apartment for twenty minutes when my phone started ringing. It was my best friend, Sadie, who wouldn't ever call me in the middle of a rendezvous with Gemini Boy—she knew I was obsessed—unless it was urgent.

"Come home," she said when I put the phone to my ear. "I need help packing. I'm going back to Arizona tonight."

In less than five hours, my college experience—as I knew it—would be over. I told Gemini Boy I had to go and would let him know my plans when I knew them. I cut through the backyards of three student houses and arrived at the nearly condemned, olive green house we called home. I took the stairs up to Sadie's room by two. The door was open, and the floor was a mess of boxes and suitcases. Tops I borrowed sophomore year for fraternity parties and our matching Halloween costumes sat on top of a bare mattress. Her speaker, the same one that we'd use to blast music when we made our pact of singleness, sat on her dresser, unplugged. Her closet was bare. The string lights were taken down. Her room was half empty when it had been full that morning, and it reminded me of the day we moved in.

I stood there in my cookie-dough-stained sweatshirt, and it all sort of hit me at once. This was my best friend. The woman who taught me that soulmates could be female friends and not lovers. She was inherent, I knew, deep within me. With us it was till death do us part. This was the person I hadn't gone a day without speaking to since the day we met. She knows everything about me. We'd only ever been in one fight. We'd lived in three homes together. Endured heartbreak and hangovers and terrible random roommates and sorority houses and watched each other fall into and out of love. Together, in Ann Arbor, we'd failed classes, cried in Starbucks, learned about what we had when we felt we had nothing else—we'd grown apart from so much but never from each other. She was my stalwart. My constant. My rock. And now, it all felt unmoored. I felt us drift out to separate seas. Standing in front of me, her strawberry-blond hair neatly parted and framing her face, I saw the girl I met in 2016 in the East Quad dining hall. I saw the eighteen-year-old, baby-faced Arizona native with the blue backpack and the highlighted study guides. The woman who refused to download Spotify and still used Pandora. The girl who changed majors four times before we were juniors. Her whole closet was the color blue. Her favorite drink was a Moscow mule and she loved Frank's Red Hot Sauce and she was my Valentine four years in a row. She hated when people sat on her bed. Drank her coffee dark and strong. Pointed out my bullshit and never missed a call when I was on the other end of the phone.

I helped her fold her bedding, which she'd had for the past four years. The familiar pattern is welded into my mind. Her baby blue water bottle, winter coat, black Ugg boots—packed away, sealed, zipped up. I understood why she had to go, of course I did. But I didn't understand why our goodbye had to be this way. I knew there'd never be a right way to close the chapter, to say farewell to the place that brought us together. But I knew there was a wrong way, and we were living it. I was blindsided by moments I'd buried away. The sound of her laugh trailing me to the big house on a Saturday afternoon. The classroom in the LSA building, where I sat when I realized for the first time that I could be a writer, a real writer. Of the day Sadie walked through five feet of snow just to get ice cream downtown to heal my broken heart. Of her birthday at the nail salon, the concerts and the casualties, the table-side fires at Garage Bar, the places she'd gone just for me. The places I'd gone for her. Now she'd go to Arizona. She had plans to move to San Francisco; I was moving to New York. When I had a spare moment, I took out my phone and texted Gemini Boy.

I'm going to go with Sadie to the airport to say goodbye.

:(I'm so sorry, he responded.

Can I come over after? I don't want to be alone.

I wanted to be comforted. To be held. For someone to put ice on the wound and remind me that I'd be okay. I wanted him to be the person to fill that space.

Sure, he said. And "sure" wasn't comforting. It didn't make me feel any better, but it was at least a green light.

At the airport we tried to make everything as painless as possible. I watched her pull her bags behind her into the terminal and silently sobbed. The car ride back to school, tears fell down my face as I drifted wordlessly back to campus. This was one of the first times I felt my heart break without romance or a boy. I had known it was going to be hard to say goodbye in May, but we'd have had closure. Graduation. Celebration. We'd have been prepared for "see you soon." This reality was uniquely emptying—a hollowness surmised best without any words at all.

I wanted to bandage the wound, and at age twenty-one I was

pretty sure I was a genius, and the object of my affection, this Gemini I'd been in a situationship with for three months, would be able to do it.

One form of love (especially when unrequited) cannot assume the role of bandage for the presumed loss of another. In my hysterics, I couldn't see that I hadn't lost Sadie, that our relationship would just take a different shape—and I thought that the temporary relief from Gemini Boy would make it all better. I'd only been gone three hours when I returned to his house, in the same clothes, my eyes freshly puffy. A plate of chocolate chip cookies sat on the kitchen counter, and he led me to his room. We sat on his bed, I cried, he interjected with the things he thought he was supposed to say. I poisoned myself with gluten and he tried to find empty space in my vulnerability for us to make out.

We weren't in any kind of a relationship. We were "exclusively hooking up"—or so I'd been told by him. The definition of "exclusively hooking up" in this context means that you are only hooking up with each other. This doesn't mean you're dating. It doesn't mean you cannot go on other dates, or flirt with other people or consider them as options. It just means that, until someone decides otherwise, you're only being physically intimate with each other.

A situationship, as this type of relationship is sometimes known, likely won't move into committed relationship territory. It starts and ends the same way: we like each other's company, but we're only committing to each other physically, and something, whatever it may be, stands in the way of us ever being anything more.

I don't regret going to Gemini Boy in shambles that night. I don't regret lying there staring at his ceiling, holding his hand. I don't regret telling him all about it.

I regret confusing these intimate moments for anything more.

Intimacy can occur without love or even without like. It is its own beast.

Modern-day dating vernacular is horrifically confusing, but I'll do my best to define it as I understand it.

Exclusive: exclusively seeing each other, but without the boyfriend-girlfriend, girlfriend-girlfriend, partner, or otherwise serious label. Being "exclusive" typically comes before you take the leap into a full-blown relationship. Supposedly, exclusivity is like a relationship trial run.

Exclusively hooking up: exclusively physical with one person, but that doesn't mean you're going to be in a relationship with them or are even heading in that direction. Usually this is for sexual safety, comfort, or reliability.

The talking stage: typically refers to the stage of a relationship before you start dating someone with labels, in a more serious way. You can be exclusive with someone and not in a talking stage (if it's just hooking up); you can also be in a talking stage and not exclusive (you're getting to know each other, but one or both parties aren't ready to stop shopping around). The talking stage is like an umbrella term for the time period where you're figuring out what you're looking for.

Situationship: the type of relationship that's a little more than exclusively hooking up with someone, but a little less than all-in exclusivity, because a situationship does not have the eventual goal of a committed relationship in the way being exclusive with someone does. It could be time, it could be logistics, it could be a desire not to get tied down. Feelings are there, but it isn't enough to get into a full relationship.

Oftentimes, we confuse situationships for a talking stage, because we believe, or would like to believe, that

a situationship or exclusive hookup could become something more. And before I go on, I should tell you that there
are people who will read this sitting in bed next to their
partner, who they started dating after a YEAR of casually
hooking up. There are people who will read this who are
engaged or MARRIED to people they were casually hooking up with, or in a situationship with.

But it's difficult to move from a situationship into a relationship, because if we start something as a casual late-
night hookup for a few months, there's a tension working
against us when trying to transition into first and second
dates.

The battle cry of the college-age girl tends to be dedicating a
semester to a fraternity boy or artsy girl she truly believes she'll be
able to take from the sheets to the streets, only to realize that it's
nearly impossible to turn a casual yet consistent rendezvous into
a future husband or wife. I wish I knew back then that it's okay to
want something casual, but it's also okay to want something more,
and to decide that I'd rather be alone and wait for that something
more than spend my time begging for someone to come around to
the idea of being with me.

Human beings have a wonderful habit of telling ourselves stories and looking for details to confirm these stories: *confirmation
bias*. I was in a situationship with Gemini Boy—which was pretty
obvious to me, but I was afraid to ask him if he would ever want
something more, because I was afraid of the answer. Instead, I told
myself that we were in a talking stage, proceeding toward eventually being in a committed relationship . . . falling in love. I searched
for details that confirmed that story to be true, although I'd made
it all up. On March 15, 2020, I decided that his ability to comfort me

in my time of need was a detail that confirmed that he wanted to be in a committed relationship.

But the truth was he was just kind. Being there for me in my time of need didn't automatically mean that he wanted to be in a relationship with me. The only way I truly could've confirmed or denied that to be true is if I had asked him.

It's common to find ourselves in the gray space with another person—not quite dating, not quite friends. There's being single, there's being in a relationship, and then there's "seeing someone" or "dating" and that's where things grow complicated. Relationships have so much nuance—for a relationship between two people to truly be successful, a lot of circumstances need to line up just right.

Still though, the middle ground—the gray space—confuses us. It causes us anxiety and keeps us up at night. We don't know how we should proceed, what conversations we should have, how to tell what someone wants with us without ever asking.

I wish I'd known that if someone was consistently confusing me, they weren't the right person for me.

Communication, though in some cases scary, is integral to pro-tecting your own emotions. I've had enough situationships and failed talking stages and successful talking stages to promote bold-ness early on. I'd rather tell the other person what I'm looking for off the bat than try to read their mind in two weeks or two months. I'd rather know what they're looking for than waste all my time trying to guess.

•

Talking stages typically commence after the first four or so dates when you're continuing to get to know someone but have started to wonder what the future of your relationship might look like.

Talking stages can fall into one of two camps: progressive talking stages, and stagnant talking stages. Before you try to de-

RULE
1

cide what kind of talking stage you're in, you should always pri-
marily decide what it is that YOU want.

Do you see yourself potentially committing to this person? Do
you want a relationship with them? Are you unsure and figuring
it out as you go? Do you want to keep seeing them, but in a casual
way? Do you want to exclusively sleep with them?

Ask yourself the questions, because you can't deduce what the
other person wants if you're unsure yourself. And you don't have
to know right away—sometimes it takes a little longer to be sure.
Just keep those questions in your back pocket and check in with
yourself as you go.

Your scripture during a talking stage: it is ALWAYS better to be
single than in a relationship that doesn't serve you. I had plenty of
experiences where I compromised my needs or my desires because
I feared being alone—if I could go back, I'd tell myself what I just
told you.

Typically a stagnant talking stage or situationship is categorized by a few things—regardless of how it started, the bulk of
time spent with each other is at home; most activities are sexually
motivated; there aren't many conversations about meeting each
other's friends outside of pregaming, at a bar, or running into a
roommate; there are no conversations about families, going on
dates, or future plans; most conversation takes place on Snapchat
or you text back and forth about meeting up out at a bar, or to
"come over and chill." If you're taking stock of your talking stage
and deduce that it fits neatly into the "casual" column or the stagnant column, I think you have to decide yourself if that's what you
want. If it isn't, then it's in your best interest to be honest with the
person and say so.

If you were hungry, you might say "I'm hungry."

If you're thirsty, you ask for a glass of water.

If you're not feeling well, you raise your concerns.

Why is it that we bury our romantic needs deep below the soil, in hopes that we can adjust our own desires to someone else's? If we do this, nothing grows from that soil. If we plant our wants and needs in the soil, and we wait, that's when we start to see a stem, and then a bud, and eventually, something blooms. Maybe it won't bloom on your first try, but you'll grow a garden soon enough.

It's hard to ask for what we want in dating because we've been told that rejection is embarrassing. We've been told to believe that if we're rejected, there's something wrong with us. But sometimes someone just isn't the right person, and this may not even have anything to do with you. When there's nothing else tangible to grasp on to, I choose to believe that every rejection is the universe redirecting me, pushing me down a well-lit corridor where, just around the corner, lies my destiny. And destiny may not even be a person. It may be the fulfilling, lifelong career you'll pour every ounce of yourself into.

Your dream life is going to knock softly on your door one day and wake you up from your sleep. You just have to be willing to open the door and invite it in.

There's no true reason that rejection, especially early on, has to be embarrassing. What I realized throughout my own dating experience is that it's more embarrassing to discard your own autonomy and your own voice than it is to simply ask and have the other person say "no thanks" or "not right now."

Dating ruthlessly and fearlessly—with haste—is something not depicted in every rom-com. We forget to give ourselves, and each other, permission to be vocal. We forget that our standard should be asking for what we want and having someone rise to the occasion the way you do for them. We forget to tell ourselves that there will be someone good. There will be someone great. We won't have to beg the someone great to stick around and hang out. They'll have already decided that they want to be here.

There will be stagnant, passive talking stages, and they might suck. Then there will be active, progressive talking stages that confirm why we all start dating in the first place: it feels really good to connect to someone else on a level several layers below the surface, below the exterior. And even if we don't end up spending the rest of our lives with that person—the human condition is all about connection. It's all about saying, "I see you; I hear you," and receiving the same thing back.

Luke's first picture on his Bumble profile was him standing in front of the US Capitol building, wearing a navy suit. He had soft eyes and soft hair, and every message he sent me radiated warmth.

We had mutual friends, we were nineteen years old, and it was the middle of a Michigan winter. He asked me to come to a meeting for the club he was president of (red flag as a first encounter), and a strange impulse pushed me to go. I told nobody of my plan to attend, put on a gray sweater, zipped up my coat, and slipped out the front door, into the twenty-degree, snow-flurried evening.

Even though it was freezing and I'd never met this man or heard of his club, some instinct urged me to walk all the way there. And momentarily, standing outside the school building when I arrived, I almost turned back. But again, that same pulse urged me to walk up the steps and open the door.

I don't believe in love at first sight. You can meet someone and look at them across a crowded bar and feel like there's a peach pit growing in your belly and still, you wouldn't know enough about them to fall in love at first sight.

But I do believe in hope and I believe in gut instincts. I believe in longing at first sight. I believe in need at first sight. I believe in knowing at first sight.

To know what? That's what you'll find out. It's just something. Something's there, hanging, between you, suspended in thin air. It looks like a miracle, and it waits for whoever is brave enough to take a step forward and grab it. Sometimes it isn't so much about holding on, but a willingness to say "fuck it" and let go.

When I walked into that club meeting, among the backpacks and strangers and open laptops, my eyes instantly met Luke's. He smiled, blushed, looked away, looked back at me, and waved. He pointed at a laptop and mouthed the words *Sign in*.

It felt like a tsunami had crashed over my insides, coating me in warm waves of heat and light. We borrowed and returned eye contact back and forth like library books the whole meeting. I don't really even remember what the meeting was about. I was nervous and giddy. I'd fallen into knowing at first sight. I knew there was something there. It was precarious and fragile and I didn't want it to fall and break and shatter all over the floor. I was afraid of the ending before we even began.

He texted me asking me to stay after so I did, and it was a little awkward, but we walked home together and I had no idea what would come next.

The next day he asked me to come study with him—as a theater major, there wasn't a whole deal of traditional studying to be done—but I packed up my things and went to the library. I was worried that he'd never ask me on a date. I was worried that maybe he just wanted to be friends. But I decided to live in the moment. We'd been flirting over text. I remember a few times stopping in my tracks on the sidewalk across from the bus stop, reading something he'd sent, and smiling to myself.

After our study date, he asked me to get brunch and go to a Michigan basketball game a week later. I was overjoyed, being that I hadn't been on many dates at Michigan, despite having one ex-boyfriend in my back pocket already.

The date couldn't come soon enough and was still eight days out, so that Saturday night I asked Luke if I could come over. To be honest, I'd been pregaming with coconut Cîroc chased down by spoonfuls of Nutella. I was wearing dark wash jeans and my favorite boots. My hair was straight, and it was then I realized Luke had never seen me at night.

This was green flag number one of our particular talking stage—he'd attempted to get to know me first. We had yet to kiss, and he had already asked me on a date, which would also be during the day. I'd only ever been involved with people who prioritized physical (sexual) pursuits. I wasn't used to someone who truly wanted to get to know *me*. Someone who'd never seen me with my shirt off or even held my hand.

I was nervous heading over to the apartment. I felt forward for inviting myself over and didn't want to ruin the very PG streak of getting to know each other we were on, but I did want to kick it up to PG-13. And not for nothing, when I was nineteen, I knew how to woo a man with the physical. I wasn't ready to believe that someone might desire me for any other reason.

That night we sat on his bed and kissed for the first time. We didn't do much else. We talked, listened to music, sat side by side. Eventually we got under the covers and just felt each other's warmth. Green flag number two: we didn't need to do anything more. We could have if we wanted to, of course—because if something is right, if someone is right, there are no wrongs. It just wasn't the right time.

If someone is the right person, it doesn't matter when you have sex with them. It isn't going to prevent a relationship from forming in the way it was going to regardless—the right person doesn't care when it happens, whether it be the first date or the fifteenth. Just like how when or if you text them isn't going to change anything either.

There are no wrongs if it's right.

But our version of right was lying under the covers, holding hands, staring up at the ceiling—nervous and giggling. I'd shown

my interest by showing up that night because I couldn't wait another week to see him. He teased me, I teased him back. That night
I left his apartment around three a.m. I couldn't stop smiling. I
waited for an Uber as soft snow blanketed my hair. My body felt
warm and energized; without a coat, standing in the quiet snow, I
wasn't even cold.

What a rush it is to fall in love.

A week later was our first date. We ate at a restaurant called
Avalon. Months later, on the last day of the semester, he'd buy
me a T-shirt from there, just so I'd never forget our first date.
At the basketball game we didn't really pay attention. We were
eager to know each other. I didn't know if I should kiss him
hello or kiss him goodbye. We walked home from the stadium
and his mom called him and he answered. They spoke for a few
moments, and then he said, "Sorry, I have to go, I'm with Eli, I'll
call you later." Green flag three: he was speaking to his parents
about me.

After that date, we spent all our spare time together. We talked
through the day, made plans to run 5Ks and attend each other's
formal functions, and maybe visit each other come summertime.

RULE
3

I remember one day Luke hadn't responded back in a
while and I feared he'd changed his mind out of the blue.
Eventually, I double texted and he apologized for not replying earlier—his text back to me hadn't gone through. It
turns out, there are no rules for texting. The right person
would never think it was weird or change their mind if
they heard from you. They'd be thrilled you wanted to
just say hello.

Not two weeks later it was the night before spring break. We'd known each other for almost three weeks, but it felt like longer. I didn't even have to ask, because we knew where it was going. We both just knew.

RULE
4

Even when something is going extremely well, as it was between Luke and me, I didn't end things with the other people in my peripheral vision until he and I had a serious discussion about not seeing anyone else. Don't abandon your roster until your star player proves they're serious about the team.

I went to his apartment in the late afternoon to say goodbye. He was going to Florida with some friends, I was going home. It would only be ten or so days, but we had something so fresh between us, we wished we were both just staying in Ann Arbor, lying side by side, eating breakfast across from each other.

Before saying goodbye, we slept together for the first time. The condom broke. He lasted sixty seconds. He Venmoed me for the Plan B, told me the condom had been sitting around for a while. I didn't care about either sexual faux pas because I was infatuated by him. I knew the sex didn't have to be good the first time. It just had to happen. There were no wrongs if it was right. And in that moment, it was so right.

Walking to the CVS through empty Ann Arbor streets to go get a pill to make sure I wasn't pregnant, I couldn't wipe the stupid smile off my face. Anything could be heaven with the right person. Even bad sex.

We spoke nonstop over spring break. When we returned, I went straight to his apartment. We had better sex, in his walk-in closet, because his roommate was home.

A week later, on his twentieth birthday, he asked me to be his girlfriend while we lay in bed after all the celebration had quieted. This was the easiest yes I'd ever given someone at that point. We'd had a blissful talking stage. One that made me realize that long-term casual hookup "talking stages" that last two months probably aren't going anywhere.

When someone wants to be with you, and you want to be with someone, it doesn't look like a "u up" text or a late-night Netflix and chill. It was breakfast dates, shitty first times, lying beside each other staring at the ceiling, going to an event and only being able to focus on each other, doing something boring like studying and it still feeling like the best day of your life, telling your parents and friends about each other like a little kid sharing a secret. And both just knowing.

Luke and I didn't work out. But the end goal of every relationship isn't forever. This one just showed me how it could look to feel right in the beginning.

I held on tight to the memory of that feeling. I told myself: *This is what you've always deserved.*

•

Not every successful, progressive talking stage has inherent, unspoken answers like mine did with Luke. Sometimes it IS going to work out, and the talking stage is progressive, yet it isn't clear. And it may be unclear for several reasons—perhaps one or both parties are inexperienced or nervous about reciprocation, perhaps someone takes a bit more time to warm, perhaps someone goes out of town and it becomes difficult to get to know each other with haste.

Don't panic. This is normal.

RULE
7

Though this seems highly technical, the talking stage is meant to be fun. Tease the person, play a little hardball with them, be silly and flirty and coy. This is your time to follow your flirtatious impulses and build the tension (sexual or romantic) between each other.

My typical rule of thumb is that if you're at least a month in with someone—and you've gone on at least six dates—you've entered the "What are we?" territory. We should always remember that it takes roughly a month to form a habit, and this is vaguely the amount of time, then, that you'd need to deduce what you

RULE
8

want with someone too.

Let's think of other times we ask directly for what we want.

We ask for what we want when we order dinner at a restaurant. Sometimes we say—"I can't decide, what do you think?" But, typically, when we know, we know, and we're going to ask for exactly what we want.

Can you imagine, if instead of ordering what you want, you ordered exactly what someone else ordered just because they were having it, even if you didn't like it or want it at all? That's what we do when we let someone else decide what a relationship should be, or when we keep our wants and desires with where a relationship is going to ourselves.

Typically, when I have to say something that makes me nervous to say out loud, I write it all down first. Then I'll practice saying it out loud. Finally, when I'm about to say it, I count down from three in my brain, take a deep breath, and just let myself say what I want to say. The apprehension of saying the thing is always more difficult than the aftermath.

About the question "What are we?":

1. There's no actual answer to this question. If you ask someone "What are we?" and you're not in a relationship, it's difficult to find the words to explain.

2. Everyone hates this fucking question and going forward we're not going to ask it—at least, not in these words.

To get clarified answers, we need to ask clarifying questions. No good answer ever came from a shitty question, and "What are we?" is a shitty question.

And there are three ways to go about figuring out where you stand with someone without asking "What are we?"

1. The sexual safety trick. This is for my less-confrontational, sneaky types, who might not feel comfortable being super candid about what they want, but still crave clarity. Before you're sexually active with this person, in the moment things are heating up, pull away and say, "I wanted to let you know I got STI tested last week at the OB-GYN and I'm not actively sleeping with anyone else."

Even if you've already slept with this person, you can share sexual health and safety information with them, in hopes that they'll say back to you, "I'm also not sleeping with anyone else" or "Thanks for letting me know; out of transparency, I'm still seeing other people."

First and foremost, your sexual health is important, and any person who makes you feel weird or uncomfortable for sharing that information is not worth sleeping with. Second, it's healthy to be forthright with each other when you're being sexually intimate. It isn't weird or an overstep to simply inquire as to whether that person is sleeping with other people; if I'm sleeping with you, I want to know you're using condoms with other partners, or what your feelings are about sex.

I also want to pull back and let you know that if you DO have an STI, there's no stigma around that. There are other ways to ask if a health complication makes the aforementioned manner impossible.

2. Ask all the right questions without actually asking *the* question. Try "Out of curiosity, what were you looking for right now?" or "What were you looking for when you joined Hinge?"

This person might say, "I'm just looking for something casual, and I still am!" (there's your answer). They might say, "I was just keeping an open mind and am interested in finding someone to be in a relationship with if the right person comes along."

This opens up the conversation for you to tell them what you're looking for, or for you to ask, "Do you see us heading in that type of direction?"

Another way to ask without asking is, "What do you refer to me as when you talk to your friends?" when their friends come up. Try to deduce if they're saying "my friend, X" or "the girl I'm talking to," or "the person I'm dating."

3. Share what you're looking for and see their reaction.

For example, if you say something like, "I wanted to let you know I've really loved getting to know you, and I'm interested in continuing to see how this progresses," that could give them an open opportunity to say, "I feel the same way."

I know this isn't easy. It isn't easy to let yourself start falling for someone and then open yourself up to the reality that they might not be falling back. It isn't easy to put yourself out there and then find yourself right back where you started when you thought you were progressing forward. Might I remind you: nothing easy ever became anything great. We have to work toward what we want and when we really try, with a little luck and a little hope, we'll get it eventually. And when we get what we want—when things feel all nestled into place, that's when you say "my hard work paid off," and you relax on your couch with a glass of wine next to someone who really loves being around you.

A tough pill to swallow: whether or not you ask, the person you're asking knows the answer to this question. In the same way you know the answer to this question. So by not asking, you're only leaving yourself in the dark. Once I recognized that no matter what I say or don't say, no matter how I say it, the other person already knows the answer, I realized my not asking was an act of self-harm—it was perpetuating the waiting game. A game that felt interminable and contributed to anxiety about dating.

When I asked Noah, I had a pretty good idea that we were on the same page. On our second date, we sat with our knees touching at his kitchen table. Out of the blue, he announced that he wasn't looking for something casual but wanted to get to know someone more seriously. We'd only just met, and he wasn't necessarily inferring that he wanted to get to know *me* more seriously. After around six dates and the one-month mark, I wanted to know where his head was at. I knew what I wanted. I wanted this to be different. I wanted it to be a situation where I either got out early enough that this became a single-spaced diary entry and not a whole chapter, or that I got to be in the driver's seat, and take the reins.

So I did. And when he said, "I feel the same way, I really want to keep seeing where this goes too," and leaned over to kiss me while a Pixar movie droned on in the background, I couldn't believe how easy it was to be open with the right person.

When you set up your direct ask softly—without confrontation or accusation—the other person is going to meet you where you're at. Even if the sentiments they express aren't the same, they're going to follow the tone of the conversation you set.

For this reason, we always have to brace ourselves to accept their answer, whether or not it's the one we hope for. I'm not suggesting you enter into a conversation like this expecting it to crash and burn when, if you've been observing the relationship and telling yourself the truth about how it feels, it'll likely go in your favor. I'm suggesting that when we ask—when we're brave enough—there are many possible answers that lie on the other side.

Some of them may be the answers you want to hear, others may not be. But at the end of the day, no answer is an unfavorable one. Either the universe is telling you "this is where you need to be right now" or "this isn't, let's go find that place."

This person's response, whatever it'll be, is out of your control. What's in your control is how you react to their response, and how you proceed when you walk out the door, if that's what you decide to do. You only have your feelings. And your feelings are big and warm and good. They're real and valid and they tell you the truth. Don't forget that.

Our brains are so overexposed to the idea that we won't be okay alone that we often date to be selected by someone, instead of dating to select someone for ourselves, or dating to see what happens next. When we date to be selected by someone, we approach dating like we're waiting for someone to pick us, and we'll be grateful when they do. We treat ourselves like a number in a numbers game and not an individual. And I understand, because it feels good to be chosen. It feels good for someone to say, "I want to be with you over anyone else." It feels good to be someone else's special. It feels good to be a best friend or the first person someone runs to when they just need a pair of eyes at the other end of a table, or a voice at the other end of a phone.

But we can survive alone. In fact, solitude and the state of being alone is our baseline. It is what we had the second we got here, and what we'll walk away with. It is our job to find comfort in solitude.

I'd been waiting and waiting and waiting for other people to come to me, when I could just get the fuck up, splash some water on my face, put on my Snoop Dogg T-shirt, and go to other people. I'd classified myself as someone who waited on others to make decisions, who waited for others to take action, who waited for a text from someone else to make plans, and waited for a Snapchat from a guy to feel good about herself. I'd always seen myself as motivated and independent and talkative and sincere—but I wasn't rising to my own expectations in the ways I wanted to.

I'd entered a perpetual waiting room, locked the door, and lost the key on purpose. I was hoping someone would find it for me.

I promise you, when you find that place, it's all going to make so much sense. When I found that place for the first time, I felt like Dorothy approaching Oz. I needed glasses to cover my eyes. I had never seen something so bright. I became so glad that my love stories and talking stages didn't work out with so many people. I realized, in fifteen seconds, why everything else hadn't worked out. I am so glad everything fell apart, I thank everything for falling apart, because I now know what was waiting around the corner— waiting to fall together. The reasons for every no had finally made themselves known.

When we're trying to tell someone how we feel, when we're asking for what we want, when we're expressing our utmost needs and desires—step one is to believe that you deserve the good shit.

Step two is to get yourself out of the waiting room, and onto the train. To be in transit is to go toward, and simultaneously to go away. Forward momentum. We all need that. The train has been waiting for you in the station this whole time. Your only job is to get on when it's time for you to get up and go.

If you want to text him, text him. If you want to go for it, then go for it. Get out of your own perpetual waiting room.

When we don't know what the answer is going to be, we feel out of control. But don't assume their answer before you ask. Don't overthink each possible outcome and decide on which is the most probable before you even ask.

When we boil it all down, I want you to count down from three and then say what you feel.

3, 2, 1. (Don't forget to breathe.) *I really like you and I want to be with you.*

Easy as that.

Rules for Sex

1. The mood should be decided and set beforehand. Is this going to be slow? Is it going to be wild? Are we going to experiment?

2. Use your words.

3. EFF like a man does. If your partner is going to ask for what they want, you should too.

4. COMMUNICATION. IS. SEXY.

5. Spray PERFUME on the HIP BONES.

6. Hotels are king for spicing things up.

7. Showers can be a swing and a miss—be smart about them.

8. Utilize the man manipulator 9000.

9. You should be fed after. Period.

10. Plan out the rest of the evening ahead of time so you're not just sitting there looking at each other afterward.

11. Toys"R"Us. Specifically vibrators.

12. NO is a very powerful word.

13. Your lingerie is your power. It's not for them, but for YOU and your confidence.

14. Make a collaborative sex playlist with your friends so everyone can add in their little tricks and treats.

15. Go to the bathroom first, then cuddle.

As an interlude to this chapter, I'd like to be transparent that my personal experience is as a straight cis woman having intimate relations with cis men. My colloquial language and experiences reflect my identity. With that said, I've aimed to be as inclusive as possible when speaking about sex and gender, remembering that the baseline is not cisgender heterosexuality and my experiences are just those of one person.

LOSING MY VIRGINITY was the most anticlimactic thing that has ever happened to me while naked. It was December 2015 and he was my high school boyfriend. We never had the boyfriend and girlfriend label, and ended things before senior prom, but someone told me he was referring to me as his "ex-girlfriend" when he got to college, so I've decided to accept the title we never formally placed on our relationship.

On the day it happened, I was so nervous I remember trying to stop my hands from shaking on the drive over, my sweaty palms gripping the steering wheel of the white Jeep Wrangler as I put the car in park. We weren't in love. We were pretending to watch *That '70s Show*. He made me feel comfortable and never pressured me into anything. He asked me over and over if I was okay, which I appreciated. I'm pretty sure that I lost my virginity in cowgirl . . . à la Lady Bird . . . apropos of a future dating and sex writer. I don't know who the hell loses their virginity in cowgirl but add me to the list.

We were on a basement couch of faded canvas plaid. Scratch that, it was a reclining armchair. I'm pretty sure we could hear his parents' footsteps in the kitchen upstairs the whole time.

I made him fill the condom with water after to make sure it hadn't broken. I drove home with my sweater inside out. I was so paranoid the next day that I drove four towns over, went to a CVS, and took Plan B in the parking lot, blasting the original cast recording of *Evita* at full volume all the while, which in hindsight is likely an indication that I wasn't ready to be having sex at all if I thought a condom plus the pullout method required the additional usage of Plan B.

My entrance into the world of sex was not romantic, it was not *special*. It was simple, comfortable, and quiet, which is honestly exactly how I'd want it to be if I could do it over again. I don't regret a minute of it, and I never have.

For that, I'm sure, I'm one of the lucky ones.

The expectation of a first time winds up harming us when we don't meet the high standard we yearn for. In fairy tales and romantic comedies and smutty beach reads, virginity is a passionate, moonlit, crazed extravaganza—he has a six-pack, your hair looks perfectly soft, you both finish together, and then you lie on the floor and say something melodramatic afterward like "This was perfect, I love you." Then he proposes, and even though everyone else in the world has credit card debt and six roommates, we latch on to the idea that losing our virginity could be that flawless. We latch onto virginity as a tangible concept—something that has to be "special" instead of the heteronormative trope it is. Of course, you can plan for losing your virginity to be intimate, sweet, safe, and comfortable—but the expectation of perfection is a recipe for disappointment.

I wanted mine to be normal and safe and quiet. I didn't need it to be special, I figured there'd be plenty of special sex in my life—I wanted to only go up from the first time. Like taking the training wheels off my first bike in the driveway of my childhood home, I was sure to stumble, and maybe to fall. How can anyone expect you not to? You've never done this before. In the fantasy, we both finished at the same time and my makeup still looks phenomenal. In reality, it's a plaid couch, the "are you all right?," a drive home, a little bit of pain. Sometimes you have to work for fireworks. I'm glad I did.

After my first time, I told two friends and made them swear on their college acceptances not to tell anyone. On the converse, he told the entire baseball team, and someone then took to YikYak and wrote something along the lines of "Tony hit Rallo first." If you don't know, YikYak was an anonymous Twitter-style social media platform that circulated my high school for a brief three-day stint in the winter of 2016. I told Tony to get the post taken down, but of course, our public high school social worker saw it before he could, and I got called to the office and asked if I'd been physically abused or if anyone had hit me.

Imagine you're me, trying to explain to the vice principal and school social worker that the YikYak didn't mean I'd been physically hit, but that "hit" was actually a sexual innuendo.

Congrats on losing your virginity, mazel tov, now it's blasted all over the internet and you're having to explain it to a balding forty-year-old man with a clipboard and resting bitch face.

Tony was the first and only person I slept with before I went to college.

•

I learned about sex from three sources: Sunday school, health class, and my parents.

The first, which we called CCD, or Confraternity of Christian Doctrine, is a Catholic Religious Education course started in 1562, created with the intention of educating children on Catholicism.

Quick religious history of my family: my mother was raised Roman Catholic. My father is half Jewish (maternally) and half Catholic (paternally). My 23 and Me results said I was 27 percent Jewish, but after my grandmother passed away from breast cancer while my dad was in college, he removed himself from any reminders of her, including Judaism. So I spent the first thirteen years of my life raised Catholic, and then my brothers and I mutually decided we didn't feel very connected to Catholicism. So now we celebrate Christmas, and I grapple, daily, with whether or not to believe in God.

I had a bad track record in CCD, beginning with the chastity pledge I was forced to take when I was in the fifth grade. At eleven years old, I was told to write a pledge to God that I'd wait until marriage on a small slip of paper and place it in a red box at the front of the classroom. I am 99 percent sure the box was just a repurposed shoebox, but they'd convinced us that our pledges were going straight to God. In classic Catholic fashion, they guilted me into believing it was my hand to the shoebox, then straight to God's ears.

So there I was, eleven years old, sitting in front of my little sheet of paper, and already self-aware enough to know that I probably wouldn't wait until marriage, and also that I feel guilty lying to God. So I take my piece of paper and write, "I will try to wait until college," and sign my name. Genius.

First of all: girl boss. Second of all: never sign your name to something without negotiating your terms first.

Now I know those papers definitely didn't make it to God and I'd love to know what my CCD teacher thought when she read mine.

To be fair, I tried to wait until college. But I failed. And failure is an integral step on the path to success. If I'm going to hell (if there is such a place) for having premarital sex, most of my favorite people will be joining me down there, so it shouldn't be so bad.

In eighth grade, the same CCD teachers showed us graphic photos of STIs to scare us out of having sex à la *Mean Girls*. First, this perpetuates a harmful stigma about STIs. Second, it doesn't work. Sex is going to be had, regardless of an attempt to villainize STIs. And third, the proper approach would be a discussion on safe sex to lower your risk of contracting STIs, or educating us on how STIs can be treated, and how they differ. I was convinced chlamydia would kill a bitch, and not that it could be cured with a single pill. When half my friends got chlamydia in college, it was easier to treat than when they all got the norovirus and spent a week throwing up.

The second way I learned about sex was from the New Jersey public school system's required sex education courses in middle and high school, which were actually very informative when it came to using protection, pregnancy, anatomy, menstrual cycles, and STIs. I'm incredibly grateful I was so well educated on sex from a biological standpoint, because I know many people don't have those same privileges. (I explained the very concept of ovulation to Luke, at the ripe old age of nineteen.)

The third way I learned about sex was through my mother, who read me the infamous American Girl book *The Care and Keeping of You* and *Where Do Babies Come From?* when I was in middle school.

I regretted to inform her that my more advanced friend had already taught me about what sex was via a dirty joke about a snake and a garden one day at lunch.

I felt pretty well educated on sex from a procreation standpoint from these sources. But a few important points were never covered: how to talk about sex, how to have sex for pleasure, any education on nonheterosexual cisgender sex, how to say no, how to be vocal in the bedroom, and what hookup culture would be like in my young adult life. Nobody taught me how to like sex.

Popular culture and media were actively teaching my male peers how to like sex, and they were talking about it. But I was left in the dark.

Nobody told me: here's how to say "please go down on me more often." Nobody taught me that sex was about more than male completion. Nobody taught me that I was allowed to enjoy sex, and not feel embarrassment or shame. Nobody told me that I was allowed to make my own definition for the word *sex*. Nobody told me that I was in the driver's seat. Nobody told me there were things that would scare me, and there were parts I might hate, and that I didn't have to feel shame rise in my cheeks for things I actually loved.

It's no one person's fault that I never learned about these things. We live in a society that views sex heteronormatively, for male completion—not for female completion or pleasure, and not at all for anyone other than heterosexual cisgender individuals. If we trace it back to the days of Daphne Bridgerton, women couldn't have sex before marriage or even SPEAK about sex before marriage, or she'd be seen as dirty and unclean, and her father would have a difficult time transferring his "property" to a suitor, who'd probably been having sex with half the "unclean" women in their city. Subsequently, in many cultures and religions, women aren't taught about sex until their wedding day, when they're expected to give their bodies to their male partners for the purpose of procreation.

From this standpoint, sex is scary, foreign, and anxiety inducing.

Though I was educated on sex from a biological perspective, I was never taught about how I could form my own relationship with intimacy. Nobody ever handed me a vibrator, taught me about pleasure, or instructed me on how to be confident in my sexuality.

Nobody ever taught me how to feel sexy. I never felt like I had permission.

•

When I got to college, at my first sorority hangout, all my newfound sisters were talking about the sex they'd been having with older guys and all the crazy things they did over welcome week. I'd never had good sex, and I wasn't sure it existed. I thought we all just pretended like it was fun and hot. The world's best-kept secret. I'd hardly gone past kissing people in sweaty basements, and it dawned on me how incredibly behind it seemed I was in the world of sex. I'd only had sex with said high school boyfriend Tony all of five times in high school. Now I was seeing Ezra, the college sophomore, and told him we had to wait until after sorority rush to have sex—because I was worried about being blacklisted from a sorority for sleeping with an older guy. This was a lie, but a good way to buy myself time. I was so anxious about having sex that I lied my way out of it, believing it would be weird to tell him my honest feelings. I wish I had simply told the truth—I was inexperienced and nervous and didn't even like sex.

When it finally did happen, on a lofted dorm room twin bed (romantic, I know) I felt so fucking terrified. I remember sitting on my bed while Ezra was on his way over, spritzing myself with a Bethany Hamilton perfume from Billabong, drinking small sips of water, and taking shallow, controlled breaths.

He could tell that I was terribly inexperienced. We used a condom brand called Shabari, and I will never forget the way that specific brand of latex smelled. But he was nice enough to me during it, and after a few more times with him, I felt more confident. Sex *is* like riding a bike. Once you get the hang of it a few times, you can ride down the street like a pro and you'll never really forget those motions.

But the confidence I felt in bed with him was derived from the way it felt to pleasure him. The confidence was derived from his affirmation—the times he called me sexy or moaned in a specific way or told me that what I was doing to him felt good. And I was desperate to please, to have the affirmation he had given me to fill up my gas tank. I was running on blue raspberry Svedka and dining hall cereal and his between-the-sheets affirmation.

I felt gross or ugly unless he was being pleasured by me. I didn't dare ask how he felt about returning the favor. I would've sooner burst into flames. He would occasionally ask me what I liked or what felt good, but as hard as I searched for them, I couldn't come up with the words or the voice to share them. So I just stayed quiet. I remained convinced that women liked sex because of the brief high we got from the affirmation, which sustained us until the next time. I remained confused what sex could look like, truly, for anyone other than a straight cis man.

·

There are many things that men can talk about and make cool but when women talk about them, they are seen as dirty or unladylike. A prime example would be female pleasure in the bedroom, masturbation, and sex in general. It wasn't normal or comfortable for me to talk with my girlfriends about sex or orgasms or masturbating, because I was taught through a lack of openness by women around me that this was shameful. If I couldn't speak about it with my friends, I didn't feel comfortable talking about it in the bedroom, either.

The first time my friends brought up vibrators, we were sitting on our couch watching *Love Island* and drinking shitty white wine. It was my junior year of college. A few of us had them, others didn't. Nobody had used one during sex, or even considered doing so. We were mostly single, save me; I was dating Luke, who I often had to plead with to have sex. He told me he didn't find sex special if we did it more than once or so every week to ten days. We had vastly different libidos, and I realized that when sex couldn't be used to derive affirmation like it had with Ezra, it became a transaction that I hated. And after testing the waters and dipping a toe into the casual hookup pool, I realized that hookup culture also wasn't working for me.

It seemed like every other twenty-year-old living in Michigan *loved* casual sex. It seemed like something I was supposed to like too. And when I didn't, when I was left feeling hollow and irritated, I figured there must be something wrong with me. But truthfully, for the most part, we all know casual sex is an entirely different beast than sex with a romantic partner, or someone you're in a relationship with. And that different may be good, it also may be bad. It's up to you to decide what you like and what you don't like—what feels great and what doesn't.

In college, surrounded by people who seemed to enjoy casual sex, I felt like an outlier. I felt weird or off or different for struggling with casual sex when it seemed like other people thrived in casual flings.

For me, in casual sexual settings, it was difficult to feel comfortable—a general lack of communication and transparency made me feel even more out of control than I already did. I like to know, before someone literally puts their body inside of mine, who the hell they are and what they're looking for, or at least a last name. I want to know if you're going to try and cuddle with me or ask me to spend the night before I take my pants off, because I'd like to do neither. I almost need a sexual intercourse constitution drafted up before I even so much as consider sitting down on your bed next to you. But I never felt like I could quite make my voice loud enough to say so. I never felt like I had permission to speak up. But by trial and error, I learned that sex is inextricably linked to emotion for me. Intimacy is intimate for me, and when sex is devoid of intimacy, I often feel left searching for the emotion after it's over, and when I realize that emotion doesn't exist, I'm alone with an empty feeling deep in my gut. Starting to realize what I don't like at all encouraged me to discover what I do like. I want to make it known that if casual sex is something you DO like, then that's great too. No one kink or desire or preference is superior to another in any way.

Eventually it struck me that there is no script for how to have sex or when to have sex or why to have sex. I can be intentional about how little or how often I have sex and with whom. Just because my best friend might love casual sex, and might feel confident asking a guy she just met to pleasure her, doesn't mean I have to like that too.

Some people get almond milk in their coffee, others get oat milk. We all have our own preferences and they are equal in value.

•

I didn't reach any sort of completion during sex until I was twenty. And, by that point, I'd had two long-term serious boyfriends.

With age and maturity comes the realization that it isn't manly or cool to say it's gross to go down on a woman, or that sex simply isn't fun when it's just a one-sided transaction. And seriously— where the hell is the LinkedIn post that says I am proud to admit I had an orgasm during sex for the first time in my life.

But I wish I could've grown comfortable asking for what I wanted on my own, instead of through a partner I trusted. I wish I could've been vocal without someone asking me what I liked, what felt good, or to simply communicate about sex so we could make it better for both of us.

My wish for you is to find sexual prowess and confidence on your own, and not through the hand-holding of someone else. I do have to express my gratitude to Nate, the hand-holder who led me to the entrance of the promised land. Nate and I planned out the first time we had sex. We'd been sexting for a little bit back and forth, and I was good at sexting (still am) because I'm good at words. My favorite trick: put the ball in their court, and say to them, "Tell me everything you're going to do to me in detail when I see you next" (always works).

But in person, I simply couldn't show up with that level of heat. Instead I'd be shy and coquettish. I'd deflect.

When asked, "What do you like?" or "What do you want?" I'd say, "I don't know" or "What do *you* want?"

This isn't about the male gaze. It's about how we show up for ourselves in the bedroom, to get what we need out of it. And I wasn't showing up for myself. I was showing up ready to show someone else what I believed to be the time of their life, without taking a single thing in return. No souvenir, no consolation prize, nothing.

Some people in this life are takers. They will take and take and take and give nothing in return. Other people are givers, who tend to forget about themselves.

The best people strike the perfect balance.

Nate was one of those people.

The first time we had sex was in his Bushwick bedroom, right under the rattle of the J train, in the middle of June. His room was meticulously clean. I made fun of him for only having books on his bookshelf written by men and he promised me he'd do better. He played quiet folky music on a small pill-shaped speaker. The room was sticky with heat. He had a small fan, no AC, and he lit a candle and turned off all the lights.

"What do you want?" he said in my ear. And I was speechless. Not only had I never—not even after two separate relationships—said what I wanted, I'd never been asked right off the bat either.

My silence was stifling and sucked all the mood from the room.

"What do you want?" he whispered again, this time, with haste.

"Whatever you want," I responded, and I kissed him, trying to distract, to deflect, anything to avoid answering the question he pressed back into my lips.

"No," he murmured gently, pulling back, "what do you want?"

Deflecting again, I responded, "This, this is nice."

He realized he wouldn't get through to me at that moment, and each time he asked me another question, I put my hand in a new place, trying to be sexy so he'd be distracted and not notice my lack of response. We ended up having sex. And it was good. I wrote a poem about it. That's how good. It was kind of sticky and sweaty and slow and sweet.

It was the first good sex I ever had. Not because of what he gave, but of how he saw me—all of me in the glow of a candle that smelled like outside.

Lying side by side on top of the comforter afterward, he admitted I was the second person he'd ever slept with. I was surprised because Nate is the kind of person people write books about.

"What kinds of things do you like in bed?" he said, switching the conversation.

"To be honest, I don't really know," I replied, praying he couldn't make out my flushed cheeks in the dim light. If he could, he didn't say so.

"We'll have to figure it out then," he said, kissing me.

And Nate did his best to figure it out. And slowly he cracked me open, maybe just enough to slip a sealed letter through the door. But no more. I wouldn't let him. I was too afraid of my own sexual energy, felt too much shame about intimacy and sexuality and pleasure. No matter how desperately he tried to open me up, I hardly ever let him in.

·

Shame is meant to coincide with actions that are wrong or improper. Pleasure is neither wrong or improper, but still I drowned in shame until I allowed myself the space to explore. People explore pleasure in different ways. We all have our ways of finding our kinks or what feels good or what would turn us on. The light bulb that first lit up my dark room was listening to other women talk freely about sex. Listening to Alex Cooper on *Call Her Daddy* speak unabashedly about her sex life—and be praised for it—made me realize that I was allowed to talk about sex. From there, what helped me the most was hearing and listening to other women talk about vaginas and pleasure and clitoral stimulation and vibrators. What helped most of all was listening to myriad people, identifying in different ways, speak about their own connection to intimacy, gender, their bodies, and sex. I did this through books I'd read with a nightlight on, podcasts I'd listen to side by side with my friends while we ate breakfast in the morning in our junior year apartment, and positive influences—women I saw as fearless for being comfortable enough to talk about sex.

I'd eventually go on to learn that many cis men enjoy going down on their partners—and the good ones also center communication in the bedroom. Though it took me five self-help books, therapy, and a couple drunken hookups, I finally realized that women can, and should, have sex like men.

We should ask for things we want like men do. We should make alterations when something doesn't feel right or could feel better. We should be vocal when we're not in the mood or, conversely, are in the mood. We can and should all be seen as equals. This isn't a transaction between two people. It's a creation of energy. A shared practice. A moment in time. Whatever you'd like it to be.

Throughout my life I've often felt my voice was stolen from me or silenced in the name of manners, while men are encouraged to be dominant and vocal. But what if I reclaimed dominance and vocality? What if I asked him to go down on me, moved his hand, or added a vibrator into the mix with the same ease he makes suggestions and recommendations during sex?

Communication is hard, but it's totally normal and absolutely necessary. If a man can ask me to try a position, request oral sex, or move my hand, I can do the same.

The first step should never have been being quiet and complicit. It should've been figuring out what I find sexy. What my sexual and nonsexual turn-ons are. What my sexual narrative is. How I pleasure myself.

The second step should've been noticing when I feel sexy. Finding ways to affirm myself about my sexiness. Getting to the center and the heart of what makes me feel sexually confident.

But instead, I did the wrong step one: have sex for male validation and completion and then step two: feel incredibly shameful talking about or even thinking about pleasure as it relates to yourself, so ignore it.

When I get ready to be intimate with someone now, I take the steps necessary to feel good about it for me. I think about it intentionally—Do I want to do this? Or do I think someone else wants me to do this? Am I doing this to attain validation or to try to convince myself or someone else of something?

I put on my favorite body butter and take a good shower because that makes me feel sensual. And if I believe that I'm sexy, I open myself up to the idea that I deserve to experience pleasure. I dab perfume behind my ears and on my hip bones. I communicate about what I need and I ask them what they'd like too. We put on music and dim the lights and make sure things feel really safe and really good and really inviting.

I focus on settings and environments where sex feels the most fulfilling and safe (because that is what is most important), the most empowering and exciting—hotel rooms, for one, are an instant turn-on and always spice things up. Sometimes it's an intimate shower before or after—not necessarily shower sex (because logistically, let's be honest, it's usually a nightmare) but just an intimate pre- or postgame.

I know the positions I like. My favorite is one that I like to call the man manipulator 9000, which is essentially doggy style but the partner on the bottom lies down on their stomach instead of on all fours. I know that early on, I like to plan the rest of the evening before we're intimate, so we have a plan to watch something or snuggle or go get food after (because you should always be fed). I know that sometimes using my words has been difficult, and speaking up in bed has been hard, but the right partner will make me feel so comfortable I'll be empowered to speak up, to use my voice. I practice what it feels like to say what I need.

And because I have my little rituals, I've gotten to a place where sex can be more spontaneous. Where we can be sitting watching *SVU* in bed, our shoulders touching, and feel something between us that sort of looks like a green light and just roll over to each other, eye to eye.

It can be twelve minutes before hotel checkout, when we're finishing packing up our bags and notice we have a few minutes before we have to call the Uber to the airport. I'm aware of my boundaries and limits. Of my turn-ons and turn-offs. I communicate with partners before we have sex, and we check in afterward or over breakfast or when something feels off.

It can be in the shower or a pool on vacation or in the morning. It doesn't have to be meticulously planned, but also, it can be, and that's great too. It can be a little bit of both—the "let's have sex Friday night" and the let's spontaneously rip each other's clothes off right here and right now.

Being in touch with my own body and breaking down the iron gates around my pleasure, and making myself feel, truly, sexy opened the floodgates . . . literally and figuratively.

•

It wasn't until I dated Noah, who proposed a vibrator in the bedroom, that I was like . . . oh, okay, I could've literally just asked for that. I could've come up with that myself, and he would've said yes. And if he'd said no, then that isn't someone I want to be involved with at all. I didn't have to wait for his green light, because my green light is just as good. I wish I'd known that. And frankly, it would be pretty weird for me to ask for something very normal—pleasure, foreplay—and him to say no.

Of course I was uncomfortable at first, with the vibrator. The centering of my pleasure was not familiar to me. But if I was going to so flawlessly center male pleasure, it's only fair that mine was centered in return. If your partner is threatened by having a team-mate to help center your pleasure, they need a short lesson on the orgasm gap, or maybe to read this chapter.

The vibrator in the bedroom, and also having sexual partners who consider my pleasure to be equally as important as theirs, was when I truly started to enjoy sex and started to define it in my own way.

There are a lot of things I wish I had known when I was twenty years old. I needed someone to tell me that I was allowed to say no. That the word *no* is a powerful word. That I should practice saying it out loud—slowly and with confidence. Everyone forgets to mention that when someone is asking you for sex, and you don't want to do it, it becomes genuinely difficult to say no, especially as a woman to a man. As women, we often feel pressured to say yes in situations because we think it's easier. Because we're afraid of letting someone down. Or worse yet, because we're afraid of violence and physical harm if we don't give them what they asked for. We fear what could happen if we say "No." We now sometimes teach girls how to say no but then we don't teach boys how to ask for consent, how to respectfully react to a no, how to make someone feel safe. There's nothing wrong in not being interested right now, or not being interested at all. And someone who is normal, and respectful (the bar is so low it's basically in hell), will say "no worries," when you say no. There is nothing worse than realizing you did something you didn't want to do because giving consent was somehow easier than saying "I don't want to right now"—or even just "No." I wish I could've avoided those situations. I remember feeling like a dirty dish towel every time I said yes to a partner or a boyfriend because it was easier than just saying no. I remember feeling like I was at the bottom of the hamper, forgotten on every laundry day, when I forced myself to say yes when I wanted to say no, did things because the yes seemed a bit easier than the no, had sex because I would've rather just gotten it over with than let someone down. Each time I felt like I wanted to take a scalding hot shower and wash my sins and perfume down the drain, forget the interaction, forget their hands on me or the scent of their hair. I just wanted to be alone after all that. Consent is the most important component of sex. *NO* is a powerful, important word.

And I hated myself after, avoiding my own gaze in the mirror, because at the end of the day, even if I didn't want to, I'd said, out loud, "Yes." A coerced yes is a no. Nobody ever spoke about that with me.

With my eyes closed, I remember trying to get it over with as quickly as possible. And somehow, each time that happened to me, I felt like it was my fucking fault. I'd said yes. But nobody told me I was allowed to say no. Nobody told me a coerced yes is a no. Nobody told me that no wouldn't make a guy immediately uninterested in being with me. Nobody asked me to practice the word out loud.

And most importantly, perhaps, NOBODY told me, explicitly, that if a man decides he is no longer interested just because one night, when we were together, when I said no, then he is not worth my time.

Consent is really fucking important. Maintain eye contact while you ask. Reinforce their decision before moving forward. Make sure to be gentle, to be kind, to say "Are you positive?" Give the other person the space to say no if they want to.

It might seem simple, but as women we are taught to attain the validation and affirmation of men, even when it is at the expense of our dignity, our feelings, and our mental well-being. There are a lot of things I wish I had known. And it is nobody's fault I didn't know them. We grasp for tangible things to blame because it's easier to understand that way. But there is no tangible thing to blame when it comes to the deep shame women have been subconsciously conditioned to feel surrounding sexual intercourse, specifically with straight men. This has become so woven into the fabric of our beings, so inherent, that it takes an active undoing to truly unpack how we feel.

For too long, I accepted the bare minimum. I thought I knew what sex was—but my knowing was limited to simply how to pleasure a man. Now I realize that, for me, sex is something that invigorates me, whether it's having it or talking about it, and it's something I share with someone very important to me. Good sex means we're doing everything right for us. We talk about the sex we have, communicate our needs so that we both feel safe, try new things.

I use my token "man manipulator rules"—aka a small list of sex tips you can incorporate into your sex life to . . . manipulate a man. I'm half kidding. These rules are about finding a fun and easy way to become more confident and dominant in the bedroom, in ways that will make you feel good and additionally, make your partner feel good.

These rules include putting a little perfume on your hip bones, wearing lingerie that makes you feel sexy, executing cowgirl in the perfect way, bringing a vibrator into the mix if you want a little help, making a fun sex playlist, and saying the right things to drive him crazy and make yourself feel like a sexual goddess. When you feel good about yourself in the bedroom, you give the other person the green light to make you feel better.

RULE 13

RULE 14

Alexa, play "Good in Bed" by Dua Lipa—because these days I love sex and I feel empowered and badass and sexy when I'm doing it. But, of course, it wasn't always this way. I spent years covering the stretch marks on my boobs with my arms during sex. I spent years feeling shameful and uncomfortable. I spent years fearing the word *no*. Sex to me was about male completion. It wasn't supposed to be good for me. I didn't know it could be.

Sex is human connection and intimacy in a way that is different than any other type of intimacy—it's not superior to meaningful conversations, but another piece of the puzzle. Sex is about you, the person having sex. It is an exploration and a celebration of your body. Finding out your own impulses, the things you like, the things you'd like to explore.

Sex is about what happens after everything goes down, too. About getting up to pee while they lie in the bed. Sex is about the way he touches my hair while I lie there afterward. About how sometimes, it just makes me cry. I never thought sex would make me cry because I felt so overwhelmingly close to another person. I had only ever known it to make me cry because I wished it hadn't happened, or the person I was having sex with leaned up on their elbows afterward and told me, "We just don't have any sexual chemistry . . . like at all" (this happened to me, seriously). Sex to me is the show we plan to watch after. Or the way I lie on his chest while he orders us ice cream. It's about slipping back into the world to go on a walk. It's about how hard we laugh when there's an awkward noise or a weird bump in the road or the position we tried just . . . didn't work for us.

Someone send a copy of this to my former CCD teachers, because maybe they can incorporate this chapter into the curriculum. Not all lessons can be learned in the classroom, or the church pew, or your own living room—some need to be learned in the bedroom. I learned about sex by a lot of doing it. And a lot of doing it badly. And a lot of time spent thinking my body was a vehicle for his completion, and not a vehicle for ours, or mine.

The thing about sex is it is meant to be shared or enjoyed all alone. It is not meant to be given away. So, yes, let's talk about sex. Let's break it down. Let's stop lying to children about it and start reading from the Bible of Eli Rallo: fuck to finish or not at all, Amen.

Rules for a Relationship

1. You have to respect yourself before someone else can.

2. Communicate about your communication.

3. Play the 36 Questions That Lead to Love game.

4. Discover their love languages, and teach them yours.

5. The honeymoon phase bubble will burst—be prepared.

6. Don't lose sight of your friends.

7. Ask yourself all the big and hard questions.

8. Memorize their orders (mandatory).

9. Hard launch vs. soft launch vs. no launch—do what's right for you.

10. Therapy is ALWAYS the answer . . . usually.

11. Rewrite the narrative rule.

12. Embrace all your soulmates.

OUR LIVES EXIST in a cycle, in a series of deviations and changes that lead us from one doctor's office waiting room and apartment building and bagel store to the next. We're born. We learn to walk, and to talk. We grow through challenges. Memorize phone numbers, break bones, and climb out of windows. We move out of our parents' house and into our own. Eventually it all ends: all the happy tears and ice cream cones. Promotions and weddings. Thirtieth-birthday parties and funerals. It's inevitable—the end—just as the beginning was too.

Relationships move in a life span, too. The same exact way we do. A relationship, in a way, is a life. We raise them and care for them, nourish them and watch them grow. We celebrate their birthdays, sometimes twenty-five, fifty, or seventy-five times. Sometimes they die before they really had a chance to live—that's why it hurts so hard to go through heartbreak or grow apart from our closest friend—we're mourning the loss of a life we built together, one that no longer exists.

I had my first official boyfriend when I was a sophomore in high school. He was my gateway drug into the world of boyfriends and committed relationships—even though I fear that he asked me to be his girlfriend because I was bossy and assertive and he was incredibly introverted and shy. Not to mention, his best friend was dating my best friend. I likely coerced him into it, but nonetheless, he was my first real "boyfriend."

"Dibs," I whispered, gesturing to him walking ahead of us down Fair Haven Road the first time my best friend ever brought him to a party. We clutched water bottles full of cheap vodka in our hands and wore too much bronzer. It was early autumn. We weren't as cool as we thought we were.

We were sixteen and we acted like it. I gave him inexperienced hand jobs in basement closets. We kissed at house parties and texted under our desks during class. Neither of us could drive and seeing each other required parental transportation. I Instagrammed the roses he got me on Valentine's Day and we said "I love you" even though it wasn't true. We did what we thought we were supposed to do because that's what you do in high school. Everything I knew about having a boyfriend came from Blair Waldorf and Chuck Bass,

Rory Gilmore and Logan Huntzberger, Jess Day and Nick Miller. I applied what I learned from the TV shows I watched before bed to my life and decided that it was perfect.

I met his parents eventually, and I felt guilty doing it, because I was self-aware enough to know I didn't truly love my first boyfriend, I just liked having *a* boyfriend. I liked feeling older than sixteen years old. I liked the production of love because I'd never really felt it. I liked having someone to hold my hand.

Not only did I not love him—I realized I was too bullish, too loud, too unhinged to be with someone so kind and sweet and docile. So when I didn't feel any fiery, passionate, toxic connection between us à la Chuck and Blair, and he'd shown minimal effort to make plans about a week later, I broke up with him via text in the bathroom of my dad's restaurant during a hostess shift. I cried for two minutes, wiped my eyes, and never really thought of him again.

Our relationship wasn't anything remarkable—he wasn't my first love or my first heartbreak. It was simply the first time I wanted to be someone's girlfriend.

•

Ezra was one of the funniest people I'd ever met. He was gangly and Jewish, wore glasses and studied math. He was a year older than me, a Taurus and a stoner. You could never tell if he was being sarcastic or not, and he wanted it that way. He started flirting with me after we met in drama class. A month into my first year at college, I was out at a house party and he offered to come to the party just to walk me home. I emerged from the sweaty, warm basement into a crisp autumn night to find him standing on the sidewalk with a wide goofy smile, laughing and holding a sweatshirt for me to borrow on the walk. At first, I felt like he liked me more than I liked him, but it wasn't soon before I was utterly infatuated.

We walked down Washtenaw Avenue and then down Hill Street, toward my dorm building's back door. The next day was a Saturday football game day. We stood near the door and my heart raced when he looked at me. Neither of us wanted to break the other's gaze. Neither of us wanted to say goodbye first.

He kissed me for the first time. He pulled away, and then I kissed him for the second time.

"Good night, Eli," he said, with a certain syrupiness.

I was eighteen years old. I hadn't met Sadie yet. Hadn't joined the newspaper or even gotten through two weeks of classes. I hadn't joined a sorority, found my favorite coffee shops and restaurants, made friends or enemies or acquaintances. I hadn't smoked weed, thrown up from drinking, or decided I had the courage it took to be a writer—like a real one. All I had was that tiny moment. My freshman-year roommate upstairs. A few people I met at orientation, a purple backpack. And the way he said my name—so low and sweet it sounded like a secret. I watched him walk away and he told me later that he went back home and told everyone he kissed the cute girl from drama class.

Some days I wish to be her again, the cute girl from drama class, naive and blind.

The next morning, I woke up in his sweatshirt to the sounds of six a.m. partying clamoring outside my window. Fall Saturdays in Michigan are quite distracting, erring on the side of magic. I got ready meticulously in my preplanned tailgating outfit. I was meeting my friend to get breakfast before the pregame, so I was up a little earlier than everyone except for fraternity boys.

I left through the back door of my building, the same one I'd nearly melted into the night before. As I stepped into the chilly sunshine, there it was again—slow and silky.

"Eli?"

Walking toward me, down the sidewalk, was Ezra. He was going to pick up some beer at their tailgate house, and serendipitously we'd run into each other when everyone else, for the most part, was still asleep. I believed in signs back then. I still do. This was, without a doubt, the ultimate sign. I might have been naive and innocent and just a stupid teenager, but on that day, I loved being eighteen.

From then on, it was the two of us all the time. We met between classes at the library to study. We ended most nights out together. We watched every single *American Pie* movie. I went to his fraternity's tailgate and he paraded me around on his arm like I was his prized possession. I wanted to be that. I'd wanted to be that for someone my entire life. He gave me the job I felt like I'd both never applied for but always knew I'd land. Until then, I didn't know how good it felt to be validated by a man; though Ezra had me working overtime for validation I couldn't give myself—I still knew how to get it from him. And attaining the validation of someone who seems so untouchable, so inflated, so far away, is instantly gratifying in a way attaining validation from someone honest and open isn't.

At that point, I felt like I wasn't pretty enough to receive validation or affirmation—from any men—and I had watched my prettier or cooler friends drink affirmation like warm tea throughout high school. Now I wonder what's worse: having the affirmation from men, or having none at all.

I just loved how special and desired I felt as his. I'd never felt that way before. I wished I'd known then that those tiny moments of bliss—when he called me sexy, or acted proud to be with me, or slung his arm over my shoulder in public—were moments I could give myself. I had to find a way to be that person—sexy, proud, supported—on my own. I couldn't rely on someone who was only giving me goodness so I would give something in return. There was so much to be said of inner peace, of inner happiness, and I wouldn't hear any of it.

And then, the weather turned cold.

On the night Donald Trump was elected we were drinking at Ezra's fraternity house, waiting for a Hillary Clinton win that would never come. He accidentally splashed a shot of vodka into my eyes. He walked me home like he always did. But suddenly there was an angry, frustrated, vindictive edge to him. He developed a hobby of saying things just to hurt me: "You're not like my ex-girlfriend," "I've been in love with her forever, and you'll never be her," "Could you stay home tonight? When you're around I don't get to hang out with my friends who are girls." He'd go a day without texting, leaving me wondering when I'd hear from him again. He'd make excuses and my insecurities would soar to the moon, in tandem with my need to be validated by him. He'd tell me what was wrong with me and send me away to go fix it. He was a drug, and I needed a fix. This is the origin of my anxious attachment style as it relates to romantic partnership—the more he pulled away, the more relieved I felt when he came back. Without him I didn't have much—not a thriving social life or any self-esteem—and instead of going to find out what I could have, I clung on for dear life.

We spend so much time asking the person being manipulated why they stayed—where their self-respect was, why they didn't end it. We spend less time asking the manipulator what they were doing to make them stay. When someone tells you, when you're already naive and insecure, that every shortcoming and challenge in the relationship is your fault—and that you can go and fix those things, and if you do, everything will be wonderful—you might just believe them. You might do what you have to in order to feel secure.

So there were moments I was wrong, but there were moments of clear power dynamic, toxicity, and manipulation—a sticky spider's web I was stuck in.

Most of our relationship was lived after it ended. I was determined to get him back and he was determined to use me for my body and nothing else. We spent a semester breaking up and getting back together. He spent days saying it would work and would yank back the promise like a magician doing a trick. We spent a summer blocked from each other's phones, me checking if he viewed my Instagram story. He manipulated me in my worst states. I spent my time wishing I was good enough. Blaming myself. Wondering how he would feel if I was thinner or more beautiful or more interesting or more self-assured. I tried to patch up my need for validation with an air of feigned confidence, and every bit of self-improvement I embarked on was for the goal of winning him back. When we got back that fall of my sophomore year, we met for coffee and sat outside. He told me he did shrooms and hiked a mountain and I gave him a letter I wrote him with everything I didn't have the courage to say to his face.

It took two months, but we started seeing each other again in November. I thought we had a chance. Maybe in another world, we did. The last time we saw each other, in February, he gave me the flu. I finally decided to give up on trying to get someone back who just didn't want to be with me. I decided to try and get to know myself. Eventually I told him to stop contacting me. Eventually we both moved on. Eventually we both grew up.

We never said I love you to each other. He told me that right before he broke up with me he was going to tell me he loved me, but just couldn't. He told me that when I looked at him in the eyes, he started falling in love with me, so I shouldn't.

What a burden it is to hate the color of your own eyes because someone once told you it hurt to see them.

He would've done anything not to fall in love with me. And when we made it to the other side, both of us, I think, felt love but never said so. We said and fought so much, we went down like a house on fire, engulfed in flames. I think he knows, at the end of it all, that I did love him so very deeply. And I think he knows now that I know that part of him loved me, too.

Even after everything he put me through, I don't regret a minute of it. All the abuse, all the manipulation. Our relationship was a push and pull. An endless tug-of-war between a lost eighteen-year-old from New Jersey and a charismatic, narcissistic "comedian" from Texas. It was hell and it dragged me lower than I've ever been dragged. Getting back up and finding my way to a light switch was a truly beautiful becoming.

There was so much I wish I knew.

I only stopped seeing Ezra when I met Luke, who I felt for so truly and deeply I realized why it was called *falling* in love. I couldn't stop it. I couldn't anticipate it. Gravity did her thing and suddenly I was flat on my face, wondering what I'd tripped over and when I'd stopped paying attention.

Luke was the gift of being nineteen. His existence proved I could love again, after spending a year filling up my notebook with melodramatic diary entries saying not only that I would never love again, but also that I didn't want to. I couldn't bear it. The thought of anyone else before him made me sick with wanting.

I was thrilled to feel for him, and even more overjoyed that I had the ability to feel twofold what I once had. And I loved to hear it from him: I love you. Like sirens racing down the street or the jingle of an ice cream truck nearing—intensity and urgency. He loved me he loved me he loved me. And I loved him back. And it felt thick and secure, concrete.

I loved his softness. His sensitivity. I loved all the things he had that Ezra lacked. He was exacting, punctual, wanted to be in journalism, and wore pressed shirts. He took school seriously, maintained a very coveted 4.0 GPA, and made me want to sit in the front row in class and pay attention. He used big words and had big aspirations and his motivation was magnetic. We were polar opposites but when your heart gets involved, everything else goes to shit—including your motor skills, decision making, and intuition.

We spent the summer apart, just two months after we started

dating. He visited me in New Jersey and met my family, and we took a day trip to New York City. For a while, that day slept in my memory as the best day of my life. The weather was perfect— early summer in the West Village almost always is. We ate outside, drank espressos, held hands, and swapped happy stories. The love I had been waiting for was finally mine, and I would've done anything to keep those feelings exactly where they were.

Little did I know then that in any circumstances, and in any life, I would always come in second place, and sometimes even in third, on Luke's list of priorities. He reminded me a lot that his career and school were always his main focuses, and I was too in love with him and too scared to admit that his words hurt. Because even when I knew we'd never last, I still wasn't brave enough to let go yet. I wasn't brave enough to speak up when I felt scorned, or to tell him he made me feel small.

I wish I knew that love sometimes isn't enough. We're told it is. We're told love conquers all. That it lifts us up where we belong. And I'm all for being hopeful and romantic—but a relationship is a life, and a life needs more than love. It needs communication, healthy problem solving, priorities in tandem, enough water, and two people with similar schools of thought.

Luke called me crass when I told him I wanted to write about sex and dating for a living. He often told me I was facetious. We weren't on the same page about politics, and he slung around big words to make me feel small and eventually I countered by ending it all.

Love is a powerful drug. It'll totally blind you. It'll knock you out. The comedown is brutal but the come-up is bliss. You'll keep going back even when all you have left is your name. And when you finally see it for yourself, when the fog finally lifts and everything appears exactly how it is—when you finally break the surface—the blood drains from your face. You realize you lost everything for someone else. And then you waste your minutes blaming yourself, when it was never your fault for being brave enough to feel the right thing for the wrong person.

It wasn't that I didn't love him. Because holy fuck did I love him. I loved him with everything in me. I wanted to fix someone broken who didn't want to change. I was naive to believe I could. It makes me wince to think of that girl, on those early fall nights, tucked into his bed in Ann Arbor, who thought she always would. But love wasn't enough. It would never be enough. We'd never make it.

And having to walk away from someone I loved so much because we weren't right for each other was the most harrowing experience of my life. And when I walked away, I saw who he really was so much more clearly. And as the years faded from our 2018 relationship to 2020, and further and further, his identity became so much clearer. It was the right choice, one of the easier choices I've had to make, but the fallout was acutely painful.

•

The term "rebound" always sort of bothered me, because it feels like the minute someone moves on from one relationship and gets involved with someone new, it's written off as a rebound, even if that wasn't the intention.

I knew that people thought my relationship with Nate, which started only two months after ending things with Luke, was a rebound. I'll admit it was, at first, a distraction—but I'll also admit that in another time and on another plane, we could've really been something together.

Nate was also the guy I told Luke not to worry about. The irony is, Luke started dating the girl I wasn't supposed to worry about—a beautiful girl with a perfect VSCO feed. Nate and I were friends who'd met in a class. When we met, we were both in serious relationships. We had the same interests: poetry, reading, creative arts, and great food. We laughed at the same kinds of jokes. He was a gentle and kind person, and everything between us had always been entirely platonic. So when Luke brought up his dislike and insecurity of me having a male friend, I promised it was nothing. And I was being honest. Perhaps there was a coquettish edge to our friendship every now and again, but I never in a million years thought that anything could exist between Nate and me beyond friendship.

When things crashed and burned with Luke, I felt comforted by chatting online with Nate about books and music. We never hung out one-on-one; when we saw each other it was at rehearsal, a theater party, or in class. We'd answer each other's Instagram stories of books or poems, but again—the stakes were very low.

We made plans for my third night back on the East Coast. We went on a first date; it was 20 percent talking and 80 percent kissing. He was my great New York City love story. The one that looks like a movie but doesn't end like one. I was twenty years old and thought I was twenty-five. It was a dream the whole way through.

The kissing in the rain. Making breakfast together. Swapping writing and having sex on the floor and the flowers he'd buy and leave on my bed while I was showering and he was in my apartment alone. He looked at the bright side so often it almost annoyed me.

Nate was from Michigan. He loves both John Mayer and Taylor Swift. He took me to an Avett Brothers concert once. He was a goofy drunk who fell asleep on the subway sometimes and had a special relationship to popcorn. He told me he liked to budget but never beat himself up if he was spending his money on books.

He is someone I wanted, so badly, to love.

We never fought. There was never anything to fight over. It was June and then July and then August. He told me he loved me in a 7-Eleven parking lot. We were eating Cheetos from a family-size bag and kissing, waiting for an Uber.

I said it back because we both needed to believe it was true. He had to believe he could love someone other than his beautiful ex-girlfriend and I had to believe I could accept love from someone like him.

I told a therapist I could never figure out why I was intentionally pushing him away. Why I was being bitter and mean to him on purpose. She told me it's because I couldn't bear to end something with someone good. It was almost like I wanted him to do it for me.

I hated her for being so right.

•

You don't necessarily have to love yourself before you love someone else—but you have to respect yourself before you can accept love from someone else. I believe the most brilliantly beautiful love stories and relationships happen between two people when both parties are a little lost, both parties are searching for a shred of light, both people are a little hungry for something new.

No one ever says you have to love yourself before you can have friends. So why do we hold ourselves to a different standard when we're looking for a romantic partner? It's almost as though we say "everyone else can see us at our lowest, at our most broken, but we must truly love ourselves to have a romantic partner." To me, it's kind of bullshit.

Total self-love, and I'm talking seven days a week, twenty-four hours a day, active love for ourselves, is unrealistic. I work on self-acceptance every day. Accepting my body for how it is, and for all its miracles. Accepting my work, my energy, my mood, making slight alterations to challenge myself and to grow. I do have an underlying love for myself, but it isn't this persistent, pulsating, constant love. My relationship to myself is the most important one

I have, and challenging this relationship to be perfect every single day would crack me in half.

So instead, the challenge is to respect myself every day. In my relationship with Ezra, I relied on him for both validation and affirmation—I didn't know how to give that to myself, and hadn't even pinpointed my derivation of validation from men as an issue. If anything, I thought it was the right thing to do.

When he walked away from me, I was left with nothing. With no source of external or internal validation or affirmation, I had no way to measure my successes and my failures. Emptiness overtook me, and my days blurred together. I knew that the next relationship—and the one after that—didn't have to feel this way. It took a lot longer than I thought to get there.

I couldn't handle the way that losing someone became losing everything. I thought he took me with him when he walked out the door, but really he never knew me to begin with.

I wanted to go into my next relationship intentionally. I wanted to believe that it was enough to be proud of myself. It was enough to feel confident about how I dressed and where I spent my time and what I put out into the world. I wanted to believe that the right person would see me being who I am at 100 percent and be excited about the potential to know me, to love me, even.

My reliance on Ezra for validation turned into his resentment toward me. Just like I would never rely on one single friend for 100 percent of the emotional support I need, I couldn't rely on him for it either. It had to come from me first, and then everyone else could supplement it—little by little.

Human beings are like magnets—we gravitate toward the good energy we give out. When we're trying our best, respecting ourselves, and feel open and ready for goodness we know we deserve, that's what we attract.

The push and pull in my relationship with Ezra caused my insecurities to skyrocket. I've worked through this in therapy, and I actively work through it on a day-to-day basis, but it's important that my partners know that I am secure in validating and affirming myself, but I carry with me baggage that requires my partners to affirm our security.

I wish I could be 100 percent trusting, but it's a very difficult road for me, and a lot of people, to walk. I want to believe that the great person who treats me wonderfully and gives me no cause for concern isn't going to suddenly turn on me and end things, but after what I've been through, it's tough. Letting someone know that I need them to overemphasize the security between us, or encourage them to consistently share their feelings with me, is a standard practice when I enter any kind of relationship that could become serious.

With Noah, I wanted it to be right because it felt comfortable in my chest from the start. I wanted to lay it all out on the table, but I didn't want to come on too strong. I wanted to be like couples I idolized—though I knew, behind closed doors, they, too, had their own sets of challenges. It's much easier to pretend there's a way to get it all 100 percent right. I guess accepting that you never will, and every relationship will be in some way flawed, is the first real step.

In 2015, the *New York Times* published a piece titled "The 36 Questions That Lead to Love." The article discusses a grouping of thirty-six questions psychologist Arthur Aron created to make two strangers fall in love in his laboratory.

The questions are increasingly personal and intimate and after reading the study and then the questions, I became fascinated by them. While I'm not sure if I subscribe fully to the questions' ability to make two strangers fall in love, I do think they are without a doubt the best way to facilitate a deep conversation within parameters and guidelines. They help make deepness, toughness, and emotional vulnerability a little bit easier, a bit more regimented.

Noah was coming over one night, early on in our relationship, for margaritas and my ex's mother's infamous feta avocado dip (which I've co-opted and made my own) and I decided to propose we play the "36 Questions That Lead to Love" game. He agreed.

We had yet to sleep together or learn much about each other's family backgrounds or lifestyles. I knew how many siblings he had, where he went to college, and what he did for a living. I knew some of the things he liked and had met a few of his friends. But deep, true connection couldn't be manufactured or cooked up overnight. We'd have to work on it, and going through these questions and bouncing into sidebars and stories helped us both to feel comfortable communicating our needs, fears, desires, and anxieties.

To be open with someone is to be brave. Vulnerability is inherently brave. It takes strength and a willingness from both parties—one to give and the other to receive. I've now played the "36 Questions" game with my closest friends and my entire family.

In a relationship, specifically one that will last, you'll constantly learn new things about your partner as things mold and change and grow, and as they enter new phases and stages of life. Setting the precedent for healthy communication in the beginning will only benefit you in the stretch ahead. It's hard to interrupt a honeymoon phase with a level of severity, but it sets up the posthoneymoon phase to be just as blissful in an entirely different way. Learn the person's love language—ask how they like to receive love and how they like to give it. Find ways to support them and give them that love in the way they need it. Ask them to do the same for you.

A honeymoon phase, typically the first three to four months of a new relationship, is drunken bliss—you're doe-eyed and infatuated, thrilled by every little thing they do, engrossed in them, desperate to spend all your time together. But as all vacations do, the honeymoon phase will end.

During the honeymoon stage, a relationship exists in a bubble—

RULE
4

it feels like you might as well be the only two people on Earth. You're protected from all the terrible things that exist outside of it, like jealousy, sadness, hurt. And when the bubble bursts, there might be a little shock at first, but that's truly when you build something special. Something worth sticking around for. And if you can make it through that reality checkpoint, some days will feel like a honeymoon all over again.

Some days will be a walk in the park and some days certainly should be. Other days are going to be slightly more difficult, with work to be done. It'll end up being worth it if the walks in the park outnumber that work.

When getting into a new relationship, it can be hard to remember all the important happenings outside of it—especially during the honeymoon phase. Of course, you'll have a percentage less time to dedicate to everything else, because you just decided to give your time and energy to a new relationship, but you shouldn't let yourself slack on the rest of your relationships, your passions, or your life. Your friends are the people who, at the end of the day, will truly always pick up the phone. Your friends are your soulmates, your anchors, and your lifeboats. Don't lose sight of them.

And if you notice a friend in a new relationship slipping away—caught in the rip current of a honeymoon phase—put out a limb. Gently remind them that you're so happy for them, but you really miss them, and would love to see them soon. If they don't take the limb, or they refuse it, then sometimes you have to be patient until said friend comes to the realization themselves that they've neglected your friendship. See if you'd like to accept an apology.

I've been on both sides, and it typically plays out in the same way, though it's entirely avoidable. Engulfed in my honeymoon phase with Luke, I failed to consider the hasty transition from spending 100 percent of my time with my friends to splitting my time between him and them. It's our responsibility, when we get into relationships, to place the ones we had before on the same, or higher, pedestal as we do our romantic relationship. The first few weeks of a new relationship are going to be exciting and invigorating—but we can't forget the people we've already built such beautiful lives with— the people we know better than we know the new person we call our partner or boyfriend or girlfriend.

As a trusting person myself, I've always wanted to trust that I was getting involved with people who I knew were good people, who I knew it was going to work out with. But at the end of the day, someone you've known for a few months or weeks isn't someone you truly and deeply know, and it's important to keep yourself alerted to anything about them that doesn't fit the idea of a serious partner that you have in your head.

For example, perhaps you find out that your new partner really likes to sleep in and you like to wake up on the earlier side. This is likely negotiable—something you can compromise on easily.

But perhaps you find out that your new partner plans to move to a country or a state you never see yourself in, and you're both 100 percent certain that you won't budge on your future plans for where you'd like to live. This doesn't sound like something that could be negotiated and might end up being a deal-breaker.

We all want to trust the wonderful person that we just started to call ours, and we should, but we also cannot proceed as though we know everything about them: every detail and every specificity, right at the beginning. Take cognizant pauses as consistently as you can. Ask yourself the big questions about this person.

RULE
7

Do they have opposing political views or life values? Do they have any hobbies or interests that are important to them that you don't ever see aligning? Do you have opposite lifestyles and goals for yourselves?

We don't need to be thinking in terms of absolutes or forevers, but everyone deserves to have their time respected and energy preserved. Ensure that you're putting yours in something you believe in. Sometimes we want to blind ourselves to the deal-breakers because we want a relationship on the precipice of something to work out. But trust me that you'd rather know early on and be disappointed than be heartbroken in six months or even years.

I've been known to have trouble at the beginning of a relationship, immediately feeling ready to dive in headfirst, falling incredibly quickly, and being unintentionally blind to red flags. I am a trusting person who likes to believe that everyone else is good. And I'm proud of that. I'm proud of how I carry myself and how I love. But at the same time, obsessing over my future wedding and children and lifelong happiness with someone I've been dating for a month isn't the healthiest practice. Reason one: it puts an unnecessary pressure on the relationship to succeed and go in a certain direction. Reason two: the end goal of every relationship isn't forever. The end goal of MOST relationships isn't forever.

**Nothing is going to work out until
something does. If you date ten people,
only one of them is going to be a forever.**

That completely reframed my mindset when it comes to relationships. Something is allowed to feel really right in the beginning, and not feel that same way in five weeks or months or years. Something is allowed to feel like it has potential at the start and blossom into something much more. Just because a relationship ends or doesn't work out doesn't mean it was a failure or a waste of time. It's still a lesson. It's a part of the journey.

The end goal should never be forever. Instead, our outlook should be a consistent hope that we learn something, about ourselves and about others, and that each connection we make to another person is a step in the direction toward the goodness we deserve. Our outlook should be that we are lucky to feel for someone, even briefly, even if it's ever changing, even if it lasts for just a blip in time, and even when it hurts when it's all over.

Each person I've committed to, in some way, taught me something. Ezra led me to learn about myself. Luke taught me what it was to truly and deeply care for someone else, but also to set boundaries and be brave enough to shatter yourself so you can rebuild again. Nate taught me how I seek to be treated. The respect and grace he gave me, the kindness and thoughtfulness—it was the right lesson, the right gift. He was the right person to give those to me, just the wrong person to continue on with when we'd run each other dry.

•

I think when you're so in it—you won't feel like you're the only two people to exist, you'll feel like everyone else exists, too, but nobody else has felt something so sensational, so warm and orange and bright. Getting to know someone intimately is a wonder of the world. It's not so much about the big, grandiose details but the little things—how you like your coffee and if you like your toast burnt or golden brown. Your favorite fast-food restaurant and what temperature you like your burger cooked. Visiting their hometown for the first time and relearning them through the eyes of their childhood, their grandmother's carpeted floors, photo albums, and the quilt on their bed.

And slowly you'll decide to show your faces to the world—to come out from under the covers and say "we're together"—and it becomes a little more real. First to our friends in person, perhaps next to our family or other important people, and eventually, for most, on some form of social media.

On social media, there are two ways to launch a relationship:

A hard launch: when a person posts a picture for the first time with their new partner, without having teased their new relationship online at all, making it a shock to that estranged relative, middle-school classmate, and sorority sister you now have nothing in common with.

A soft launch: when you've been teasing a relationship or a partner via Instagram stories or suggestive TikToks—peppering in details of a new relationship before posting a full-frontal hard launch for the first time.

I don't really see one as more superior than the other. I do think that if your relationship is something that may surprise a lot of people (you're back with your ex, dating your ex's best friend, dating someone you knew in another chapter of life) it could be dramatic to hard launch, and I live for drama. But ultimately, the way you handle your relationship as it relates to social media doesn't really matter.

If anything, I think a lot of times people, specifically celebrity couples, amp up their social media coverage of each other right before they announce a sudden breakup. We, sadly, as a society, see social media as a confirmation of our relationship—a validation that it exists, that it's special enough, that it's perfect. Ultimately, social media doesn't have anything to do with your relationship, and nor does any opinion you didn't ask for.

When you are excited to be with someone, and excited about a new relationship, there's a certain thrill in posting about it—but when I reflect on my social media behavior as it relates to my past relationships, I wish I'd remained more private. The amount that I was posted on someone's Instagram, or the amount I'd posted them to mine, had and has nothing to do with our relationship—its longevity, health, or our happiness. It was a way for me to have other people validate an "us" they had nothing to do with. It was almost a cry for help.

Social media is one of the most incredible and most toxic vices of our lifetime. It's an amazing resource and can simultaneously be incredibly detrimental. I once had so much fun posting about my relationship and including my partner in my content. But ultimately, strangers online found it appropriate to comment on my partner, be cruel or bully him, make assumptions about my relationship, or wish harm to my relationship. After I faced the harsh reality of being a public person and showing my relationship online, I wished I had never posted about it at all. I can handle any hate that comes my way, but when someone I care about, who doesn't have a public social media presence, is sent hate or harm, it crosses a line and becomes my job to protect that person.

From my point of view, there's a delicate line as it relates to social media and romantic relationships, and every person and every couple is going to navigate it differently. I wish I had known, when I was pining for a boyfriend or a romantic connection and watching other people online have exactly what I thought I wanted, that everything you see online is curated, and that being envious and jealous of someone else's happiness—wishing they didn't have it or that I had it instead—isn't healthy. For every beautiful photo of two people in front of the Eiffel Tower, there was an argument, or a weird gut feeling, or a challenge you didn't get to see. I also wish I'd known that my relationship was no less valid or real if it was kept offline. I wish I'd known that because my relationship lives between my partner and me, we're the only key players—Instagram comments and TikTok likes don't matter. It's just about the two of us.

•

When you get past the honeymoon phase, past the harsh lightning bolt of reality, and you finally settle into something with someone, a relationship really starts to take shape. You see someone as a normal person, a human being—not the fluffy, inflated version of themselves you first got to know. And they see you in that same way. Then we decide if we can choose to love each other as human beings, in our realest, rawest form.

Oftentimes we overinflate or overidealize a person in the beginning—we put them on a pedestal, and regard them as perfect, and when the rose-colored glasses come off and we realize that they're just a really great but normal human being and not a prince or a princess or royalty of some kind, or we see that they do have flaws and mistakes, we panic and decide to run for the hills. I'm not suggesting you should ever compromise your integrity or lower your standards, but I think it's important to view someone as a human being from the start—to recognize that they will have flaws and might not check every single box—but the right person will check the most important boxes you have.

Nobody is perfect. Not even you. Not even me (shocking, I know). And we'd never want someone else to place us on a pedestal and panic when they realize we have some baggage, or have gone through a few things, or have a habit we've tried to break but have cut our losses with.

Your perfect person, your forever person, might bite their nails or hate doing laundry or have no sense of style, but they may make you feel like the most important person on Earth, love you unconditionally, and show up for you in a way nobody else has.

Meet someone where they're at. See them for everything they are—because the shitty parts of us, the hard things, the trials and the tribulations, are what make us unique. And love is the willingness to give and receive joy despite the bad things—through the bad things—to love someone as a whole being, even when they feel a little half-hearted or unformed.

My parents have been married for over twenty-five years. To commit to one person with that longevity, after also only knowing said person for two years prior, isn't an easy thing to accomplish. If there's anything I've learned from watching my parents' marriage sustain over decades, and simultaneously witnessing my grandparents, who started dating at thirteen and never parted in the over sixty years since, maintain their relationship, it's that relationships are work.

Love is work. But when you both work, and choose to work, and commit to work, every day . . . It works.

I'm not suggesting that relationships need to be hard, or should feel hard. They *are* hard. That's the baseline. That's why they're so special. Why they're so worth it. Why they feel so good. And the right one, with the right person, will feel easy even when it's hard.

I've always been a proponent for being in therapy, as individuals, or even as a couple if you need it, because it helps us to understand ourselves more, and subsequently to empathize more. Throughout my relationship with Ezra, I think I would have benefited from therapy, but I didn't think I needed it at the time. Being in therapy now, during my relationship with Noah, has ultimately and irrevocably changed the way I empathize, meet him where he's at, and work on being a better person, so I can be a better partner.

No human being is above a little therapy.

Even when I'm truly happy. Even when my relationship with Noah is the best it's ever been, and I think the best it'll ever get— there are still challenges. There are still good days and bad days. The good days outnumber the bad days. And the energy I gain from being together with him is far greater than the energy we expend keeping our flame alive.

But there was a time, after all, when I figured I'd never have that peace. I thought after things with Nate fell through that I didn't deserve love, because if I couldn't fall for someone who seemed so right, who was so kind and gentle—why would the universe give me another chance? I accepted, at twenty-one, that I wouldn't ever have a great love, that I'd lost my chances to find someone.

The story I told myself was one thing that was completely in my control. I spent a year crafting a pretty tight narrative that I'd lost my chances in love. That I'd never be in love, never find someone, and that it was my fault. I crafted a narrative that I was unlovable, undesirable, a body detached from any flowery mind or poignant soul. I stopped believing I had something within me that someone else could ever find lovely or want to spend their time on.

But that was a story I was writing for myself. I held the pen and ink. It was my mind that was coming up with all the little thoughts that convinced me that I was unlovable. So I could also get the whiteout. I could get the eraser, and I could start with a clean page. I could rewrite the story I told myself.

What if I just erased the self-loathing, erased the story of a sad girl with no potential, no opportunity, no ability to see that if I wanted love, I could always have it. It would be in the places I least expected it and all the moments I didn't know I needed it most. I could write a story where I was resilient. Happy all alone. Where I went to bed and felt at peace without anyone beside me. I could write a story where I wasn't afraid of not finding love, but was afraid of wasting my potential. I could write a story where I wasn't worried I'd die alone, but worried I'd die unfulfilled. I could write a story where I was open and ready for whatever was coming around the corner. I could write a story where I saw myself as beautiful, courageous, and kind. Where I deserve good things and could recognize all the good things already in my life, and not just the absence of good things.

You always have the ability to start rewriting. To make the end turn out a little differently. That's only something you can do for yourself.

•

I don't believe in a soulmate, I believe in soulmates, plural. Many of them. Potentially an infinite number of them, wandering the earth, trying to figure it out. Let's put a number on it, and say we each have five hundred potential soulmates.

Think about your soulmate like a winter coat. You buy a winter coat and it keeps you warm for a few winter seasons—sometimes it'll be the perfect winter coat, and you'll keep it for ten, twenty, thirty years. Other times you'll grow out of that winter coat, you'll lose it, you'll realize it isn't your style anymore, some buttons will fall off, or you just won't be able to find it when the weather turns cold again. When that happens, you go to the store and you find yourself a new winter coat. There are thousands upon thousands of options—coats that could fit you, that you could love, that you could wear for a few months or a few years or forever.

There's always a winter coat ready to keep you warm. And because our end goal isn't forever, when we grow out of a winter coat, we still have the fond memories of the winter that it kept us warm. It still served a purpose for us. We have the photos, the memories of wearing it on the day it snowed so hard we couldn't make out each other's faces on the walk home.

You have an infinite number of opportunities to find a soulmate. To find someone to keep you warm. And you may get lucky and meet a few of them, and spend a few winters together. I'm certain I have.

You may want to live in Florida, and never really need a coat at all. We all find our own sunshine.

I also believe in infinite soulmates because I believe that soulmates come in many forms, and they aren't just romantic partners. Soulmates can be our friends. Our mothers. Our siblings. The people who tie our sails when we can't seem to catch the wind. The people who carry us across the finish line, and cheer for our victories. Our soulmates can come in the form of art and artists, our guiding lights, our mentor pieces, the music that lulls us back to sleep.

I wish I would've known that there isn't just one. That I am a person with an abundant life and abundant opportunities to live. There are winter coats for sale every season, and I'll find one that I will want to wear indoors, all year-round, even sometimes to bed.

I wish I would've known that you should never get into a relationship just to be in a relationship. We should never settle for a partner because we'd rather have someone than be alone. It's always better to be alone than in an awful relationship, a relationship that feels wrong, or a relationship that doesn't serve you. And being alone isn't lonely. It just is.

•

People ask you all the time, when you're in a long-term relationship, if you think your partner is "the one"—and I never know how to answer, because I don't think the question is very clear.

Anyone I choose to date, I see myself with in the future—I can envision a life together, the experiences we may take on together and the potential we have as a pair. If I didn't, I wouldn't be with them. But ultimately, I can't predict the future, and neither can you. So I take the pressure off.

Noah is my one for now. For this week and next. We have plane tickets booked for an upcoming trip and plans for the next round of December holidays. He's going to be the one through all that. And I hope with everything in me that he'll be the one for ten or twenty more December holidays and plane trips. He knows he's my one for now, and he knows I hope that he'll be my one every single day as long as I'm me. He tells me he feels the same, and kisses me on the nose.

I try to be realistic because our realism is healthy. It keeps us floating between the ground and the clouds together. Together we can hope we're meant to be. But nobody truly knows anything, we all just guess and check. Guess and check. Once upon a time, I thought Ezra, and Luke, and even some days Nate, was the one. I didn't just wish Ezra was the one—I was utterly convinced that he was. But if I hadn't lost Ezra, there would be no Noah.

We are in love for now, we are the best things in each other's lives for now, and even though we don't know what's to come, I do know I'll always love Noah, because the time we've shared together has been too big and brilliant to ever truly lose. For once, I feel freedom in love. It's possible to rewrite your narrative, to relearn yourself and unlearn someone else just to learn, for the first time, someone new. All I wanted, through all the relationships, and all the pain and all the really good nights, was to just want to be with myself. All along, the most important connection was the one I had with me. And that affinity for myself snowballed. It snowballed to Noah, to us pressed up against the cool window, his glasses on the bedside table and his arms warm around my waist. The key to us was mine the minute I unlocked everything I'd buried away, everything I didn't want to admit and everything I always wanted to accept, but just couldn't. You, solitary and alone, are the only route you can take to find an us.

I like to tell a lot of people about how I manifested Noah. In grad school, I met with a woman named Terry, a witch and psychic

medium for celebrities—even a couple of US presidents—who today is known for helping young women steer clear from danger
on New York City streets and subways, when she could tell that a
man around them had plans to violently handle them in some way.

Her apartment was on the seventh floor of a walk-up building with a winding, wrought-iron staircase. The building had been
renovated since Terry moved in, but she told me that she requested
her apartment be left alone.

Her stove was a vintage Chambers stove and her dining chairs
and table were made of a soft, dark wood. The walls were lined
with collected trinkets and books and envelopes and postcards. It
smelled of fabric softener and firewood and reminded me of wher-
ever Jack and Jill were going to fetch their water in the nursery
rhyme. Cool light streamed through the lace curtains and there
was a claw-footed bathtub in the kitchen. She could tell you where
each trinket came from. Where she was when she read each book.
How she made her first magic wand and broomstick, which hung
on the walls.

I told Terry that I felt stuck. Uncertain. Unclear. It felt like while
everyone else could hit the gas and go, I was stuck in an interminable car, parked. It wasn't that I was unmotivated, more that I
wasn't sure where my energy was meant to go.

I was a grad student, nannying four times a week, single, and
a little lost. I was killing myself in journalism school but something felt wrong—I felt like I was working three times as hard in
my classes but performing three times as poorly. In other words, I
wasn't so sure I was a good breaking-news journalist. In my classes,
during workshops, I pored over my classmates work, wondering
why my brain couldn't wrap my head around what we were learning in the same way.

I was worried I'd never work in journalism, or if I did, I'd never
do very well. Nevertheless, I'd been pushing forward, day by day,

killing myself—propelling myself forward with too much force—
with a little pocket of anxiety buried somewhere behind my ribs.

"You have to just be still and wait."

"What?" I countered.

"Be still and wait. Something's coming. Many things, actually."
She laughed. "You don't want to know. Trust me. You want to be
surprised."

"I do?"

"You do."

And that was it. I packed my things and took the winding staircase down to the streets below, feeling ever so slightly different. I
crossed the street and ducked into the cheery bakery, playing holi-
day music and smelling of butter and lemon.

Be still and wait.

I didn't know what it meant, yet it was only four words. I ordered a gluten-free cupcake and sat down and tried to undo the
words in my mind. I settled on letting it mean exactly what it
should—stop pushing so hard to find what's right. Stop pushing
so hard to find where your energy is supposed to go, or who it's
supposed to go to. That's when I started manifesting and journaling. I started writing down all the things I wanted out of life. I
started believing they could come toward me. Tales of love, career
aspirations, and goals I'd been working toward filled the pages of
my notebook. Most prominently, I switched my mindset. I started
believing that future me already had the love of her life, the book
deal, the career milestones. Current me just had to work toward
those and believe they'd come true.

Just enjoy the ride, do your best, and work hard. Let the universe handle the rest.

Part
3

Rules for Heartbreak

1. TIME. HEALS. ALL. WOUNDS.

2. Wallow. You have to feel everything, especially the hard things.

3. Pull 'n' Peel Twizzlers, Phish Food, and Sour Cream and Onion Chips. Eat your heart out. Lean in to comfort.

4. Set an END DATE to your wallowing—two weeks, three weeks, end of the month. I don't know what your prerogative is.

5. Heartbreak glow up time. But do it for YOU, not for them.

6. Make out with someone else first, then go on a first date, then consider sleeping with someone new.

7. If at first you don't succeed, don't screw your ex.

8. Block, unadd, unfriend. Throw out their things.

9. Positive mentor films, books, and music: keep it positive and Girl Boss-y à la Elle Woods.

10. The end goal of a relationship isn't always going to be forever.

11. The switch rule: when this person enters your mind, switch the thought with a positive one.

12. You don't miss them, you miss the feeling they gave you.

MAY IN ANN ARBOR is the best version of May I've ever lived. It's 45 degrees in the morning, 71 degrees in the afternoon. When the sun dips below the clouds, the sky looks like it's holding its breath. It turns a phosphorescent purple. We used to dress like it was summer, just because it wasn't 15 degrees anymore.

It was my first May there, and I was packing up my things to move out of my dorm room. Sitting cross-legged in the space between the room's two beds, I folded up my clothes, some for cardboard boxes to live in a storage unit for the summer, others for the large black suitcase at the lip of the bed.

The night before, Ezra had come over. We hadn't seen each other since March—his idea, one that I followed begrudgingly after a night where he invited me over just to force me to enter through the fire escape on the second floor, sleep with me, and kick me out afterward.

"I didn't even want you to come over," he said that night, to my half-naked body wrapped in his sheets. We'd been lying side by side for an hour when he sprang out of bed, decided that he never wanted to see me again, and harshly let me know.

"It isn't my fault," he continued, with a hint of soberness, to show he meant it, "that you've never experienced hardship before and can't handle us being done."

"Why are you doing this?" I asked, in a small voice, the loudest I could be.

He had no reply. He just threw my jeans at me. I barely caught them. He told me to get dressed.

"Get the fuck out," he kept saying, over and over and over, as though he hadn't been the one that invited me there. As though he hadn't spent the last hour tracing the goosebumps lining my arms and shoulders, as though he hadn't kissed the top of my head.

It wasn't his "get the fuck out" that hurt. It was the way he looked at me and said that, as the only person at school who knew about my Thanksgiving, that when I went home and to my surprise, my mother wasn't strong enough to get out of bed.

I dressed quickly, his gaze burning down at me from where he stood, in the frame of the door. It was two o'clock in the morning. Twenty degrees outside. I had no jacket. My body was shaking as I tried to zip my pants, trying to wrap my head around why he wanted to hurt me so badly.

"Go" was all he said, while I looked up at him, trembling like a terrified animal and not an eighteen-year-old girl.

"Why are you doing this?" I whispered. He just turned, giving me the space to squeeze through the door frame. I knew I wasn't allowed to walk downstairs, past his fraternity brothers and friends, out the front door. So I walked down the fire escape, my fingers burning as I gripped the frozen iron handrail. I could hardly feel the cold; everything in me felt like liquid. I was afraid my legs wouldn't work when I got to the concrete below. I could see my breath outside. I let the cool air sting my bare arms. I wanted to feel something other than hurt. I sobbed as I headed down the sidewalk, my eyes turned down to my feet. I wasn't upset that he'd said those things to me. I wasn't upset that he terrified me, or threw my clothes at me, or said "get the fuck out." I was devastated that no matter what I did, he still didn't love me. I was devastated that after weeks of endless yo-yos and games, I couldn't win him over. I'd gotten so close—most weeks he'd tell me I earned him back, only to decide days later he didn't want to be with me anymore—he'd give me a list of things I'd done wrong, a list of reasons why I wasn't good enough, and I'd go into the world on a wild frenzy trying to prove him wrong. I almost always did. I wish I'd known that it was never me, and there was never anything I could've done. The ritual was sadistic and manipulative, but the only wrong thing I did was believe I wasn't good enough for him, or anyone else.

People ask so often why I went back. And I struggle to find the words. I think we need to stop asking those manipulated why they went back, why they had no self-respect, and start putting the onus back on those who manipulate—what they do to force someone to stay, or how they managed to make someone feel so worthless.

In the months we spent apart, I struggled to heal. Everyone told me that our breakup was for the best. Everyone told me that after that night, I couldn't possibly go back. But people forget—when you're in an emotionally toxic or abusive relationship, you often can't see what's happening clearly. People are so quick to judge or place blame, but I couldn't help the way I felt—and even when he hurt me, or dragged me lower than I'd ever been dragged, I was in so deep that I was blind—I couldn't just stop loving him. I was told, by him and a voice inside me, that this was all I had. A tiny piece of me knew if he called, I'd answer. I was ashamed and sick and depressed, but I couldn't help it. I felt like he was what I deserved. I'd tried to derive affirmation from any other source—from running half-marathons, my classes, or blond-haired fraternity boys with kind smiles—but it hadn't worked.

Now, months past our breakup, I was shattered, heartbroken, sitting on the floor, thinking about the night before, when I'd let him come over—same sheepish smile, same goofy jokes, same all-encompassing spell over me. We sat facing the wall, our legs brushing, our feet hanging off the edge. It was almost cosmic, the way that we hadn't seen each other since that March night, and when he asked to see me, I hardly hesitated. It felt like something had woken me, after weeks of darkness. I didn't want to say or do the wrong thing, so I let him lead. There was a kinetic force between us, an undeniable level of chemistry. I didn't want anyone to know he was there because to admit that would be to admit that I was weak. That I couldn't possibly be a feminist or strong or brave if I had this horrible, crippling vice. I wish I knew that it could be true that I shouldn't have let him in, but also that I had been deeply emotionally manipulated, to a point where being at his will felt natural. Both could be true at once. I wasn't a weak failure. I hadn't lost. I was lost, and I wouldn't understand this girl until I was found.

He kissed me and told me there was nobody like me—told me that nothing felt the way we felt together. Lying there after we slept together, thinking I finally had him back, he pulled the rug out from underneath my optimism and told me he'd been seeing someone—a sweet nursing student with a diamond cross necklace and Bible verses in her Instagram bio.

On the floor, packing up my clothes, I felt empty. He undid me. Took everything and kept trying to take and then went back into the world with all of me, like it was nothing. I folded a sweater that smelled of a night we had spent in Detroit. Us in the car, listening to country music. I had fumbled with the buttons on the front in the dim parking garage, peeling it off as we shimmied into the back seat. Now I packed away jeans with love spots on the knees from wearing them over and over; they had so often spent the night on his carpeted bedroom floor. I considered donating piles of tank tops with lace trim or ties on the side that I wore when it looked like everyone belonged except for me. Maybe I'd been spending time in the wrong places, wearing clothes that looked like a costume I'd wear if I was a character in a movie about my own life. On my neck I felt a bite mark, a red spot that felt tender when I grazed it with my fingers—a reminder that I wasn't even my own. I threw out the half-burned candles from a Homegoods off campus. I had a panic attack when I was buying them, standing in a sea of floral scents and wax, because he'd blamed our arguments all on me, told me everything was my fault. It was one thing to be heartbroken, and another to be heartbroken without any control.

We'd gone back to being strangers for two months, and then I invited him back in the second he asked, with no hesitation, easy as that—with the effortlessness of blowing out a flame. I wondered what it would be like to ever say no to him. Now I was lost, stranded in the ocean, and the lifeboat he captained would hover nearby but never save me. Every time I tried to climb aboard, he pushed me off the edge and watched as I drowned.

It's hard to place a feeling you've never had before, but there's only so many explanations for an emotion that makes you want to crawl out from under your skin.

It was crushing, gutted, brokenheartedness.

•

"I want to end up with someone actually Jewish, not just someone with a Jewish dad who has a name that sounds Jewish."

It was ten a.m., we were in a Catholic church parking lot, and I was just eighteen.

And to Ezra's defense, honestly, wanting to be with someone who shares the same religious beliefs is valid and I understand. I get it. If I was raised religiously Jewish, perhaps I'd want to end up with someone religiously Jewish too. That's his right, his religious preference, and something I'd always respect.

But what really hurt was what followed the first statement.

"I always told myself I'd make an exception if the person and the relationship was absolutely exceptional . . . but you're just not." He looked at me like I was dirty snow under his boot. Ann Arbor was gray and broken. Everyone was getting ready to go home for the holidays. I would soon be faced by a cacophony of questions: How do you like college? Is it amazing? How was the first semester?

It was ending with a bang, that was for sure.

"I always knew this too. So maybe I should've said something earlier." He rocked back and forth on his feet, and I tried to focus on anything else. The backdrop of this entire charade was a Catholic church on one side, and his fraternity house on the other. Bliss.

But you're just not. The words rang in my head like church bells. I couldn't even hear what he was saying. I just watched his mouth move.

He started sniffling, then, like it hurt him so badly to back over my heart with an eighteen-wheeler. Like it pained him to insult me. Like he was a good guy, a nice guy, a guy who wanted me to be okay. I remember asking myself what my mom would say to do— would she tell me to fight back? To be honest? To cry with him? I couldn't think.

"Just stop" was all I could muster. Then I turned around defiantly and marched back exactly the way I came, down a small alley I often traversed to go from my dorm room to parties at his house. I walked briskly, trying to catch my breath, trying to remember the way his face twisted at me when he said "and you're just not." I waited until I was out of his line of sight before hysterically crying. I remember thinking it was really bitchy and cool of me to leave him crying in the parking lot like a pathetic asshole. But I didn't remain cool for much longer. I felt my world tumble around me—the brick house I'd felt so comfortable in was knocked to the ground in a matter of thirty seconds. He said it was over, but I knew it wasn't true. It should've been, but for the next year, neither of us could let the other go.

I mean, after all, this was my first heartbreak. At eighteen, I was baby-faced, with long brown hair with dead ends and a penchant for patterned sweaters. I looked like a deer learning to walk for the first time. I wore tops that revealed intentional skin and laughed superloudly so people would notice me. I lied my way through sorority rush because I was afraid I wasn't cool or interesting enough to have friends if anyone found out I liked to spend Friday nights reading, that I was in the drama club in high school. I thought I had what I wanted—the sorority sisters, the packed social schedule, the attention from a gangly older boy. But the one thing I didn't have, or even know, was myself. Losing him meant losing most of what I had, and not even being left with the idea of me.

It sounds dramatic, but when you're eighteen years old and are heartbroken for the first time, your world shatters. Because many times your world is the five times he told you that you look so pretty and the way it felt to be on his arm in the basement fraternity. I won't patronize my past self—her world was over in a way mine wouldn't be now. But that was her world then.

I didn't realize that love could expire and then evaporate. I thought about my parents, who met when my mother was twenty-one years old. I thought about my grandparents, who met when they were thirteen. I felt blindsided and stubborn, like I couldn't accept that we could be holding hands walking to class on a Thursday, and everything between us could be null and void forty-eight hours later. I didn't understand why he fell for me, why he even wanted to be with me, if he knew, all along, that it wouldn't work out.

In the back of my head, though, still small enough for me to quiet it, a voice suggested that I could make myself exceptional, in the way he wanted. It seemed the easiest solution.

Where does the love go when all is said and done? I asked myself, as I walked slowly to a Starbucks, with muddy snow caking the toe of my Ugg boots. I convinced myself it couldn't go anywhere—that if there was something between us, it would stay there. That way there was a shred of hope. It never occurred to me that it could just be over. It hurt too badly to face that dead-on, so I didn't. Instead, I decided the pain would be temporary—the pain would subside once we both got our heads on straight and fixed what went wrong. I wanted it all reversed by the same person who started its engine.

I felt hungover. I remember asking Sadie what to do. We'd only known each other for two months then. I found her around the same time I found him, and I trusted and loved them both equally, until she seamlessly pulled ahead. She'd stick around even though the breakup made me legitimately insufferable to be around and stay through everything that came after, too.

I waited for hours to tell her because saying it out loud made it all feel real. Finally, I texted her, and she told me to come over. Her dorm room was a mile away, and the journey included passing Ezra's house. The sky was black and a snowstorm had ensued, but I couldn't sit inside any longer, so I walked to her dorm room and we sat on the couch in the common room and ordered pizzas. I hadn't eaten all day; everything tasted like wet cardboard. I told her it felt like an elephant was sitting on my chest. It felt cruel and heavy and distressing. We couldn't yet know anything that was to come for either Sadie or me. We hardly knew each other, and I hardly knew myself. For the rest of that year, we'd sit on my lofted bed, sip on drinks, and pretend to be happy. Through it all, we'd always have each other. I wish I would've known to focus on the love I did have, and not the love I'd lost.

"You're going to kill me," she said. "But the only thing that really helps is time." She looked up from her laptop, and I nodded, but I told myself I'd live to convince her she was wrong. In my brain I figured that the beautiful, audacious girls would tell you that "time heals all," but things came easier to them so their advice had to prove false. But of course, she was the wiser of us two, and I, drenched in naivete, decided to prove her wrong anyway.

When I got back to school in 2017, I was filled with vengeance and false empowerment. I made it look like I was doing fine—I joined all the clubs I procrastinated joining when I was caught up in fraternity parties and having a boyfriend. I started to write again, even though most of it was syrupy and sad.

I went out every night. Guys touched my waist, spilled beer on my jeans, blew smoke in my face. Maybe I'd get in bed with them. Maybe I'd become friends with the girls dancing near the DJ. Maybe I'd just go home. A feigned scripture lived in my bones. I said it over and over: *You're fine. This doesn't hurt.* I pushed away the pain because facing the pain, and the heartache, meant accepting we were through. But no matter what I did, where I went, I searched for Ezra in the crowded corners of every college bar.

On Instagram—on the exterior—I did a decent job of convincing everyone (and myself) I was fine and avoiding the truth. But behind the closed dorm room door, it wasn't so easy. I struggled, lying in bed, wallowing, eating Pull 'n' Peel Twizzlers by the pound, and listening to the Bruno Mars EP, specifically "Versace on the Floor," for whatever reason, until I'd finally get up and defiantly lie to myself that I felt better. I wouldn't let myself feel for too long, or in front of anyone else, because to feel was to accept reality's cruel truths.

There are so many things I wish I'd known back then. I wish I had felt everything—especially the hard things. I pushed those bad feelings so far away that when I finally felt ready to face them, I had to dig them up from under everything I stacked on top. I held in so many tears, so many breakdowns, and so many emotions because I didn't want those feelings to exist with me, in the world. I figured if I prevented myself from feeling them, they'd eventually just get tired of me and leave.

But the truth is, you have to greet your pain, you have to meet the hard feelings, the desolate emotions halfway, you have to get to know them in order to say, "I've had enough of you, you can go now."

You have to hold something before you can let it go.

Give yourself a few days, or weeks, or at least a weekend of watching your favorite romantic comedies, eating ice cream, and just feeling sorry for yourself. It's an integral step in the healing process. And then you give yourself a date for the wallowing to be over—you take a shower, clean up your space, go on a little walk, and put one foot in front of the other.

Today, I would go out and do things to actually mitigate the pain a little and not make that pain worse. Back then, I didn't know that random hookups and hangovers would compound every-thing I was already going through.

Today, I would remind myself that there's no timeline. No "sup-posed tos." No one correct way to handle a breakup or heartbreak. It's allowed to feel awful, and it's allowed to be strangely freeing. It's allowed to be devastating even if you were the one to break up with them. I'd go out and do something for myself—a haircut, some (nonimpulsive) bangs, some fresh highlights. I'd make my-self feel a little refreshed, in a period of newness.

I would take it one step at a time. I wouldn't start dating until I was ready to start dating. Maybe first I'd dabble in a dance floor makeout, then go on a first date with a stranger, and eventually sleep with someone new when the time felt right. In 2017, I fig-ured that dates and sex and distractions would eventually remedy me, bandage up a wound that wouldn't stop aching. The heart is a muscle, and when you pull a muscle, the doctor will tell you to take some time off—to not do anything that hurts, to stop and rest when it does.

It's the same with your emotional heart. Don't do anything that hurts. When it hurts, stop and rest.

The night before we broke up he had an improv show. I thought his improv group was a very glorified and cool group of losers. The exact type of company I so often craved. It was December. I did my hair pin straight without heat protectant and sat in the sec-ond row. I was giddy and proud. It sometimes embarrassed me to watch him perform for some reason. But he was funny. He often told me I wasn't funny at all. Interesting, because my dad would disagree with him, but I digress.

After the show, I went up onstage to give him a hug. He asked me if I was too tired to come to the after-party and I said of course not. It was stupid of me to forget he'd returned a bag of my things a day earlier, claiming his roommates asked him to "declutter" their room. No man's roommates have ever asked him to "declutter" the room. So if your boyfriend says that, make sure to call him out on his bullshit.

The weird thing about feeling heartbroken for the first time was realizing how uniquely painful heartbreak is. It doesn't sound or feel or empathize like any other pain. It doesn't manifest like any other kind of sadness. Just when you thought you understood the range of emotions humans are capable of feeling, a new kind of empathy fills you, a new kind of hurt knocks you over. It is a special and intriguing beast. After our breakup, I would cry on the bus that took me to class, shield my eyes with Ray-Bans and act hungover and cool. I refused to let myself wallow because it seemed pathetic to be so sad over someone who broke up with me in a church parking lot after saying I wasn't Jewish enough for him, and that it embarrassed him to be with me.

What I wished I knew then is this: heartbreak hurts so badly because love feels so wonderful. Like a pendulum, the range of human emotions is ever expansive and dizzying to ponder on either side. We only have the capacity to love because we have the capacity to hurt.

I'm not sure if I believe in "getting over it" because getting over something, anything, implies that you were once somehow under it. I never got over him. I just grew out of him. I grew into a different version of myself—after spending a year trying on different people. I eventually gave it all up and decided to just become myself. But the girl who fit him would always fit him, and the boy who fit her would always fit her. I had to leave her behind. I left her and her need to be a glorified loser vacuuming up the pieces in East Quad.

He ended up apologizing long after, but it didn't matter. We are so far past what that time was, and what it meant, that his apology, and the words *You were always right, it was never you* meant nothing to me. It was simply kind of funny.

If I have any advice for heartbreak now, it's to tread water until you reach the shore. Because the shore always comes, and your arms are strong enough. Put your head down and fucking swim. Sometimes you'll just drift, other times you'll find a patch of land and take a break. But I know you can get to the other side, because all around the world, every single day, people do. We're all either heartbroken or in love or somewhere in between. When you're stuck in a rip current, they say you have to let it take you first. You're supposed to stay calm. You can't fight it. You just let it take you out to the sea. And then you call for help, start swimming parallel to the shore. You'll almost give up fifteen times before you realize life is too worth it to just stop swimming. When you get there, it'll feel like you've been to hell and back, and you'll be proud of yourself for standing firm on the earth.

When I think about Ezra, and our fallout and the aftermath, I know that my biggest mistake was not that I didn't feel everything, and not that I couldn't accept it, and not that I couldn't see my own value. It was that I thought I could and should get him back.

I did it all because I was afraid of what losing him meant: having to find myself.

But here's the truth: we cannot convince someone to want to be with us. And furthermore, we shouldn't beg to be someone's maybe when there's someone else out there waiting to look at us and say "fuck yes." We shouldn't have to beg someone to be with us. So go where you are wanted. It's simple, but ultimately, it's the key to not crawling backward into the arms of an ex-boyfriend who will never want you the way you want them to.

I blocked Ezra on everything—including GroupMe, for good measure—except, apparently, email. He sent me a letter as a Google Doc and said something that I will truly not forget.

"I fear I will never have sex this good again" (this is word for word, just to be clear) "Eli Rallo: 1, every other girl: -100."

Also, if you've ever made a "pro/con list" in your iPhone notes, attempting to decide whether or not to end something—you've already decided. End it. Stop starving yourself so they stay fed. Throughout our relationships we all change. Sometimes your person will change into a someone that doesn't look like who we first fell for. Sometimes it's just a feeling. Follow it.

Ask yourself, if nothing happened between us, would I choose this person again today?

We so often fear the end because it can be sloppy and it sucks and we're left walking through the snow in Ugg boots all alone to go take a jar of Nutella to the face. We forget who we are for a few weeks until we start remembering again. We fear the end because the only thing that comes after it is a new unknown beginning. We lean into comfort and familiarity because it is easier than getting to know someone else, or, even scarier, ourselves. But that doesn't make it right to move backward.

•

Years passed, and eventually I was boxing up another bedroom, heartbroken once more. The spring of 2019, my apartment was on the same street as my freshman-year dorm room and this time I could pinpoint exactly what I was feeling. I was heartbroken, and this time it felt so much fucking worse.

Every serial dater knows that what was once love will eventually hurt like a bitch. That's like, the laws of gravity, or something. Thank you, Isaac Newton, you son of a bitch. Even if you end up with someone until the very end, there's an end—and love always ends up hurting. It's sort of beautiful that we continue to go after it with the force and the intensity that we do, even though we know how much we stand to lose.

The thing about heartbreak is that it generally hurts more in proportion to how much you loved and were loved. Being heart-broken is actually a lot like being in love. I see them more as twin feelings than I do as foils. Heartbreak is an all-consuming torrent of unavoidable emotional devastation, but it does not exist without the presence of love—making it, in some twisted way, a gift.

I'd ended a relationship with the second person I've ever loved, Luke, who was the first person I imagined the rest of my life with. Something about having future plans makes a dissolve-ment tougher to swallow. We had an unfinished bucket list in my phone notes. Days that we would never spend together. I'd ended things that May and spent the following summer hot, lonely, and wounded, wondering if I made the right call, filling up my days with another person who I unfairly wished would distract me. This time I was the one on the other end of the breakup.

Luke and I had been dating for about six months when things started turning sour. We were in love, and we were naive enough to think that would get us through. But our priorities weren't the same—in fact, he told me, to my face, I'd always come second to the rest of his life (at least he was honest).

I spent my time begging him for a slice of the pie that made up his life—an occasional date night, effort to come see the play I was producing, or desire for me—but he could hardly give me a crumb. As time went on, I grew famished, and the reality came into focus—this is how it would always be with us. This is how it would always be with him.

And I wanted it to be different because I'd never felt that way. I was so deeply in love, I would've done anything to fight for us—to fight for our happy ending. I tried to meet him halfway, or even a quarter of the way. I gently asked for a little more effort here or there—asked for him to make me feel more desired.

I wondered if this was as good as it would ever get, too. I wasn't being emotionally manipulated like I'd been with Ezra. But there was also an obvious lack of effort from Luke. I ended it in May but would've done it earlier when I realized our priorities weren't the same, and neither was our output into the relationship—but I was afraid, terrified that this was as good as it would get.

I wish someone had told me I would've rather been alone, single, living my life for me, than in a relationship that didn't serve me. The last time I saw him, I went to his house, punched in the door code, and we sat on his bed. I had one of the bandannas I always wore in my hair back then in my pocket, spritzed with my perfume, and a letter telling him I loved him but that I couldn't do this anymore.

He sobbed into my sweatshirt and we held hands. I tried to ask myself if this was the last time I'd ever see him when he was mine, but I couldn't make out the answers to my own questions. We sat like that for what felt like hours, just holding each other. Finally he walked me downstairs. The first floor of the building was a laundry room. It was drafty in the winter and stale in the spring. He pushed me against a washing machine and we kissed for the last time, now both through tears. I handed him the bandanna and the folded-up card. This made him cry harder.

I didn't know what to do, so I kissed him, and I left.

That was the last time we ever spoke in person.

A few weeks later I asked him if he wanted to see each other, and he said he wasn't sure. He said he wanted to "settle at his internship" and then "see what happens next." I told him I didn't want to be a maybe, especially after everything we'd been through. That he had to choose, because it wasn't fair for either of us to be interminably in the gray space.

He said we shouldn't see each other then. And it broke me in half, even though it was the right thing to say. Even though I'd ended it first. I spent every day questioning if it was the right choice and wondering if love could ever get better than something that wasn't even that good.

I wish I knew that I didn't have to settle for the bare minimum. That I didn't have to end up with anyone at all. That I could be alone and happy and content. That I could reserve some energy for myself. You are not a maybe. Neither am I.

We could never get on the same page. I kept waiting to turn mine to see if we'd ever match up.

I told myself I couldn't wallow and I couldn't grieve because *I'd* ended things with *him*. I saw myself as weak and pathetic. As time went forward, I slipped back. I wanted to wash up on a familiar shore, warm and sandy, but instead, drifted further out to an unknown sea. Seasick. Distraught. Wondering if I'd ever just stop treading water and let myself drown. But if I decided to let myself drown, I'd never love again. So I kept paddling. You have to keep paddling.

I remember once Luke asked me what the best day of my life was and I was sitting across from him in Soho eating over easy eggs. It was June, and I loved the way my body felt sitting on the sidewalk, sipping from a China coffee cup. I was wearing a great pair of pants. The sun hit my hair in the right way, and for a while after we ended, I didn't realize I could eat eggs with other people and feel special too.

"Today," I said. "I'm so happy." I used to lie a lot.

And I kept repeating it, as though I wanted, desperately, to believe it myself. *I'm so happy. I'm so happy. I'm so happy. I'm so happy.*

In the impending month, I'd go assume my role as an intern at a St. Louis theater and be all alone, getting to know myself for the first time. The summer would push me off a high dive head-first and say: sink or swim. It would be a beautiful becoming. I'd leave the summer knowing who I was, but not how Luke fit into that anymore. The best day of my life would dissolve from a faux declaration of sticky romance to running ten miles in the blaring Missouri heat, reading on a park bench all by myself, standing backstage with tears running down my cheeks as live musical theater rushed through my blood like a well-needed dose of medicine, eating tacos in my apartment kitchen, sitting next to floor-to-ceiling windows, riding my bike to get ice cream alone. He wouldn't have fit into those days. But I couldn't accept it. I loved him. I loved him, and I thought that was enough.

But it wasn't. Of course it wasn't. And then I didn't realize that sometimes the end result of a relationship isn't going to be forever. In fact, most times, the end result isn't going to be a forever. Sometimes it's a life lesson, a fond memory of him wearing two sizes two big Crocs sitting at his fireplace in New England, a city where he lives, known for it's ski resort. We should all become okay with expiration dates.

When I was missing Luke I distracted myself with Nate and cried on the spin bike at the gym.

The most confusing and mystifying part of all was that I did care for Nate. And we did have fun together. And something about our time together was love—maybe not deep, romantic love, but he taught me something valuable. I wish I had known that I was allowed to feel pain and goodness at the same time. I wish I could've been blunt about that with Nate, instead of pushing him away when our harmless fling took a turn to become more.

As that summer ended and the fall loomed on our calendars and in the air, Nate and I decided we wanted to get serious about each other. I hadn't spoken to Luke since July, and now it was late August. Nate was incredible. He was kind and thoughtful and easy to be around. We loved each other like we loved friends we'd known since childhood—something more than just friendship but less than deep romantic love. I wanted to stop feeling heartbroken about Luke so I could be truly present with Nate, so I pushed away the feelings of heartbreak, pushed away the wallowing and ignored the strings pinching my heart. Instead, we jumped in headfirst and decided to be together.

I went back to school, to Michigan, forty-five minutes away

from where his parents lived. He stayed in New York City, and he made it so easy to be long distance. Though I was running into Luke and his new, pretty girlfriend on campus left and right, I felt oddly okay, because I had Nate to call at the end of the day. Nate sending me flowers on the first day of school. Nate coming to visit for football games.

In late October, right before Halloween, Nate visited me in Michigan. He picked me up and we went to his family's home, where I'd been once before. I loved his family, especially his mom. I still think of her a lot.

We went on long runs down winding, autumnal Michigan roads and cooked in his parents' kitchen. I slept in his T-shirts and he played me guitar. The last night we were there we had sex in his childhood bedroom. The house was decorated with a slight homage to the '70s that fit them perfectly. He got up to go sleep on the couch, because his parents didn't let us sleep in the same room. I couldn't sleep, because something just felt off, so I quietly slipped into the living room, where he was awake, staring at the ceiling. I sat down beside him and started to cry. He held me and didn't say anything. He just stroked my hair. Because I think we both knew that even if we wanted it to work so badly, it probably never would.

The next morning we got up early because I had to go to work. I was a waitress. He drove me to the restaurant and we sat in the parking lot when we arrived. I started to cry again. I just knew it was the last time I'd see him and we'd be together. I don't know how I knew, or what gave it away. He kissed me what felt like a million times.

"It's okay. I love you," he said.

"I know. I love you, too," I said, and I think it was the only time I really meant it.

Before I knew it, I'd go through the stages of grief and they'd be painful. They'd be twofold, because I was dealing with the breakup with Nate and the residual and unaddressed heartbreak I'd never faced from Luke. These feelings would take an eternity to go through. They'd run around me in circles. They'd keep me up at night.

I often describe the feeling of heartbreak as someone laying fresh bricks on your chest. They keep building up until you find a way to become a bulldozer and knock them down. Sometimes it takes a year to become a bulldozer. Sometimes it takes longer. Nobody else can be a bulldozer for you, and I had never really been a bulldozer for myself.

In fall 2019, my senior year, I wasn't a bulldozer. I felt sick all the time. Sick to my stomach, sick of being hurt, sick of feeling like I'd lost the only love I thought I'd deserve. I wrote everything until I had nothing else to write, I went on dates with dentists and business students, and I put on a display of gleeful flirtation. I made a private story on Snapchat with ONE VIEWER and it was Luke. I wanted him to know I was happy even when I wasn't. I tried to kiss new people, go on first dates, find someone worth sleeping with. I posted about it to the aforementioned private story. But it all felt wrong. In therapy I asked what to do when I saw Luke out with someone else. I asked who to call when I wanted to say something nobody else would care about, when I desperately missed Nate. I made sure to always smell good. I went on long runs, and if I broke down far enough away from campus, I would sit on a curb, put my head between my knees and sob until I felt better. I would stay up all night and listen to the song "My Favorite Things" from *Sound of Music*. I did every part of healing, somehow, wrong, because it was all about how much I wished to have him back, and not finding myself independent of that void.

I tried to manipulate my own thoughts—when a thought of Luke popped into my brain, I'd switch the thought to something positive or exciting. Conscious thoughts become subconscious actions.

One thing I was finally doing right: I hurt so constantly and so truly that it made me proud. I wasn't avoiding the sensations of loss like eye contact at the bar. I was facing everything—especially the hard things, because that's the first step toward becoming a bulldozer. That's the first step toward reaching the shore. You have to get to know your demons, so you can tell them to get the HELL out of your life. People don't change unless they want to, and I wanted to. I wanted to change for me.

The commonsense advice when you break up with someone is to immediately throw away or return their stuff and the gifts they gave you. I'd been keeping Luke's things under my bed in a Steve Madden shoebox for six months following our breakup. Even through my relationship with Nate, I just didn't want to think of parting with them. But one day, after what felt like an eternity of feeling, I pulled the box out from under my bed and zipped my jacket over my pajamas. It was 6:30 in the morning and I walked with purpose out my front door, beelining to my destination: a dumpster on the cul-de-sac down the street. There was a group of men working near the dumpsters who watched me, standing there, alone, with an armful of borrowed objects. They were waiting for me to do what we all knew I needed to do. I was thinking about turning around and returning the shoebox to its home under the bed, when one of them called out: "Do it, girl! You got this!" and with his declaration, I throttled the items over the side of the dumpster, and watched, for a half second, as they sailed through the air and landed with a satisfying thud in the midst of half-empty beer cans, discarded mattresses, and cardboard. For a moment, it felt like nothing else was happening in the rest of the world, like everything had stopped. And then, the group of men across the gravel parking lot began to cheer. It's as though they knew. I turned empty-handed and walked back the same exact way I came, only this time, I felt a little bit lighter.

Later, I became friends with that pretty girl I'd seen Luke out with. I had spent so much time making myself sick with dread, scrolling through her social media, passing through photos of them out to dinners, browsing bookstores, taking trips to meet each other's families, and celebrating life's silly events. She had what was once mine, and from my view in my attic bedroom, she had it better. After they broke up, after we became friends, I realized how much of that was in my head. She told me that he still made minimal effort, punched walls when he was angry—it was the same old story. I had just made up another one based on what I saw on the screen. It appeared to me then, as I grieved the loss of someone I thought would be my forever, that she'd swiftly taken my spot, that they were happier than he and I were, that he'd changed for her in ways he wouldn't for me. It stung to watch my ex-boyfriend celebrate birthdays and anniversaries and Fourth of Julys with a beautiful girl who I felt I understood because I'd stalked her on social media. I didn't hate her. I wasn't angry at her. I resented her. I envied her.

This is a mistake many of us make, one I urge you not to. We look at someone else living out a reality we crave or think we crave from a very superfluous point of view and we destroy ourselves because of it. She had done nothing wrong. And neither had he. This doesn't make it hurt less but it takes the hurt away from the two of them and places it on the nature of how we love, how we date, how we discover people and say "you're really cool and cute and smart and I want to take your clothes off and talk to you about what you're afraid of, even if this only lasts a few weeks or months or years, it'll be worth it." They were trying each other on. I had tried him on, too, and he wasn't the right fit. Eventually, he wouldn't be the right fit for her, either. But both of them will eventually find the right fit. So would I. And it would be blissful for me to watch them do so. We all experienced unique loss and we all experienced unique love.

•

Eventually time passed, as it does, and I slipped into a version of myself I really like now. I missed Luke, and Nate sometimes, too, for a year and a half after it all ended. But I realized that I never missed either of them—I missed the *feeling* that it was to love them. The feeling I had when I loved them—a feeling I realized I would have again. And even if I was to reconnect or reignite my relationship to Luke or to Nate, it would never feel the exact same way as it did when I first loved them.

What I was grieving is a feeling that came from within me. And I knew I had the power to feel it again.

I've come to realize that heartbreak is rather beautiful and that I don't hate it. Heartbreak is complicated and innate in an admirable way. I never understood heartbreak, truly, until I realized that love does not exist without it, much like plants cannot grow without water. It doesn't make loss hurt less, but resenting heartbreak makes loss hurt more. Accepting it as the other half of the best equation to ever exist will soften a blow you cannot avoid.

•

Sometimes we tend to forget how lucky we are to feel at all. People always say love feels like you're the only two people that exist. But it doesn't feel like that to me. It feels like everyone exists everywhere, all around us, so bright and so vivid, heartbroken or in love or somewhere in the middle, and in spite of it all, we somehow burn brighter. If you had told me just a year ago that love would come and find me again, I'd have told you that you were wrong. But love always comes to find us again. Sometimes it isn't a lover, but ourselves that comes to find us. Sometimes it is a friend or a passion or a moment in time. We assume the worst, and we get the worst. So assume the best. Assume you will get through today's heartbreaks, or tomorrow's, or next year's. It is the universe's job to confirm your assumptions. Assume your heart will heal. Assume the person you lost wasn't right for you. Assume there's someone better. Better for you. Better for the love you require.

Don't just build a bridge and get over it. Take your time. Eat the Pull 'n' Peel Twizzlers and sob in your bed. Get back on the dating apps and have sex you want to have and find yourself again. You can't build a bridge until you become a bulldozer. Remember how strong you must be to heal. Build a bridge so strong it can withstand everything. Build a bridge so long you actually arrive somewhere new when you take a walk to the other side. Walk slowly. That bridge is your heart. It deserves strength. It deserves time. It deserves grace. I can give you your instruction manual, your hammer and your nails, but it'll be up to you to get to work.

So be the bulldozer. Be the best sex of his life too. Be the girl in the church parking lot and the girl hurtling his T-shirts over the side of a dumpster.

You're allowed to be all of us, and all of yourself—sad and scared and relieved in the face of heartbreak. Feel all these things, especially the hard things.

And then bulldoze the shit out of the dead weight in your way.

Rules for Closure and Getting Ghosted

1. Give it seventy-two hours, then move on.

2. We do not beg.

3. Selectively unadd the person on everything.

4. You have one hour to wallow.

5. Split a bottle of red wine with your best friend and have an EXCELLENT time.

6. Ignore the person if they reach out, which they will.

7. Revenge is success and silence. Period.

8. Do NOT be that girl, be this girl.

9. Fill all your gas tanks separately.

IN MY PERSONAL opinion, ghosting should be an offense punishable by LAW. It's disrespectful, anxiety inducing, confusing, and generally makes you feel awful about yourself, even though typically being ghosted has little to do with you (the ghostee), and *everything* to do with them (the ghoster). But no matter how we clarify or quantify or justify it—ghosting stings. No matter how many times I tell you that ghosting is cowardly, and you'd never want to be with a person who would stoop to that level, it's realistically difficult to make a convincing argument that makes it feel any less shitty.

Some things should hurt. They're allowed to.

When you finally realize you've been ghosted, a heat rises up in your chest, you feel prickly and angry and in dire need of revenge. Depending on the situation, the longevity of the longing, the intensity of the relationship, ghosting aftercare can range from a simple cleanup on aisle three to a full-blown "my friends had to drag me out of bed to shower after seventy-two hours because I thought I'd truly never recover."

When I first moved to New York City, I went on a date with a fellow Michigan alum. He had nice brown hair, unassuming eyes, and a goofy smile. He was cooler than me in college, but so were most people, so it didn't bring me much distress to harp on superfluous details like that.

We sat outside in Gramercy at a place that has since closed down. We would never get married, I could tell, but we also weren't completely and totally unmatched. We were just different, and I didn't mind it.

After dinner, once we both were drunk enough, we made out for a while on a picnic bench. There was a spark of chemistry and it felt breezy, safe. I told him I didn't sleep with people on the first date, and he said he'd rather take it slow, anyway, giving me every indication that perhaps we'd have a second date.

I figured he could be a perfect hookup or situationship for me—someone reliable, kind, and sweet who could always be there when I was feeling a little down or a little lonely—we could be the person each other resorted to when we struck out at the bar or didn't feel like going on a dating app date. I thought he must've felt the same, because he asked me to come over for wine a few nights later—*perfect*, I figured, *he sees this just as I do. We're on the same wavelength.*

We had another good time—conversation soothed by the addition of alcohol, and it was hardly thirty minutes before we were tangled together and paying each other simple, shallow compliments when we weren't busy being intertwined. I saw him a singular time afterward for a similar rendezvous—and then, never again. We texted back and forth a bit after the third meeting, and I was actively setting up first dates to see other people outside of seeing him, so when he never responded to a message I sent one morning, it didn't hit me until a few days later that I'd been ghosted.

He never answered that message, and a few Saturdays later, drunk off hard cider, I texted him "hi"; that message went unanswered as well.

Anything could've happened—he could've met someone new, gotten what he wanted from me and fallen out of interest with me; he could've, I briefly considered, died—but that was the least likely option, and after scouring the obituaries (embarrassing), I determined it wasn't the case. Still, most of us would rather believe the person had simply died and not that we'd been ghosted. We can all resonate with that ever-so-brief moment of denial, of conjuring up excuses for someone you hardly know.

But let's just rip the Band-Aid off—you got ghosted. It sucks, and it stings, but it just is.

Before him, I'd never really been ghosted before—in part because I'd made myself unghostable. If I felt like someone was going to ghost me, or was pulling away subtly, I would speak up, ask, or step in before it ended with me confused and upset, or worse, with me blaming myself for someone else's actions.

Our knee-jerk reaction when we're ghosted is to assume that we did something to warrant the ghosting, and not that the person would have ghosted us—or anyone for that matter—regardless.

The truth is, if someone you're seeing decides they don't want to see you anymore because you asked "Are you still interested in seeing where things go?" or "Have you changed your mind about me?," you wouldn't want to be with them in the first place. They're not the right person. The right person would make you feel comfortable and at ease. It's an act of self-preservation to be brave enough to confront a ghoster before the deed is truly done, and when someone is continuously making you feel anxious, or causing you to check a Snap Score or Venmo transactions, they're not the right person for you. You should always seek out clarity before you send yourself into a spiral.

And of course there's a scale of ghosting: ghosting can take place when you've been seriously seeing someone for a few weeks or months, it could be done by a serious partner, a situationship, a casual hookup, or the person you went on just one date with. Ghosting is most commonly done after one to three dates, or by a situationship or casual hookup, because they have less skin in the game, and the stakes are slightly lowered. Unfortunately, people who are less invested in you figure they owe you less respect.

As someone who knows what it's like to be the ghostee, I recommend you never become a ghoster. Of course it might feel easier and less confrontational to just never follow up with someone after one singular date, because it's true that you don't owe a stranger much, but I do believe that we owe everyone, including strangers, baseline respect. And it's baseline disrespectful to simply never respond to a message a nice person sent you, even if you just don't see a future with them, or to never follow up with them, leaving them to google your name followed by the word *obituary*, convinced you'd sooner die than rudely leave them without an explanation.

> I'll give you the green light to ghost if you go on a date or have an interaction with someone rude, disrespectful, bigoted, disagreeable, or who made you feel uncomfortable or unsafe. Then, feel free to match their energy with a ghosting—they deserve it.

If the date just wasn't great, or you really don't see it going anywhere, it takes ten seconds to type: "Hey! I think you're great, but I don't see a romantic future between us. I wish you all the best. :)" When sending a message letting someone know you're no longer interested in them, I recommend being polite and brief, and at the end of the day, not lying. No need to add "let's stay friends!" if you wouldn't be interested in that, or "I had the best time" if you didn't. You don't want to lead someone on or make them believe something is true when it's not. They will appreciate it more if you're on the level with them—give them the truth, be polite, be gentle, and then go your separate way.

But because not everyone will be up-front and direct, we have to know how to spot the ghosting before it actually happens, so we can take control of the situation and protect our own peace of mind.

After a first date, or a few dates, it's pretty easy to spot someone in the process of ghosting you—I like to think I've developed a good ghosting radar—ghostdar, if you will. Depending on how you leave the date, things will differ, but typically, when you leave there will be some kind of a discussion alluding to the next time you plan to see each other. Perhaps one party says, "Text me!" or "Let me know when you're home safe," or "We should do this again sometime!" Depending on how that conversation goes, you can decide whether or not to text the person first upon your arrival home.

After my first date with Noah, I hadn't heard from him the next morning. I also hadn't texted him when I'd gotten home, or sent a thank you via text because I'd said it in person. We decided in person that we'd have a second date in three days' time—with concrete plans to have charcuterie and wine at his apartment—so I felt pretty comfortable texting first. The plans were made, and specific, and I had no doubt in my mind that they'd happen. Additionally, I knew that he wouldn't change my mind about me based on whether or not I texted him. In fact, if he liked me, he'd be happy to hear from me. In this scenario, I felt confident I wouldn't be ghosted.

Conversely, if you leave a first date and you haven't heard from someone within seventy-two hours, I would see it as a yellow light. It doesn't necessarily mean they're ghosting you, but it definitely doesn't mean they are 100 percent into you, either. Often, I think we're so quick to decide, immediately following a first date, that if we haven't heard from them it's doomed, it's all our fault, we're ultimately unlovable, and the other person HATED us. But after a first date, we're still more or less strangers. For all you know, the other person could still be involved with other people, trying to figure out how they feel about you, or having a busy week and unable to invest time into someone they'd only met once for a few hours. Don't assume you're in the clear if you haven't received a text, but also, don't panic just yet.

If you do reach that seventy-two-hour mark, and you're feeling a little anxious that the person might be ghosting you, take the preventative measure yourself, and text them: **Hey! Hope you're having a good week, would love to do something again sometime if you're around this weekend. :)**

It is not and has never been weird to suggest that you'd like to see someone again. The vast majority of people will find this flattering, and if this person does like you, hearing from you would excite them. If they respond to your message and seem distant or vapid, I would leave the ball in their court, respond to them with a **Just let me know!** If they don't let you know, then it's time to move on. I promise you that they won't forget to get back to you or to make a plan if they wanted to make a plan with you—if they want to see you again, you'll be top of mind, and they'll get back to you in the next seventy-two hours.

Always ask yourself: *If I wanted to see someone, would I forget to reach out? If I liked someone, would them texting me deter me from liking them? If I wanted to be around someone, would the exact wording of their text bother me?*

The answer will always be no. Think about it—don't make excuses for someone else, when if roles were reversed, you'd be acting very differently.

When someone isn't giving us active or obvious signs that they're interested or that they'd like to see us again, it's up to us to be matter-of-fact so we don't waste our own time, and we can do so gently. There will be plenty of people who didn't show you explicit interest right off the bat, but with whom you end up spending a lot of time, who you end up dating, or who you even get into a serious relationship with. A lack of explicit interest initially doesn't mean a lack of interest altogether—people have different styles of dating and communicating, and it would be unusual for someone to decide they're head over heels in love with you after one three-hour date—stranger things have happened, but typically we all need to give each other grace to ease into things.

I'm not making excuses for bad communicators. I'm just suggesting to you that we should lower our first-date expectations and rewrite the narrative a little bit. A first date is two strangers getting to know each other with no expectations—it's normal not to have a decisive answer about how you feel about a stranger after only spending three hours together. If you met someone for the first time at a party and could see yourself becoming friends with them, you wouldn't call them up the next day and tell them that they're now your best friend and want them to be your maid of honor. For some reason, with dating, we're taught to see this differently. In media and pop culture, we see depictions of first dates riddled with clichés like love at first sight or immediate explicit attraction and investment. The reality is that it sometimes takes a little longer to be sure of someone, or to know how you feel, especially when you've just met. So let everyone take a beat to come up for air before deciding impulsively that you're being ghosted.

Keep an eye out for the ghoster, be vigilant and premeditated, but don't assume that just because someone hasn't professed their love to you right away that they don't like you.

If they don't respond to your message asking to see them again, assume they're not interested in seeing you again—don't make excuses for strangers. Then jump right into the postghost plan, which will leave you feeling both superior and refreshed.

The Postghost Plan

When I got ghosted after three interactions with the goofy guy with whom I had little in common, it was a bruise to the ego—and it certainly stung, but future me was grateful that I got out while I did. The stakes were low, the sting was sharp but brief, and I had fun cleaning up my own pieces after.

Don't bother telling them off and berating them for the disrespect—someone you've spent less than twelve hours with isn't worth that energy. Besides, we don't beg someone to be with us who doesn't want to be. Instead, invest energy in yourself.

Unadd them on social media—it's time to cleanse the palette. If, for whatever reason, they need to contact you ever again, they have your phone number. You don't need to keep three doors of communication open to someone who didn't have the decency to use even one to let you know they were no longer interested.

Allow yourself to feel disappointed, a little sorry for yourself. Listen to a few sad songs and indulge your self-pity, because a woe-is-me-style speech is sort of fun, in a twisted way. Set a timer for this—you get one hour.

RULE 2

RULE 3

RULE 4

If and when your friends ask about them, don't be embarrassed. Tell them the truth and invite them to accompany you on a frivolous night out. Band-Aid the sting with some pinot noir, a little baseless male attention, a carefree night with friends, and the realization that the person ghosting you wasn't right for you, anyway, and you're better off in the company of friends or just by yourself.

If they reach out again, after not answering for a few weeks, don't reply. This is what the roster is for—so we don't feel desperate.

By ghosting in the first place, this person has implicitly suggested they don't care for the feelings of others. That's no way to be, and you're better than to concern yourself with that energy. It is not a reflection of you, but a projection from them on to you, and has nothing to do with you and your character, or what you assume you may lack. Rather, it's the emotional unavailability or flaws within them, the ghoster. You didn't do anything to warrant this behavior. This is the behavior they would've displayed all along, no matter what.

It wasn't about you. It was about them.

The best revenge is success and silence. If you want someone to come back into your life, if you want the last laugh or the comfort of knowing they still think of you, all you have to do is not reach out, not communicate with them, and not try to get their attention. Focus on yourself and your success. When someone sees you looking independent, happy, and thriving while simultaneously paying them no mind, they will become engrossed by you. So go be successful, go be incredible, go be the happiest and brightest version of you. And don't say much to them about it.

·

When I was a sophomore in college I had a steamy weekend with a senior acting major who I quickly declared to be the love of my life (he wasn't). I was enthralled by him, infatuated by his looks and his stylish confidence, and I wanted, desperately, to be with him. Of course, this senior boy saw me as a one-time, maybe two-time casual fling and had given me no indication that he felt otherwise. A week after the last time I saw him, I walked into a party and saw him pressed against a wall, talking to his gorgeous ex-girlfriend, their faces close enough together to smell each other's shampoo. After about twenty minutes of making rounds through the near condemned two-story house, I couldn't handle being in their proximity anymore. I grew drunker, staggered through the kitchen, and felt their heat like a flame on my neck. They kissed, he brushed her hair from her face, and they looked like a perfect match standing together. I was mortified that I'd ever even thought that he and I could be good for each other. I was mortified that I would ever think he'd choose me.

I got up, grabbed a friend, left the party, went to Buffalo Wild Wings, drank a vodka Red Bull, and crafted a delusional, intoxicated five-paragraph essay in my iPhone notes, berating him to shreds, and sending it to him before my fries were even delivered to my table. He replied at four a.m., clearly confused, told me he wasn't hooking up with her, but even if he had been, would that be an issue? Had he led me on to believe he was interested in being with me?

I never responded, mortified to see his response to the message on my phone the next morning. I wished I'd never sent it at all. Please, learn from my mistakes: do not hit send.

·

Of course, my advice regarding reaching out to someone who has ghosted you differs if that person happens to be someone you were a bit more invested in. In any relationship—casual, hookup, or otherwise—spanning more than a month with regular meetings and a genuine understanding of each other, ghosting becomes more than disrespectful; it becomes really hurtful, and a much harder cross for the ghostee to bear. If you've been led to believe someone is genuinely interested in you, and then they one day just cease communication after weeks or months of consistency, it can be really damaging. While I've never been ghosted by someone I'd been seeing regularly, dating, or having more of a consistent relationship with, per se, if I was, I would 100 percent call them out on it.

I wouldn't do this looking for closure so much as to ask for an explanation and some clarity about what happened. I believe closure can truly and honestly only come from ourselves, from within and not from external forces.

If a week had gone by without hearing from someone you're dating, or hear regularly from or spend a good amount of time with—I'd send a message saying, **Hey, can we talk soon? If something changed between us it would be really helpful if you could let me know. I hate feeling confused and would love to just address this over the phone or in person.** Be direct and up-front. Demand the respect you deserve. Be your own hero. Save yourself when nobody else can.

If this person isn't willing to give you the decency of even a five-minute phone call explaining what happened, I promise you that you can do better. There are better orgasms and better sex out there from someone who respects you enough to give you the communication you deserve. You deserve a slice of the pie; stop begging for a crumb.

And remember, once you're done telling them off: success and silence.

I would be lying if I said I hadn't lain on my back, staring at a ceiling fan, typing out a message to someone who didn't deserve to hear from me, which read something like: **Can we talk soon? I just need closure.** When my friends asked why I was giving someone my time—again—who didn't deserve it, I'd say closure, because the word *closure* just manages, every time, to cover up the truth.

But what even is closure—and why are we so obsessed with having it? When something abruptly ends, it only makes sense that it would take our brain a little bit of time to readjust and catch up—to experience closure. But the person who initiated the end cannot be in charge of opening the door to your new chapter, your new room. That's on you.

And of course it was true that I needed closure. From every relationship, every life situation that ends, we need some form of finalization. But the unfortunate truth is that nobody can give us closure—not even a partner we dated for five years, or a best friend we knew our whole life. It isn't their job, or their responsibility, to give us closure. It's something we have to gift ourselves.

I'm sorry if this comes as a disappointment, but I'm urging you to put down your phone and block their number before asking them for closure. Asking someone else for closure has the opposite effect—the more you see them, the more contact you have with them in the aftermath, the less sure of yourself and your decisions you'll be, and the less you'll be inclined to make sense of everything that happened.

I learned the hard way.

My second semester of sophomore year of college, Ezra and I hadn't spoken in a month. One day, he asked me to get coffee and catch up. It was out of the blue, random, but it didn't matter. I would've dropped anything and anyone to go, to have that *closure*.

But if you're looking for closure in someone else, it's never closure you're after. We can tell ourselves that all we want, but truthfully and deep down, when looking for closure in someone else, we're actually looking for hope. We're looking for reassurance that they're pining for us. That they're lonely. That they're worse off without us. We're looking for a window back inside. The way you know when you're emotionally over someone is when you wouldn't say yes to a "closure coffee date" because you know nothing ends well that way.

We went to coffee at four p.m. the next day. He picked out a place I'd never been to before, and I got there first. I tried to look casual but also pretty enough that he'd think I looked nice. I ordered a black coffee, and sat in a booth trying to act calm while I waited. When he got there, he ordered, and slid into the seat across from me. Despite my stalking of his Instagram and Snapchat over the last month, there were details he shared I didn't know. He had a car now, which he drove to our meeting. It was tough to find parking, he said, and that was why he was late.

He asked about my family, my burgeoning summer plans, my class schedule, and seemed to care about the answers. We bounced a few inside jokes back and forth and I hoped he didn't notice that the whole time my hands were shaking. Our conversation lasted an hour, and then he said he had to go. He was pregaming that night to go out to an upperclassman bar. He didn't offer to drive me home.

I felt vacant and aggravated as I watched him leave.

I went looking for closure, and I left hysterical. I cut across the center of campus, trying to hold in my tears. My roommates weren't home when I arrived back at the sorority house, and I went upstairs, ate half of a stale Rice Krispies treat edible, and sobbed all my makeup off in bed.

Three hours later, he snapchatted me from the bar and asked me to come over. I washed my face, redid my makeup, turned off my location, and told nobody where I was going.

I wasted so much time looking for closure in outside forces, in exterior places—when the work to achieve closure was something only I could do for myself. And I had all the tools, all the skills. Every time I went out to look for closure, I got a UTI instead. And that's 100 percent my fault.

Maybe this is hard to hear, but wandering to your ex-boyfriend's apartment at ten p.m. on a Thursday night will never bring you closure. And I'm not telling you to not go get the coffee with your ex or to not have phenomenal sex with them after things end. But after a breakup, there is no conversation or amazing sex or phone call to be had that can bring you up the muddy hill and down the other side to closure. Not even reading the words *You were right, and I'm sorry* can bring closure. So have the breakup sex if you want it, but don't think it's going to close the door for you. Because, like I said, we cannot rely on the other to give us what we need to find ourselves.

You wouldn't drink poison if you were thirsty. You wouldn't light yourself on fire if someone else was cold. You wouldn't pay for someone else's rent so they could build a home. Loneliness is a feeling, not a state of being. It is not permanent. You can do this alone. No coffee date can mend what went wrong in the first place.

Once you realize this is just between you and the world, you are free to move ahead. You have to start by making the choice to sit down and unpack your bags—to let it be okay, or shitty, or sad, or amazing that something is over. That it won't ever be the same again. The only way to experience the next best day of your life, the next great love, the next best friend, and the next wonderful experience is to let this one quietly rest its head. All good things end. If they didn't, there'd be a lack of diversity in our good things, a lack of color, of nuance. And after you unpack, you'll see that one step forward will become a mile, and then a mile will become ten. That's all life is, anyway: one foot in front of the other. And eventually, it'll just be a fond string of memories you're grateful brought you to today.

A common misconception in looking for closure is that it should happen quickly—that it should be found in one conversation. In one night. It doesn't happen that way, and that's okay. Sometimes closure takes forever. It's like an interminable microwave minute. True closure is a long, dirty road, and you walk it alone. Sometimes we take so many breaks it feels like it takes an eternity. Drink enough water, rest when you need to, and look straight ahead, but always remember what came before you. What came first.

In August 2020, I moved to New York City. I had an idea in my mind that if I could focus on deriving my happiness and contentment from my graduate program at Columbia, going on dates and trying to be the person I figured I was supposed to be, I would forget about Michigan and unfinished business; the chapter would close on its own. It would have no choice if I became someone and something completely new.

> This is so often a mistake we make: we decide to become a version of ourselves that isn't even attainable, instead of realizing we already are that girl we needed to be. There's no such thing as "that girl" or an unattainable woman you could become. You are already you. You are already whole. Anything that comes into your life should be an addition.

RULE
8

Nonetheless, full force ahead, I tried to transform, and I looked like a bit of a fool doing it—I put so much pressure on so many of the wrong things to bring me to the new chapter that I ran in the opposite direction. Hiking back was like déjà vu.

But what I learned—through months of failing to feel anything more than anxious—is that you cannot rely on one sole thing as your source of happiness or your respite. You cannot rely on one thing to give you what you need—not closure, and not joy, and not love, and not contentment.

No one person, career, hobby, family member, or graduate school will ever succeed at making you 100 percent content and happy. They're not supposed to, and we cannot rely on them as though they could. What we're left with, then, is disappointment.

So I had to reframe my mindset. I was acting like a boyfriend could make me 100 percent fulfilled, or that grad school would fix all my problems. But the truth is we're all machines with lots of different and specific gas tanks that need to be filled. One of these tanks is my career, the other is romantic partnership, another is my education, and another one after that is my mental health. I'm composed of gas tanks for my family life, my social life, my hobbies. Some of them are self-serve, others can only be filled by someone or something else.

If I relied on my boyfriend to fill all my many tanks, he'd never succeed, and in turn, we would crumble. If I require him to fill just the gas tank of partnership to 100 percent and supply all my necessary oxytocin, he will do that if he's the right person for me. I can confidently say he's the only person I've ever dated to not skimp on the gas. It overflows. And I overflow his tank that's been reserved for me. That's why we work. If sometimes one of us is running low on gas, that's okay too. He's given me enough this far I can make it when he needs a little push, or vice versa.

Same thing with grad school. Grad school didn't exist to fill all the tanks. It filled the one it was meant to fill. Once I stopped relying on grad school to remedy loneliness and anxiety, or a boyfriend to put a bandage on the whole damn thing, is when I started to live. That's when I realized closure couldn't be forced. It would happen to me just like everything else would. I had to be patient. I had to walk forward. I had to make love to the emptiness. Become familiar with the loneliness. I had to honor my life every single day. And eventually it wouldn't hurt so much anymore.

You're the only person who can close your own door. You're also the only person who can open up the next one. Other people are always going to disappoint us, to a fault. We cannot rely on them to close and lock our doors or open up the next. Unfortunately, they just don't have the right keys.

Where you end up is your choice. Nobody else's. Nobody else is capable of rewriting your story, of rewiring things behind the scenes. And there's power in that—in all of it. You're lucky to have a voice, and a means to hit the gas and go. Autopilot can only take you so far—and what would you be willing to do, to see, and to go out and grasp, if I told you that after fifteen failures, you'd finally succeed?

Well, for once—you would be in a rush to fail, that's for sure. You would be excited for things not to work out, because you'd know that around the corner, something was waiting to work out.

Rules for Friend Love

1. Our friends are our soulmates.

2. Date your friends intentionally.

3. Institute a rotating-host Thursday night dinner party.

4. The chosen-family rule.

5. To thine own self be true.

6. Three-person friendships don't have to be messy if you don't make them messy.

7. You have to be a friend to have a friend.

8. The romance and friendship 180—start viewing your friendships like relationships.

9. Friendships take work, but when it works, it works.

10. Quality over quantity, always.

11. The Facebook grandma rule—use social media to your advantage!

I WAS LUCKY enough to live twenty-two years on this earth before receiving a hasty phone call from home, delivering news nobody wants to deliver and nobody wants to receive. My mom called me—it was a Monday night in January—but when I picked up the phone, my dad's voice was on the other end, signaling to me that something was wrong.

My mom's best friend since grade school, whom I'd grown up knowing not just as my mom's best friend, but as Aunt, had passed suddenly, my dad explained, as my mother attempted words in the background.

This was a woman who'd been a part of my life for as long as I had memories. She was a constant. A rock. My mother spoke to her every day. They never lived more than a ten-minute drive away from each other. When I last saw her, she slipped me a $100 bill and a ceramic pig (the same gift she gave me on my third birthday, which I still have and cherish) for helping her son with his college essay. She tossed me a wink, put her finger up to her lips, and mimicked *shhhhh*.

"You're going to do big things," she said, with a sweet squeeze of my shoulder. We told each other we loved each other, because we truly always have, and always would.

My Upper West Side bedroom squeezed and contracted around me, feeling smaller than it ever had before. A numbness chilled me, starting in my toes. I searched for words but couldn't find many. Whatever came would be the first words I put out into this hellish, new reality.

"What?" is all I could come up with. It wasn't what I wanted to say but what I needed to. I was confused.

My aunt and mom both often said they were each other's soulmates—always had been, always would be. They said they'd retire in Nantucket, sitting in matching rocking chairs, drinking wine and people watching. That was their idea of paradise. The bond between them, they felt, couldn't be re-created or manufactured within the confines of a romantic relationship. It was something else, something magnetic and indestructible and wondrous. It was a soulmate bond. And the power of friendship felt unbreakable between them. There was some type of scientific, kinetic bond between them—a buzzy electricity I never imagined my mother's life without.

Selfishly, as the moment settled and everything came back into view, I thought of Sadie. My best friend. My soulmate. She used to tell me if something ever happened to me she'd drop out of Michigan.

"No use being here, if I'm not with you," she said, and we laughed about it. Like it was a crazy thought. Like as beings, we were unerasable. That if, god forbid, one of us went, the other was sure as hell not staying at the place that brought us together. But we laughed because it was a crazy, far-off thought. We laughed because a few times in my college career, it felt like she was my only friend. We laughed because thinking of that actually happening hurt too much.

But now it had, just not to me.

But underneath the joke was a truth—neither of us would want to exist without the other. My mind circled around Sadie, and how it would feel to receive a phone call that she was gone. My throat squeezed tightly. My mother's hell was twice that. Three times that. I felt white hot with something that was half guilt and half rage.

My brain snapped back to the phone against my cheek, my present reality, the conversation—I was on the other end of the phone, wordless, wondering how my mother could possibly take even one step forward.

When we hung up the phone I wondered what I should do. Was I supposed to get up, keep watching *The Bachelor*? Was I supposed to get on a train home? The only discernible emotion I felt, other than deep sadness, was worry. I was worried for everyone in her orbit, everyone who would bear this loss, everyone who would have no choice but to take one step forward, into Tuesday, into the morning, when everything was irrevocably altered in the most horrifying of ways.

I unlocked my phone and sent a message to Daphne and Sadie. My best friends. I told them what happened. I told them how much they meant to me. I told them I'm sorry if I ever took them for granted. They keep me buoyant. They keep me alive. I love them.

I also texted my childhood best friend. We grew apart toward the end of 2020. Things happened, mistakes were made. I carry the weight of our friendship with me every day, along with a lengthy list of "what ifs" that I've tried to stop wondering too hard about. The rift was an obvious juxtaposition from how we grew up: attached at the hip, our names used together in a singsongy way as we traversed hallways and our first parties and life's little events.

It didn't matter that we hadn't spoken much or seen each other recently. It didn't matter who was upset with whom or who did what. I just wanted her to know that when it came down to it, I'd do anything for her. If she needed something, there would never come a point when I wouldn't pick up the phone. If she ever paused to ask herself if I love her, I wanted her to know the answer, indisputably, would always be yes.

I hated—loathed—that a loss so immense was how I realized it. We see our friends as a given. While we worry if our boyfriend will break up with us, or if the girl from the bar will text us back, we operate under the naive assumption that our friends will always be there to pick up the pieces. They are as inherent to us as our morning coffee. There is no other relationship we expect to always remain. Except for, of course, siblings, who become friends we happen to share DNA with. But beyond those two, there are no other pairings we expect to always just have. Friends are our gold. Isn't that what they told us in Girl Scouts?

We forget to remind them we love them. Or check in with them or ask them "How are you . . . really?"—in earnest, the way we do with our significant others.

My mother lost a person who stood with her, beside her, experiencing her, from the time she was ten years old—through high school and then college, through engagements and weddings and birthdays. She'd seen more of my mom than my dad, or even perhaps my grandparents, ever had or would.

And a heat rose in my chest as I tried to comprehend it all. Like a stone thrown through a glass window, creating a jagged little keyhole to see through—something beautiful had to shatter to force me to look beyond what I once thought to be true.

There is no state of being more indispensable, more concrete, than to be, or to have, a friend.

.

Whenever I tell people I've never truly experienced a long-distance relationship, I'm sort of lying. My relationship with Daphne is both those things—it's just that it's platonic love. And it's proof that with the right person, long-distance relationships can work out just fine.

She moved to London when I was a senior in college. She initially went for a gap year, but she fell in love with the city, and though it broke me when she told me she was extending her stay to finish her degree at King's College—her happiness, the glint in her eye when she told me, the edge to her familiar voice immediately repaired whatever had broken inside of me. If this move was going to bring her joy, it was going to bring me joy too. That wasn't even a question.

No matter the distance, it wasn't a question of what would happen to us. We'd both do what it took. She has been more like a sister than anything else. We both grew up with only brothers.

Daphne is a bit of a genius. I don't say this to hype her up, I say it because it's impossible to ignore. She knows everything about everything—if you wanted to know what Halsey's claim to fame is, or what the implications of the Mormon undertones of the *Twilight* saga are on modern society, or the undercurrents of drama in Netflix's latest cooking competition reality show—you ask her. She was also a math major, that's right, MATH, at NYU before transferring, and her knowledge of pop culture, media, marketing, and music are equally as impressive as her skills in math and sciences. She is naturally book smart, but even more street smart. She gives advice like a therapist who has lived for five hundred years and will never die, wears great shoes, and uses expensive hair products. She opts for voice memo instead of texting, joined the drama club in high school for no tangible reason, eats sushi six times a week, and knows how to cook homemade sourdough bread.

We often joke her life is like a movie. I've never been more grateful to be cast in a supporting role.

There is nobody on this earth who has been a bigger cheerleader for me. And nobody ever will be. No boyfriend or future husband or anyone else. I wouldn't want them to be. When I wrote my first play and it was going to be produced in a studio at Michigan, she took a flight and two lengthy car rides to come into town and be one of very few audience members. She wept the whole time.

Once we were driving down Ocean Avenue along the coastline of the Jersey Shore. I was telling her about how I thought sometimes about getting back together with Luke. Eventually I pulled into a Dairy Queen parking lot and, through choking sobs, told her things I wouldn't tell other people. She didn't judge me for a moment. She didn't even think to. She listened and listened and listened.

She told me that it wouldn't matter what her opinions were of Luke, even if I'd asked for them, because she was my best friend, and she was going to support whatever choice I made, because her allegiance is to me always. Me first, always.

Unless a romantic relationship you're in is causing you any sort of emotional or physical danger, a true friend's allegiance will be to you.

In that moment, with or without Luke or anyone else, I knew my soulmate, the other half of me, was in the passenger seat drinking a Dunkin' Donuts iced latte, playing Taylor Swift through my car's speakers. I could do without him, as long as Daphne was there.

"It's you and me, Lili," she always said, her name for me. And it was. Over miles of currents and dark sea. Over time differences and whatever else. It's you and me, V. It's you and me.

Whenever I was with her, I never focused on the love I perceived to lack, only the love I had—the love of a female friend, and that love was abundant and more than enough.

•

Though I regret participating in sorority rush and going through the Greek system at Michigan, without that experience, there would be no Sadie. And without Sadie, I'm not sure what I'd have, really.

From the day we met, we haven't gone twenty-four hours without speaking. It's a daily tradition, a meditation, a fact of life. I've always felt like our relationship mimicked a romantic relationship's honeymoon stage, sans the sex, but equally intimate in other ways.

In college, we spent most of our days texting back and forth, unless we were together. We hardly grew tired of each other, hardly argued. We still tell each other how much we love each other all the time. We plan elaborate evenings together for just the two of us. We're brutally honest with each other, and with Sadie I feel the same sensation you do when you fall in love.

It's the epitome of friend love. A level of platonic intimacy that can't even be replicated in a romantic relationship. A feeling I waited eighteen years for. With our significant others, we plan date nights, special anniversary outings, and Friday night dinners and movies—however, we often find ourselves lazier with planning these special outings when it comes to our friends. But our friendships deserve date nights, too—one-on-one dinners, cooking together, movie marathons, wine nights, hot girl walks, workout classes followed up with coffee—these types of dates keep our friendships alive and afloat. They help stimulate early friendship—help us get to know each other, and reinforce friendships we've had for five, ten, twenty years. Don't sleep on dating your friends. Of course, dating your friends can also mean lying in bed talking shit and watching TikToks for several hours. What I'm trying to say is that effort is important. And the people who you love, who love you, will notice this effort.

Center these people.

I started dating my friends more seriously—intentionally—when I was in college. We'd plan dinners for just the two of us, set aside hours at a time to binge-watch *Love Island* and order takeout and eat Twizzlers, to plan brunches or long drives or study dates.

I'm glad I started dating my friends in college, because nobody quite prepares you for what happens when the structures that formerly govern your lives and uphold your friendships (classes, clubs, sports teams, Greek life) fall away and you have to support them on your own. It's okay to realize that without those structures or groups, someone you were once close to becomes someone you don't see often. It is okay to realize that with the time you do have to socialize and dedicate to friends, you'd rather give to others, now that there aren't weekly practices or meetings sustaining a friendship. It happens to all of us in our twenties, and yet we don't talk about it.

In my adult life, especially in a place like New York City, it's impossible to keep in touch with anyone unless you (1) live under the same roof or (2) are sleeping together. Dating my friends has become more imperative than ever. We make plans weeks in advance to go on pasta dates, or browse the MoMA or the Met, to see a free concert or walk through Central Park. Not every plan or meeting with my friends has to be premeditated, but in the hustle and bustle of adult life, sometimes preplanning two weeks in advance to ensure you're centering your friends is important. Of course things are allowed to be spontaneous and serendipitous. But it's important that we're investing similar effort for our platonic ones as we do for romantic date nights. Sometimes the only way I can see my friends—with our disparate and busy schedules—is to put a date on the Google calendar three weeks in advance. Those who love me meet me where I'm at, and I them. Our friends deserve this from us, and we deserve it from our friends too. Sometimes, when we're overwhelmingly busy, our time spent with our romantic partners is reduced to pillow talk and the inherent intimacy of sleeping beside each other, which on the occasional busy week can be enough. But we can't necessarily have that same intimacy with our closest friends, and if we feel overwhelmed and busy and like we've been neglecting them, we just have to take a moment—communicate, and plan something, even if it's twelve days away.

My friends from graduate school and I live different New York lives with different schedules. Some of us are in the East Village, others the Upper East Side, Hudson Yards, Midtown, Downtown, and Brooklyn—some of us don't live in New York anymore, but Dallas, Vermont, or Laguna Beach. We plan FaceTimes, visits, phone calls, and a simple text to check in goes a long way.

I'm glad we don't expect for our friendships to be consistent without effort—to just happen. When we were young and we'd see our friends every day at school, friendship was inherent and easy. In our twenties, postcollege, it takes a little more work. But that work makes it more worthwhile to see them lounging on your couch with a glass of wine, or at the other end of a dinner table.

RULE 3

Biweekly, my friends plan a little dinner and game night. Pretty consistently, we bop from apartment to apartment, bringing homemade desserts, bottles of wine, our dietary restriction dishes, flowers, and blocks of cheese with us. We laugh, we drink red and white and sometimes champagne, we catch up—all of us, on the same living room floor.

Throughout our weeks, in between our little Thursday night dinner parties we see one another one-on-one, or in smaller groups. Sometimes we do dinners or happy hours or go on walks. Nobody is ever threatened by the way we strengthen our individual relationships to one another—we know it makes us stronger as a whole.

And just like in romantic relationships, communication and trust is what got us to a place where we aren't threatened by one another's individual friendships. If anything, it brings me joy when Jen comes home and tells me how her movie night with Sophie was, when I may have been off shopping with our friend Macy—we strengthen the limbs of our collective oak tree, and we're a force when we come together as one.

> Community is how we survive our twenties. Especially in big cities, the community we build is equivalent to a trust fall or a home-cooked meal—comforting and assuring. It is imperative that we build community and have chosen family (even if we're lucky enough to have a wonderful biological family). It'll keep you alive.

RULE 4

I think there's an idea that the minute we graduate from college, our time to "make friends" is sort of up. That we have our arsenal of friends, our group, and if we don't have great or close friends yet, our window to make those friends is closed.

Being that I met some of my best friends when I was twenty-two years old, in graduate school for journalism, that couldn't be more off base. Though school does make it easier to make friends, I was in graduate school virtually, on Zoom, in 2020—and we had class once a week with seven other students, socially distanced. I'm living proof that you can meet a best friend on any day, any moment, any year of your life—so long as you keep yourself open to the opportunity.

I met Jen in graduate school, and though it was only two years ago—now I feel half whole if I don't talk to her every day. She is the most emotionally intelligent and self-assured person in my life. Jen knows how to articulate her emotions and experiences in a way only writers really can. She loves turtles, pasta with a home-made lemon sauce, red wine, this little stuffed animal that sits on top of her well-made bed, organizing closets, calling her mom, and breaking in new loafers. When she tells you a story, she gives you details regular people don't remember to include, and she makes you feel like you're right there beside her, in the car in a Sonic parking lot, or at her senior year house, or studying abroad in France.

Jen puts a weighty significance on friendship. I've never seen someone put such a significance on friendship, and it's taught me to do the same. She emails me when we spend time apart, and she bakes cakes for people on their birthdays. She isn't just the type of friend who is fun to go to happy hour with, or go dancing with—though we do both those things often. She's also the type of friend who you can do nothing with, for days, and feel like you've traveled the entire world together, had the wildest night of your lives, and had your annual fill of adrenaline. Doing nothing with Jen is like doing everything I've ever dreamed of doing without ever leaving our living room.

Whenever I'd undertake making friends in college, I always did so on guard—anxious that the people I was letting into my life wouldn't accept me for who I am or wouldn't want to be friends with me just as I was. I feared that being myself would ward off new friends. Being yourself might thin out the eligible contestants, but it also ensures the quality of those friends—and their desire to be in and a part of your life—is much more elevated.

I'll never forget the way being loved by Jen makes me feel, and I hope I never have to. Because not many people have ever made me feel that way—utterly and honestly lovable, just as I am, right in that moment.

Before Jen, meeting new people meant, typically, a mask, a facade, a game of pretend, where I'd stuff myself away and be who I thought other people would like. Now, I know that I can come as I am. I can show up with my heart stitched right on my sweater sleeve. I'd never want to go through the dance of tricking someone to befriend someone I'm not. I'd rather know that the people who want to be my friend want to be my friend truly, when I'm barefaced and have nothing to me but my name.

Our time knowing each other has encouraged me to reach new depths with other people. We've cried together over lovers the other didn't know, talked through our greatest anxieties and our smallest worries, and if I was told I could have dinner across the table with Jen every day for the rest of my life, I'd ask you who's bringing the wine.

Many people assume, or are taught, that three-person friend groups never work out, because there's no way that three people can all be best friends without one person being left out.

I may be here giving you the rules, but there are no rules when it comes to friendship—other than, throughout my relationships, I've learned the integral lesson that everyone should be taught a bit more explicitly: you have to be a friend, to have a friend. We gravitate toward people who make us feel like our insides are on fire. We gravitate toward people who keep us warm. I gravitate toward people who quell the social anxiety bells ringing in my brain.

The first step in a successful three-person friend group is transparency and trust. If you trust that your friends, both of them, have your best interests at heart, and you have theirs—and you'd always communicate with one another if something feels adrift—you have a pretty good foundation. It's natural for everyone within a three-person group to have their own relationships to one another—their own inside jokes, their own topics of conversation, or places and things they bond over—but ultimately, at the end of the day, when the three of you are together, there's no drama or negative energy.

Everything is just really good.

There isn't a one size fits all to being a friend. To having a friend. To going out and seeking out friends. I think that's a rule all by itself—groups of three don't have to be a toxic mess, friendships are allowed to strengthen and then fall short and then strengthen again in the future. We're allowed to change and grow with our friends, we're allowed to set boundaries with our friends, we're allowed to communicate our needs, we're allowed to grow apart and we're allowed to grieve that growth.

Relationships end for a variety of different reasons, but one of them is when both parties have grown and changed, but in a way that no longer complements the other anymore. We view friendships as far more indestructible than romantic relationships. We don't allow our friendships the leeway or agency to have those same transformations and transitions, and in that we create an expectation that change will be really bad for our friendships.

In reality, friendships aren't much different than our romantic relationships. Sometimes we are going to experience friendship heartbreak. Sometimes we are going to grow apart from someone. Sometimes we will grow back together with them. Sometimes we're going to surprise ourselves with a new friend who is so different from us . . . but somehow we work. Sometimes the nature of our relationship, the nature of our needs, the nature of ourselves will change—and that could damage or strengthen a friendship.

Drifting apart from friends, though often troubling, is also normal. But even in times when you haven't seen a friend for a while or heard from them—because you're both busy and you're both figuring out how to navigate life and you're both going through something—it can be worthwhile to reach out, to drop a line, to touch base every now and again. You'll be grateful, when your schedule is a little more cleared, that you kept that flame with them alive.

And when you do experience a friendship breakup, I implore you to treat it how you do a romantic breakup. Breakups suck. Heartbreak sucks. Losing someone sucks. If we start treating our friends like we treat our lovers (we have to build something together and then we have to keep it alive, or else it won't be sustainable), we won't feel so out of control and lost when going through a friendship breakup. We'll feel sad, and emotionally on edge and maybe a little bruised, but we'll know to navigate the loss of a friend like you do the loss of a lover. It hurts more sometimes, to lose a friend—especially if and when you fought for that friend, and you fought for your relationship to work out.

When you feel a friend drifting, you're allowed to—and I encourage you to—confront them about it, albeit gently. Asking "I miss you, is everything okay? You seem distant lately" puts the ball in their court to share if they have something to share with you, or to let you know they're just busy.

Just like with romantic partners, we need to learn to respect and understand our friend's boundaries as well. A good friend listens to listen—not to respond and will respect the boundaries you set (gently, or even silently). Whenever I've set a boundary for my mental or emotional health, the closest people in my life have seen that boundary as something to respect, because if I improve—we improve. Your good friends will be your biggest cheerleaders, and your joy will be theirs.

I wish I knew to view my friendships like I do romantic relationships. These relationships aren't that different, and yet, we view them like they're polar opposites.

·

Making friends—especially when you're starting from complete scratch—can be daunting. If I'm being honest with you, as I promised I would be, I struggled with it a lot in the past.

The fear of how I'd be perceived almost consumed me whole, coupled with social anxiety—I lived in fear of introducing new people into my orbit. In many ways, I also feared I'd just let them all down. But through a lot of inner work, and therapy, I've steered myself to a new shore. The truth is I'm a good friend. And a good person. I know these things, and I've grown to believe them. I constantly remind myself of what I know to be true—not what I think other people MIGHT believe about me.

The truth is, at the points in college where it was true that I had one friend, that was enough for me, because she was more than ten shitty friends combined all in one person. The number of friends you have, or do not have, does not dictate your worth. The truth is I am worthy of friendship. The truth is I have to assume that people would like to get to know me. The truth is I trust a little too much, and give too many second chances, but my heart is bigger than the moon, and I'm proud of that. The truth is I've made mistakes in friendship, and I've been hurt. I've lost friends and gained friends and regained friends. The truth is I haven't always been the best friend, but if and when that's true, I'll do whatever I can to fix it.

I live for my friends—even when they are small in numbers. Even when we haven't spoken in a little while or have something straining against us relentlessly. I live for the morning coffees we grab once a month, even if that's all the time we have together. I live for reconnecting to someone after months apart and feeling like we never walked on opposite sides of the same street. I live for their laughs, their joy, their little quirks.

Friendship has made me anxious before, and then one day I realized that the right people, in the right settings, wouldn't make me feel that way. I had to believe I was worthy of the great people who are worthy of me. But before we get to all that inner peace and inner work, we need a group of people who make us feel really good to be around as often as we'd both like.

The Facebook Grandma Rule

RULE
11

Luckily, as a society, we've come up with a thousand ways that one can make finding friends a little bit easier. There's Geneva, an online community forum built by creators who have dedicated followings, looking to meet one another. There's a website called Meetup, boasting thousands of community-generated clubs, groups, and Meetup opportunities. There's Bumble BFF, which, if we're looking at our friendships like we do our relationships, is a totally normal way to socialize.

And, if you're anything like me, there are Facebook groups—everything from "Moms for Trader Joe's" to book clubs, to a Facebook group I created for my followers, where people have a space to connect with one another.

I recently met a girl in the locker room at the gym who told me she met her roommate through my Facebook group. I've met girls who met their best friends in the group—and together those best friends took a trip to Paris. Sure, it's unconventional to meet your best friends on a Facebook group or an online forum, but in a world that's become totally online and socially distanced, we have to make do with what we have.

> And to find a wonderful someone you wouldn't have found otherwise on a Facebook group sounds like a no-brainer.
>
> The worst-case scenario, when putting yourself out there, is that you remain exactly where you are now. And where you are now is pretty good. The best-case scenario is that you change your whole life in the most wonderful way.

In high school, I had a pretty big friend group. By our junior year, it'd amassed to about twenty-two girls and an adjacent guy friend group of a similar size. It was regularly incestuous and these were the people I spent all my New Year's Eves, football games, and Friday nights with.

As it is with a massively sized friend group, despite our best intentions, we formed smaller groups and became closer with some individuals than others. Problems arose because of intentional exclusion—someone in the group would throw a party with upwards of fifty invitees and intentionally leave out people in our friend group. Sometimes I was the one left out, other times I wasn't. And it was high school—it's a runway for pettiness and exclusion and attitude checks, but it always just rubbed me the wrong way.

I also had a problem with the insular nature of the group. As I branched out and made other friends in the drama club, or at my after-school community theater, or in cross-country, I'd be left out of my friend group's outings. I never wanted to subscribe to one place, or be just one thing, or spend time with just one type of person. I liked the variety and color various groups and activities brought to my life, and it seemed silly that at the expense of that variety and color, I'd be excluded from parties or the friends I'd always had.

When I went to college, I abandoned the idea of having a friend group. I feared the same would happen—that if I had a friend group, I'd feel locked into or barred from exploring other things. And though I often felt like the "weird one" for having different friends in different places, once I realized that nobody truly cares what I do with my time or who I spend time with, as it does not impact them, I started to do exactly what made me feel good. So I never had a friend group. Instead I had many people in many places, all who filled my cup.

To me, more often than not, friend groups stifle growth in many different directions. They prevent our branches from pulling east, west, north, and south—touching various and different parts of the sky. I've always liked to have a small group here or there, but have my friends spread out—reflective of me, someone who feels like she's always been a little eclectic, a little colorful, a little eccentric.

If I'd pushed and subscribed to the idea of a friend group, filled with people who didn't really like me—and who I didn't really like, either, I wouldn't have made so many of the friends I have now. I wouldn't have tried so many new things. I wouldn't have developed a deep bond with Sadie, one that has her tethered to me. I wouldn't have been able to explore so many of my different passions, or I would've felt guilty doing so and "breaking from the group."

And eventually I realized, at the end of the day, it doesn't matter, as long as the people in my life know I'll always pick up the phone (I sleep with my ringer on) as long as they'd say the same.

In college, I had friends from classes, from the *Michigan Daily*, from my twelve different theatrical ventures, from the three publications I wrote for on campus, from my sorority and from friends of friends of friends. I had friends from ex-boyfriends and ex-flings. I formed friendships with girls I'd only met because we shared an ex or, at one point, a crush.

When I stopped forcing myself into boxes, into little groups, I started to expand and grow, and fill my life with people I never would've otherwise. I don't fit in a little box. You don't either. Don't put yourself in one just to be normal—there is no normal, there's just life and we might as well live it.

If a friend group works for you, I'm so glad it does. But in my adult life, I've realized they just aren't practical for me. I wish I'd known that when I was eighteen. I wish I would've known it's normal to keep a small circle, or to feel like you only have one friend. I wish I would've known that nobody gives a fuck who I spend my time with. I should be doing what makes me happy, not what I arbitrarily believe I "should be" doing. I would've saved myself so much time spent worrying that I was lame or uncool or out of the norm because I didn't have a friend group like I thought I was supposed to.

·

There were some points in college, some weeks and months, when it felt like Sadie was all I had. That I only had one person I could truly trust. Certainly, I had loads of acquaintances and surface-level friends here and there—but I only had one true friend. One friend I knew would last.

I think about it like this—if you were pulled out in a rip current, desperate to be saved, would you rather have ten people who might consider saving you if it's convenient for them, or one or two people who, no matter what, no matter where they are, or what they're doing, would dive into the fucking water and save you?

I'd always rather Sadie come save me, because she thinks I'm worth saving. Because we've almost drowned together. Because she'd never leave me out to sea and go back to the shore herself. Because if the rip current took me out, she wouldn't hesitate, fully clothed, to come get me.

The quality of our friendship is unlike many things I've ever experienced. It runs so deeply, so entrenched in the ground beneath our feet, that it's second nature to me—it's inherent. She's someone I know, as long as we're both here, will always be there to pick up the phone.

In 2018, I ran the Detroit marathon. It was October seventh and it was 28 degrees when my brother Jack, Sadie, Luke, and I got up the day of the race. It was my first marathon, and my family couldn't make it (save my brother Jack) so I was counting on my cheer team to carry me through the race.

Sadie jumped in at mile 20. She ran the last 6.2 miles with me. While my toes ached, she told me stories and tried her best to keep me afloat. She and Luke had been in a fight, in which he was in the wrong. I felt slightly guilty when I realized she'd sacrificed a weekend to freeze her ass off with my horrible boyfriend and my little brother, but it eased when I remembered that this is what love looks like. When she started running with me, I asked her if she could just promise that the nine-minute-mile pacer group wouldn't pass us. I wanted to run a sub-nine-minute race, and I was on track.

The end was brutal: there was a slight uphill, which culminated in a sharp right turn, and then eventually a left turn. About six hundred feet away from that left turn was the finish line. My lungs burned, my feet ached, my eyes were crusted in sweat and tears, my nipples were chafing against my purple striped sports bra.

I picked up my pace, eyes on the finish line. The race had thinned out, and we weren't surrounded by many people, or much noise. The shouts and cheers of spectators were still about four hundred feet away. Everything else was pretty much quiet, until Sadie started screaming.

"YOU FUCKING DID IT! YOU FUCKING RAN A MARATHON! YOU RAN A FUCKING MARATHON! YOU RAN A FUCKING MARATHON!!" She grabbed my hand, and she kept screaming, and as we got closer and closer and closer I started to sob.

I did it, I ran a marathon. And the person who had been by my side, cheering me on, was right there with me. We stepped over the finish line, I was handed a medal and a silver cape to insulate the little heat I had left. She grabbed me and wrapped me in a hug and we jumped and screamed and celebrated.

There is nobody I'd rather cross a finish line with.

•

You don't have to have many friends to have a good friend, or to be a good friend. You don't have to have a boyfriend or a girlfriend or a partner to have a soulmate or a love of your life. You don't have to have a thousand friends to be cool. You actually have nothing to prove to anyone but yourself.

And I beg you to prove to yourself that you deserve good love, friend love, and go out and claim that. It can come from one person, or three people or ten people. It doesn't really matter and it's up to you.

You don't have to have a group chat on do not disturb with thirty members in it to have a bustling, lively, and full-of-love social life.

When it comes to true, beautiful friendship—the kind of friendship that saves your life over the phone, the kind of friendship that runs you to the end of the race, the kind of friendship that says *I don't like him, but I fucking love you and I'll stand by you through it*—it really only takes one.

So treat your friends like you would the love of your life—because it is when we water our friendships and see them grow that we realize the true meaning of love, and the true meaning of life.

Rules for Honoring Your Life

1. Make a goals list.

2. Leave the romanticizing behind.

3. Ask yourself the tough questions.

4. Facts before feelings—always put the facts of a situation first.

5. YOU ARE THE CEO. Make your executive decision.

6. Don't be someone's cup of tea, be your own shot of tequila.

7. Journal it out—ten minutes in the morning, ten at night.

8. Before you go anywhere, remember: you're too hot to be sad.

9. Failure > Complacency rule (you'd rather fail!)

10. Always follow the ideal version of your life.

MY FIRST WORD was *wow*.

I was six months old, sitting on my grandfather's lap while he watched a basketball game. Everyone has always called me an old soul, from the beginning. Something happened during the game, something shocking, and my grandfather said, "Wooooow." And I tilted my head back, looked at him, and repeated him.

"Woooow."

Wow. A short, three letter word. Like my first name. Such a small word for such a big sentiment, if you know what I mean. Such a small name for such a big personality.

Wow: expressing excitement or adoration, a sensational success.

Words have always been important to me. A throughline, a lifeline, a means of making sense of the world. They course through my blood and keep me awake at night, staring at the ceiling fan. They sleep in books under my pillows, stack around me in journals and hasty Post-it notes. And my first one, the one that started it all off—a sensational success. Expressing excitement or adoration. To impress someone greatly.

How the fuck was I supposed to live up to that?

I guess I feel the same way about my name. Eli—Hebrew, conventionally a boy's name. Meaning high or elevated, but it can also mean "my God" when it's a derivative of biblical names like Elijah, Eliezer, and Elisha. My parents chose the name before I was born. When I arrived, July 22, 1998, around four p.m., right in time for happy hour (naturally), they cycled through similar, traditionally feminine options—Mia, Eva, Lily.

Nothing felt as right as Eli, so despite the very small percentage of girls named Eli—a percentage that excludes cases where it's used as a nickname for Eliza or Elizabeth or Elanor—my parents put Eli on my birth certificate and decided I'd just have to live up to it.

As a child, I hated my name. Every classroom I walked into from preschool to fourth grade, I was expected to be a boy. When my classmate's mom requested the class list from the teacher to invite all the girls to a birthday party, I never got the invite—she figured I was a boy. I wanted to be feminine, to be pretty—I wanted to be Isabella or Elizabeth. I wanted a name that looked nice when you wrote it in script. I wanted to be longer, thinner, prettier from day one. Go figure. My name was flat, short, stubby. When I wrote my first book in the second grade, it was a short novel about twins named Elizabeth and Isabella. I told my parents when I was eighteen, I would change my name, and they'd have no say in the matter.

At some point, I changed my mind.

The girl named Eli had a nice ring to it. I'd never change it. Eli allowed me to be memorable without trying. To be unexpected. To show up with a talking point before I even opened my mouth.

Now, I just had to figure out how to live up to the name. That, and my first word.

Wow.

•

I've never believed in the idea of romanticizing your life—because I believe it causes us to create false expectations, false realities, and leaves us feeling helpless and a little deflated.

I always say guilt is reserved for when we do something wrong without repercussions, and I think often, we feel guilty when we don't reach our arbitrary romanticized scenarios, our New Year's resolutions, and our superfluous goals. We spend so much time with a red pen, crossing out our imperfections, and so little time recognizing how realistic it was to ask ourselves to attain the unattainable.

The romanticized version of my life looks more like my favorite movie than it does reality. And the reason my favorite movie is my favorite is because the ending is always happy. The emotions are always controlled. Everyone ends up feeling good, being successful, and winning in their own right. I watch movies because they are an escape from reality. They can simultaneously hold a mirror to reality, to reflect a strange truth or an untold message, but movies will never *be* reality. They can't be. They don't exist in the same cycle of obstacles and trauma and sadness. They have a script. They have a director. They have a plan, and it's followed precisely to elicit a specific emotion.

Of course, your life has a script too. But you're writing it as you go. It's never locked, it's never a final draft. I believe we arrive on this earth with a rough draft of how things could go—and through our decisions, our choices, our free will—we end up writing the next draft. We have no red pen, no eraser; each draft is written in permanence, and only our next choice can change our fate based on what's already written. That's what makes life a little different from a movie. We'll never know when we're forced to put the pen down and look up.

With expectations come pressure, and with pressure comes disappointment. At the crux of it, when we're romanticizing our lives, we'll never actually attain what we want to attain. The pinnacle of our romanticization—the end goal—is one that will never actually come true, because we aren't basing our goals in reality, rather, a picture-perfect, movie-style happy ending.

> RULE 1
>
> End goals put a cap—a ceiling—on our potential. Make lists of things you hope to accomplish—I urge you to (you know I love to manifest), but remember there is always something more, something new to add to the list. Maybe you'll surprise yourself. I sure hope you do.

Just because I've struggled with the idea of romanticizing life doesn't mean I don't understand why some choose to believe in the message. Romanticizing your life is a way to find happiness and fulfillment in the mundane, in the nine-to-fives and shitty family gatherings and tasks we don't want to do. But simultaneously, it can come with disappointment, so I'd like you to throw away romanticizing and instead adopt the phrase "honoring your life." Because I do believe in choosing joy. In your experiences being brighter and more colorful, even when they seem regular.

Honoring your life, to me, means grabbing your current reality exactly as it is, and finding a way to elevate it. It's looking at your current reality, and saying, "How do I, within my current means, take what I have and make it something really beautiful? Something really lovely? Something I really feel proud of? Something I really like?"

RULE
2

Honoring your life means recognizing that while the sky's the limit, we don't need to reach the sky tomorrow. We can take baby steps. We can move slowly. We can honor our Tuesday, or our week or our month in a way that feels affordable. That feels realistic. That feels tangible. We don't expect to meet the love of our lives every time we go out with our friends. We don't expect to make the dream a reality today, or stumble into a million dollars tonight. We can just expect to put a routine in place that ensures we have an amazing time, that ensures we make memories, that ensures we're proud of ourselves. We don't expect that the next date we go on is with our Prince Charming who's here to *save* us. We start doing the work so we can figure out how to save ourselves.

Romanticizing your life is often conflated with a single story. A single story that looks like one thing. It looks like a societally beautiful person, a thin person—a person with a charming prince, a person with wealth and affluence and really expensive clothes. A person with all the success in the world, who is somehow void of any negative feelings. Romanticizing your life suggests that we all coexist in lives that look like the end credits of a rom-com—but for most of us, that's not the case, and never will be.

We have razor bumps, cellulite, bad skin days, fights with our parents, jury duty. We don't know how we'll pay our rent, we stain our white sweater with coffee, we aren't all in the most privileged of positions and we cannot assume life to be as such. We get parking tickets, go through breakups, and have stomach issues. Sometimes we get too drunk and say something we didn't mean. We grow out of our pants and into different ones, we fuck up at work, we consider quitting. We turn to our vice and then we ask for help. We nearly drown making it to shore. We're out of breath and our hair is stuck to our cheeks in jagged little strips.

We can have all those things—be all those things—and still honor our life. We can be imperfect, a little bit of a mess, a little bit unfinished or undecided.

Our ambition can be undecided, too, and we can still honor our life. That's why I take control of my life, because it's my life, not a version of one I saw in a storybook as a child, and it can be a total mess some days and still be elevated in a way I can grasp.

There's no wrong way to live your life to the fullest. To make it feel really fucking good for you, as often as it can. There's no single story to anything. To anyone. To any place.

Wow.

·

I always got in the way of my own ability to honor my life, distracted by the way others saw me. I spent twenty-two years focused on the perception others MAY have of me. Others' possible perception of me ruled my life. I left no time in my day or in my week for my life to be lived—for my life to be honored—because I spent all my time concerned with what other people were thinking. My concern was not: Am I enjoying this ride? Am I working toward my goals? Am I living in a way that feels honest and good to me? Am I a good person with realistic goals and unrealistic dreams?

But rather, it was: What does everyone else think about my choices? My clothes? My hair? My job? The way I look when I walk into a crowded room?

I wasn't making choices I authentically wanted to make, just choices I figured everyone else wanted me to make. Or the choices I thought would put me in the best place to be liked or loved. And since those people don't actually care about my choices, it was unfulfilling when I made them and they didn't feel good to anyone.

I figured that if I gave the world what it wanted, it would give me what I wanted back.

I don't regret a minute of the past—truly—but damn, was it exhausting to try so hard so someone else would call me pretty.

Here's the thing about the world. The world doesn't give a fuck what you do with your time. You have dazzling autonomy. You can do what you please. You can ignore something until it eats you alive. Or you can face it. Only you can choose.

I remember sitting in my sorority house bedroom, deciding if I wanted to go abroad for the summer of 2018, or go intern in Missouri. I thought everyone wanted me to go abroad, but I wanted to do the internship. I thought everyone would judge me for choosing Missouri over Europe, and it was swaying me in a direction I didn't want to be blown toward.

What if, I wondered, sitting at my desk, picking at my nails, *I just made the choice I wanted to make?*

I sat there, considering it. A tough question, but a worthwhile one.

What would happen if I made the choices I wanted to make for myself? What would happen if I allowed myself to be the CEO of my own life? Either way, I was paying—for my abroad summer or my internship housing and flight down to Missouri. Who could genuinely and informatively tell me I was wrong about the way I pursued my own happiness?

RULE
4

I try to make things as simple as possible. To put the facts before my feelings, and then decide how I feel once the facts are all laid out. The simple truth: this is a big choice, there is noise, I am going to mute the noise, because I am in control.

I am in control. Wow.

RULE
5

I tried it out: making choices for me, taking control. I made my executive decisions, carefully at first, starting with low stakes choices: How *I* wanted to dress. What *I* wanted to eat. Where *I* wanted to go. What *I* wanted to do. I asked myself the questions I asked other people when they came to me for advice—How does that make you feel? What do YOU want to do? I know you said that's what you think you should do . . . but what do you *want* to do?

I threw out the little trendy tops that I wore because people said I should, because I was told they were trendy. My true uniform was eclectic, lots of turtlenecks in the winters, patterned sweaters, lived-in jeans, blue sneakers—I didn't need anyone else to tell me what was right for me to wear. I wanted to show up in this life as I

RULE
6

am. If you think my outfit is ugly, I truly pity the five seconds you wasted to tear someone down inside your own mind. Listen, I'm not everyone's cup of tea, but that's because I'm actually a shot of tequila. I wanted to attract the people who liked the version of me that rose from a tangle of sheets at seven in the morning, ready to do her best. You don't have to like me, I am self-aware enough to understand that not everyone will, but you should aspire to respect everyone in your path. It is a shit show otherwise.

I lost a lot when I gained myself. Inhibitions, phony friends, men who used to pay attention to me. But in some ways, I gained the world—*my* world. A world that I was proud of. A life I was building day by day. I gained the respect of people watching my autonomy, shocked and thrilled that I had the guts to stop listening to all the noise. But mostly, I gained the love of myself. When I honored my life, when I honored what I have here, the draft I'm writing, the hand of cards I'd been dealt, the only thing that truly changed: everything eventually grew a little brighter.

•

A few months later, I was lying awake on New Year's Eve, allowing myself to be honest. Allowing my brain to think whatever it wanted to think. Allowing myself to write it all down, not push it away because I didn't want to believe it, not hide from it because I was afraid to tell myself the truth. I wanted to honor my life, and it started with finding myself opened up, all alone.

It was all of me. Inconsequential, raw, on a pretty notebook page.

December 31, 2018, I wrote, staring at the wall. Journaling makes me cry. I do it every day for twenty minutes. Ten in the morning, ten at night.

A tiny spider crawled slowly past my eyes and up to the ceiling. It was just the two of us. No party, no boyfriend, no kiss. I didn't look at the time but knew it was midnight because outside my room and outside the house and outside myself I could hear euphoric screams and drunken firework displays and it just felt like midnight. I felt that in my bones.

I started to write.

I whispered happy new year to the spider and then I burst into tears. There was some kind of electricity sleeping next to me in bed. I knew everything would change in 2019.

Time is like music except there's no option to skip and no option to shuffle. It just throttles forward. We have sex with losers, make deals with the devil, eat ricotta toast, go for runs, max out our credit cards, regret the cigarette smoking abroad or the text we sent when we should've said nothing at all. And time, our sweet little demon, keeps checking herself out in the mirror and being a huge bitch, in spite of us needing a second to breathe sometimes.

3, 2, 1 . . . Happy New Year.

All the New Years that came before that one, I did whatever I thought I was meant to. I let my anxiety be the captain of the ship, I let my self-doubt be the president of my country. I made resolutions I'd never see, and beat myself up for never attaining—five pounds I never lost, a gym membership I didn't use, books I didn't read.

I wish I'd known any day can be your New Year's Day. I'm here writing this, and you're in your own world—your own life—with your own pen. Get up and start writing.

I spent most of the moments leading up to 2016 on the cool concrete floor in a suburban New Jersey basement storage room, my blue sparkly dress tangled around my legs. It was a PG-13, 17-year-old's display of sloppy makeout affection but I felt like Aphrodite. Feeling wanted was a currency back then and it made me feel rich.

I spent most of the moments leading up to 2017 remembering the year before—the concrete floor, the television, the prosecco. Now in college, we all looked at each other like we'd learned so much. Like we were mature and jaded. All I had learned is that people would beg you to let them in, and then they'd leave without saying goodbye. The words *I love you* meant nothing to me and I ended the night sitting in the grass, letting it cool the backs of my bare legs while my cousin threw up champagne beside me.

A year later, my hair was shorter and I felt worse. I clutched a bottle of moscato and avoided eye contact at the party I attended. I wanted to act distracted so nobody would ask how I was. I texted Ezra and asked him to keep things casual with me in 2018. He said yes. I felt like a champion for five minutes, until it all hurt so much again.

Two thousand eighteen was a year I wouldn't redo but I wouldn't undo, either. It would teach me what love was. It would suggest that maybe I was a pretty decent writer. I wouldn't want to stop time, but I'd wish for it to move at .5x speed. Because I was having fun. Because things felt good. I uncovered the truth about being attractive—about being hot—hotness, which I had craved so deeply. It was all about confidence. Having utterly fuckable energy, utterly hot energy, it was all about the attitude. I changed little, but liked myself more. It showed. I whispered to myself in the mirror when the hurt beckoned—*You're too hot to be sad.*

We want slow motion when things are good, a pause button when they're confusing, and a fast-forward when they suck. But a year later, on the eve of 2019, as I watched the spider crawl up the wall and I put my palm to the same wall and felt the vibrations of celebration outside. I wasn't upset to be in bed. To be alone. To be without him. The truth came to me like a secret whispered in my ear.

I just wanted to finally live a life for me. A life I liked. A life I honored. A life I watered like a well-kept plant. Even if I had to lose love to do it. I wanted the feeling I started to discover—of choosing me.

I just didn't know where the hell to start. First, I knew I would lose love. My first love. I had to walk away from him to walk toward me. And it wasn't easy to realize at the expense of him, I'd be there—bruised and delicate, but ready to begin.

I'd suddenly be twenty-one. Suddenly back in Michigan. Suddenly waiting for my life to begin again. I knew I wanted it to, but I didn't know how.

Truthfully I just had to be open to it. And I had to be a little selfish and a little brave. I had to go outside by myself, and let the rain wash me and the wind dry my clothes. I had to realize that if I tried and failed, I'd be happier than if I stayed put. Failure would always be more attractive to me than complacency.

I started to ask myself who I wanted to be, when nobody else was looking, when nobody else was listening to the sound of my voice. I wanted to be the word *wow*. I wanted to be a sensational success. I wanted to feel excitement, to feel adoration, most days, or some days, or the majority of days, when my eyes opened to my alarm or just the sun coming in like streaks of paint on a canvas through the blinds. I wanted to say, to be, *wow*.

The questions that arose within the ashes, within the cup of cold coffee, at two in the morning: How do I live a life I'm proud of? Am I just another woman who wants to fit into smaller pants? Am I shoplifting someone else's heat to keep me warm? Do I like my life? What the fuck am I doing? Should I eat less? Should I feed myself more? Should I ask for help? Should I grow out my hair and move away? How do I rebuild a relationship with myself? Where do I begin? Was it all worth it? Am I proud of myself so far? Is it okay to not know if you'd ever want marriage? How can you make a dash to the finish line, yet not move an inch? Where is the LinkedIn post that says, "I'm proud to admit I have no idea what the fuck I'm doing or who the fuck I want to be?"

For a while I felt a little like a flat, forgotten water bottle in a backpack. But you work through it like you work through anything. You put your head down and you swear to yourself that this is a beginning, that the breakdown is going to force you to look up. That your fingers will always shake when you're nervous. That you will always chase love—you will always imagine your life wildly and blissfully romantic—but you'll do it in a way that addresses all the wounds head-on. It would make no sense and it would make every bit of sense. It would be a spectacular shit show and you wouldn't let a second go unlived or unloved, but you'd be doing it in the pursuit of one person: you.

Me.

Wow.

What a gift then, to simply live.

College would disappear, so would twenty-one, and I'd assume a new role, I'd get a new set of keys, a new route to a different Dunkin' Donuts, a job here or there, someone between my legs, someone else on the other end of the phone. When you start the work and you keep on with it, goodness begins to fall into your lap. It feels confusing for a while, and you're unsure if it's even paying off without a gold star meaning you aced the test. But then, you get an *aha!* moment when you're doing your makeup, or lying in bed alone, or on a walk to the grocery store. You say I need to work on myself, and even when I've worked on myself enough, I have to keep going. And I've done it. And still I'm doing it. Brutally, we have to admit to narcissism, to nascent happiness, to occasional dread. To the understatement of the lifetime: things get better and then worse and then better and then worse, forever. But one thing stays the same: you're in control. You have the pen. You were never broken or less than.

Remember that.

•

A love story to me was *everyone* loving me. *Everyone* adoring me. Being surrounded by an excess of people and success. Not just Cinderella and the prince, but Cinderella, the prince, her wicked stepmother and stepsisters, and the mouse driving the pumpkin.

But then the winds changed, as they do, and a love story became about being alone and loving it. About not worrying if I was "too much" for a man, or if they'd be threatened by my audaciousness or desire to succeed in my own right.

What if a love story was me and a dog, in a loft surrounded by stacks of books, like the one in Greenwich Village where I took that writing class I found on Facebook?

What if a love story was me and a kid, somewhere with a lot of land and sky?

What if a love story was the run I took after you told me we couldn't make it work?

What if a love story was Sadie, running toward me in the airport, in her blue sweatshirt, crying into my hair, her laugh filling the entire terminal with the joy of familiarity?

What if a love story could be watching the world be good? The world feeling good?

A love story didn't have to mean being irrevocably and indisputably loved by everyone. A love story could be lived in twenty-six years. Twenty-five minutes. Sixty seconds or two months. A love story could be just me recognizing my own worth, me taking control.

My love story, the one I want, is one where I'm just out of the shower. No makeup, wet hair. I don't hide my vibrator. I open a bottle of champagne. I'm barefoot and wearing my dad's old sweater. I'm listening to the *Glee* cast. I won't count the calories in my dinner. I don't care about the scars on my breasts from the surgery I had when I was in college. I don't care who commented on my Instagram. I am so blissfully content. Not happy, not sad, just content. Excited about tomorrow and a little sad about yesterday. I could keep up like this forever, and even when it wouldn't be so good, I'd have that moment to fall back on whenever I needed it. That grace. That pride. That simplicity.

I wrote down my ideal version of my life once, one that was realistic but still a reach. I decided what I needed to change to get there.

The ideal version of my life is a woman who is happy. Who doesn't count the calories in her dinner. Who does whatever the hell she wants.

All I needed to change was my view of myself to get there.

I had no control over whether or not everyone, or anyone at all, would love me. Or even how they'd feel anything at all about me. I only have control over how I feel about myself. And that seems like a pretty good place to start.

•

When I started to honor my life, to prioritize my happiness, to choose me, I also confronted the reality of growing up, the rarity of anything ever feeling slow again.

I also realized that my fascination with and addiction to love didn't have to be a bad thing.

To love love is to love life. I just had to funnel that energy through the right channels. To seek love from other places besides a romantic partner. If I was my own wow, it was only a matter of time before I became someone else's, too. And even if I didn't, I wouldn't need to be.

To love is a privilege. To feel that exchange of energy—as simple as loving your coworker for picking up the slack or the lunch, or as grandiose as a white dress and a ceremony you like in the moment but regret the color scheme of ten years later—that's a privilege. It's a privilege we will all feel. A collective wanting, longing, yearning—all at different points.

I retraced the history of my heart. I thought of his handprints on my arm. The way he pushed me to the bed, the way his eyes turned pink with rage though I'd done nothing wrong. I thought of hurting someone, of breaking their heart, of the way I almost stayed to preserve their peace. I'd wonder for months if I should've just stuck around. I thought of begging him to come back, my fingers down my throat, the memorized phone numbers, saying help me and saying hold me, the nights I stayed awake begging God for answers, when I wasn't sure if I even believed he was there.

I wish I'd known that I had to choose myself, I had to choose a path, I had to choose something, anything, instead of just waiting around for someone to choose me.

So screw everyone who hurt you first. You'll forget them, because what you have is now. The losses will be your becoming. Eventually, all of it fades away, becomes the road in the rearview mirror as you start to drive toward something without having to ask for directions.

It comes for all of us, like a flood after a storm. Like tomorrow, or the tide. Inevitable. You're going to make it. You're going to choose you.

•

Trusting myself was the most difficult part of claiming my life, of allowing myself to feel proud—to feel excited. I'd convinced myself, allowed other people to convince me, that I wasn't worth being heard, that I wasn't worth believing. At some points, I couldn't tell where my belief system began and everyone else's ended. It was hard to hear anything when from every corner of my life, there was a different noise. It never gets easier to hear through the clamor, it just becomes easier to be a little louder yourself.

For a long time, my only goal was to be loved, to be adored by everyone else. I was setting myself up for failure, trying to attain the unattainable. After twenty-two years of failing, for once, I wanted to succeed.

Eventually, my desires and objectives spanned wider and harder than I had the foresight to see. To be loved, to be adored, no longer had a place there, unless the desire was to be adored and to be loved by myself.

It is in the moments we stop pressuring ourselves to be loved that we become loved.

But even if I've come far, I still have further to go. Even when I feel like I've got it figured out, I don't. I don't know everything. I don't have it figured out. I just try to feel a little better, a little lighter, each moment a bit more graceful, some heavier than others, as I go along my way.

I'm still, of course, wondering about what's next. I'm twenty-something today. When I wrote this, I was still at the starting line of my life, but strangely, on the horizon I can see a day where I'm not. I still want to play dress-up and play house and have sex on the kitchen counter and get drunk and order bagels hungover in bed. I want to host themed dinner parties and laugh so hard the memories become my wallpaper and my wallpaper becomes our memories. I want to live with my friends and love with my friends. I want us to be together always. I want to get in a fight about the living room carpet and when we finally agree the orange one is nicer, I want to order Thai food and sit across from each other on the floor because we have no furniture. I want to see the world for myself and I want to watch you as you see it too. I want to know when your heart beats really fast, and when it slows. I want a list of the addresses you'll never forget. The weirdest things that have ever happened to you. The scariest. The most quiet. I want you to tell me you like it when I move my hips and I want to live in the way you grab me in the middle of the night and make it known that we'll always just be. And maybe not always, but for tonight. I want to dance in the dining room. I want to get in the car and drive fast. I want to hold Sadie's hand and scream the lyrics to a song we loved in college. I want to write until my fingers cramp up. One day I want to have a daughter and a son. I want her to think her mom's really fucking cool. I want him to always call home. I want them to be happy and I want them to make trouble. I want them to stand up for what's right. I want to recount all the things I did, one day when I'm old, and not be able to come up for air. I want the best day of my life to happen close to the end. I want to look at solitude, at loneliness, as equal to, maybe even greater than, togetherness. I want to take pictures and draw pictures and become so beautiful and so bright that I am always alive in the pictures I once took. I want my ambition to be undecided like my grandmother said hers was. I want to understand myself, before I bring someone else into the mix—I want it to be sexy when I say to you that I'm not sure what I want, or where I'm going, or if I like myself 100 percent of the time. It's sexy not to know, because pretending you have it all together, pretending you know it all, when it's impossible to be that way, is a little silly and a little sad.

And that's my to-do list.

•

When I think about where I am, in this very second, breathing here, I think about sitting at the piano as a kid, wanting to get it right. The way it used to feel to be onstage. The guy who liked Bruce Springsteen and left his belt on my roof. Being too drunk with him on the subway, laughing about the advertisements like they were comedians. Eating breakfast after I wore your shoes, four sizes too big, and we walked to the diner on the Upper West Side. Falling asleep in Daphne's bed in London, crossing the finish line with Sadie. The day I overcame my plane anxiety to fly in the middle seat to South Africa. The time my dad said he was proud of me, and I'd always wanted him to say that. The time my mom realized why I am so stubborn—it's because I've always had an idea of how things would go. My brothers, sitting across from me at the table. All the people, who I am so grateful for, who have reached out to me, who have loved me, who have given me a hand. Everyone who has given me their kindness, my god, I only hope to always give it right back.

I think about the apartment my singing teacher used to live in. The math class I failed in college. The way it felt to leave Sadie at Michigan and the way it felt to see Jack graduate. When Jake felt brave enough to sit at our kitchen table and tell me who he was. The article I wrote about losing my virginity, published in the school paper. When I saw them walking together on a Thursday at one p.m. I thought of the pants two sizes too big and too sizes too small. All the calls home. All the watered-down drinks. Of the stories, the words, the headaches, the heartaches, the plane rides, and the blocked phone numbers.

The twenty-five birthdays so far.

The amount of times I must have said wow since the first time.

•

In a hotel room, with the moon pouring light in from a window, I think of my softness in the mirror, for once, as beautiful, but in the morning it's back to the drawing board. I don't want to float on a boat, I say, sometimes out loud, to nobody but me, I want to drown in a sea of what it means to be alive.

Love is taking someone as they are and saying you're kind of fucked-up and funny and sad and gorgeous and I love you so much I couldn't do without you. It's feeling that way about yourself. It's listening to all those songs that got you to where you are. And remembering the very feeling it was to feel back then.

Taking back your control also means being okay when it doesn't go your way. Being in control of what you can control, so when everything else doesn't work out, you still have you.

I am still learning. Still growing. There will always be growth, always be more to have out there. I'll die with goals. I have to remember that. I may as well have a little fun until then.

But I honor what that means—to grow, to change, to yearn in the direction of greatness, in the direction of a wow. And how beautiful it could be to just like yourself as you are. Even if it's not perfect, even if the laundry needs to be done and the work needs to be finished. I still like me.

One time we were lying in bed, and I told the person next to me it would be okay—no matter what. He was worried about us, about our falling apart, about what it would look like when we moved on. But I knew we'd be all right. It felt like we'd run our course. Without each other, we still had ourselves, we had plenty of love, enough love to keep us going, even if we didn't have each other. We still had our memories, our breakfast dates, the way it felt to hold hands under the sheets. The photos we wouldn't delete, the messages we wouldn't erase.

"How do you know it'll be okay?"

I didn't know it would be okay.

I chose to believe that we could go on. Because that's one thing about me, and about you, and about the heart we all have, underneath our rib cage beating us toward the pursuit of love and the pursuit of everything good and everything that could also hurt so very much. Because no matter what I have, I have me. I have my finger on the pulse of that heart. I have my little voice, and my shaky fingers, and my giant, cartoon character eyes, and I have my why and I have my wow. And I know you have the same. Because we all do. I can't guarantee much, but I can guarantee this.

"Because that's life," I said.

And life would be good either way.

And here's what I do know: If you feel good in that dress, you look good in it too. If he cheats on you, don't blame her right away, there's nuance in everything. You'll never age out of ice cream trucks. Honestly, you'll age, but truly you'll just learn more and more. If you're afraid of growing older, of phasing out, remember that one day you'll get to witness the life cycle of someone you love more than you love yourself. To be curious is to be enamored with what the world may offer you. The best could be around the corner, but so could the worst, so keep your eyes open, and have someone there who will answer the phone in case it's the latter. OxiClean can get out almost any stain, including red wine. Emotional attachment cannot indicate a healthy future, or longevity, only time can. Don't idealize anyone in a way that you wouldn't want to be idealized yourself. Feel confident when you speak your mind—you have something important to say. Take up so much fucking space the room contracts.

The expectation can, and should be, human. That will be spectacular by itself.

Choose yourself. Choose the hard road. Choose the person you want to choose. Choose to be. Don't wait for someone to swipe right on you before you choose to swipe right on yourself. What is the worst-case scenario when you choose yourself?

Maybe you go blind for a while.

Hopefully you'll become a sensational success.

Acknowledgments

If I thanked everyone I'd like to thank, we'd never stop saying thank you, and I'd also thank my local barista, pharmacist, thyroid doctor, and Chipotle delivery driver. So I'm going to keep this as short as my immense gratitude will allow.

My brother Jack is an anchor and a fishing boat. He is sustenance and life and grounding. So to Jack, thank you for the phone calls just checking in. To Jack, thank you for sitting in the emergency room with me when my heart hurt so badly I convinced myself I was dying. To Jack, for telling me it would be okay even if we both didn't know if it would. To Jack, for the secrets we shared in the city we grew in. Thank you for your sensitivity. For being proud of me. It comes in waves and it never stops coming. So thank you thank you, my sweetest brother, for allowing me the privilege to shimmer in the orbit of your amazing grace.

My brother Jake is a pain in the ass and I'd fall apart without him. So to Jake, you have no idea how much of a nuisance you are and how much I'd never be where I am today without you. Thank you for giving me someone to be proud of, to look toward for a breath of fresh air. Thank you for the creative energy we've always passed back and forth. Thank you for reminding me that before a writer or anyone or anything else, I am an older sister, I am your older sister. And that is this life's greatest achievement.

My best friend, Allie, might not know it, but this wouldn't exist without her. I might not exist in her absence either. She is the best friend I have ever known. To Allie, thank you for being there. Thank you for telling me that it hurt you to see me go back but you'd always walk with me so I wouldn't be alone. Thank you for letting me learn it myself and for not saying I told you so. Thank you for the laughter that hurt behind my ribs. The joy it was to be just us two, the formative years that wouldn't have meant much without you there. Thank you for sitting front row in every audience, come snowstorms or hell or the norovirus. You are my soulmate.

To my boyfriend who is a rock when I am a balloon, thank you for refilling the bedside table water and always telling me to hang in there. Thank you for teaching me what it means to choose us every day. Thank you for standing next to me, proud of my big mouth. Thank you for handling it all with care. For the pinkie promises, too. Thank you for reminding me what I'm capable of, for hitting the gas when you knew I needed a push, for being the calm seas and the life raft and the rip current. You are forever etched here, life's best surprise yet, and I am yours every day. I lied to you when I said I wasn't nervous, I am nervous, I hope that's okay.

Veronica is like a sister to me. She is someone I trust with every embarrassing detail. She is the other end of the greatest phone calls and the most life-altering moments. To Veronica, who is smarter and wiser than anyone I know. To Veronica for reading this before anyone else did. To Veronica for holding all my words close to her and keeping my secrets safe. To Veronica for being a best friend in the passenger seat, driving toward nowhere. To Veronica for being here, no matter where here is, and no matter when, I love you so. Thank you so much for showing up every day.

To my grandmother Gail, and my aunt Kate, thank you. I think you'd both be pretty proud. I thought of you with each word. I signed you both a copy and Mom has them on her bookshelf now. You live here even when you don't live here. You live in these words and in these pages and deep in the spine. Thank you for the female friendship, the moments I won't forget, the angel wings. I love you.

To Mia, my gorgeous accomplice, who changed my life in the

span of an email, who is the extension of my thoughts, who wants it to be the very best it can be. To Mia, for allowing me to be planted here; to Mia, for encouraging me to grow here. For going to bat for me and always scoring a home run. You're a special kind of collaborator and a special kind of friend and I am so beyond lucky to have you. (All this and more before twenty-four).

To Sarah, my feisty and spicy queen, for never taking no for an answer. For screaming at me through the FaceTime call when we got the deal. For celebrating this and for pushing this forward. You believed in the book before we even had a book. You named this book; your brain is lightning. You are the spice we all needed. I am so thankful for you. Thank you.

To Jacqueline, my editor, who I was never afraid to share with. Thank you for handling my stories with care. For being gentle when I opened myself up to you. To Jacqueline, who is the gentle whisper behind all my screaming. Who took a chance on me and always made it feel so worth it. You are the reason we are here, and I am beyond thankful for your wisdom and your grammar edits and your very being. And to each collaborator whom I've had the privilege of working with at HarperCollins—thank you so very much. Each lesson, meeting, and day has been a dream.

To Amanda and Brooke, my managers, who hear me. Thank you for your patience. Thank you for handling the missed deadlines. For understanding what I was up to. Thank you for cheering me on. For rooting for me. This wouldn't be what it is without you both. To my team at A3, for saying "How high?" when I ask to jump: thank you. I have so often felt like nobody takes me seriously when I lay out my visions or my lofty goals, but you have never batted an eye. I am eternally grateful.

To José Casas, my playwriting professor in college, who told me once to take off my headphones and listen to the world around me. Who taught me how to write a character. I took off the headphones and I finally listened. Thank you.

To my grandparents, for saving the first book I wrote in preschool, for choosing to understand my mind even when it may not make so much sense to you. For your prayers and your strength. For giving the world my mom. For every single message of encouragement. Your phone calls, your voice mails—for always believing I knew best. I love you more than I could ever conceive. Thank you.

To my friends, my communities, the people in the world around me, down the hall, down the block—burning brilliantly. You are my muses, my escape, my heart. To Kelly, Rachel, Jess, Sophie, Macy, Julia—you cheered me on when nobody else did. I will cheer for you every single day too. I love you to the end of this earth. This wouldn't be here without you.

To Sandi, thank you for always thinking I'm pretty cool. For the text messages with all the exclamation marks. Thank you, thank you, thank you for giving me the two girls who have been the closest thing I've ever had to sisters. Thank you for letting me watch after them too. They are the greatest gift. I love you. Thank you.

To my mom, I'm sorry for all the sex talk and f-bombs. Thank you for letting my mind run free. Thank you for driving me to the community theaters and the voice lessons. Thank you for letting me develop stories you didn't understand. Thank you for letting me explain them to you. You are the most understanding, most thoughtful woman I've ever known—the epitome of strength and grace, my very own Lady Di. I am so lucky I am yours, and though it isn't a walk in the park to have me as a kid, we've made the thing we have going our version of heaven. Thank you for reminding me of my worth every single day. For helping me through the bullshit. Thank you for the phone calls and the reminders. You are someone I could never do it all without. This is as much yours as it is mine and I love you.

To my dad, who said "just do it, kid" because he believed I would. To my dad, who told me to never take no for an answer.

Thank you to my dad for the laughs. For catching me when I fall. For the few words that mean everything to me, every time. Thank you to my dad for being a thorn and a rosebud. For reminding me of how I can be better, of how I can grow, and of telling me he's proud, because he is. Thank you for the tips about wine, the tips about generosity, the tips about life itself. Dad, you are the reason we are all reading this today. In my wildest dreams, I never imagined I could do it, but you always did. Thank you.

And to all of you—where do I possibly begin. Your trust. Your dedication. Your tough love and your gentle love. Your willingness to meet me where I'm at. The way you gave me what I have. Thank you will never be enough. I will run laps around myself to give you back an ounce of what you've given me. We did it. And it will be, and always has been, an us. I am more proud of each of you than you know. If you ever doubt yourself and your worth, remember that I'm on the other side of the page, willing you to go after what you deserve. It is just the beginning.